Leadership in Higher Education from a Transrelational Perspective

Perspectives on Leadership in Higher Education

Series Editors: Camilla Erskine, Jon Nixon and Tanya Fitzgerald

Perspectives on Leadership in Higher Education provides a forum for distinctive, and sometimes divergent, ideas on what intellectual leadership means within the context of higher education as it develops within the twenty-first century. Authors from across a number of nation states critically explore these issues with reference to academic and research-informed practice and development, institutional management and governance, the remapping of knowledge as well as sector-wide policy development.

Forthcoming in the Perspectives on Leadership in Higher Education series

Exploring Consensual Leadership in Higher Education,
edited by Lynne Gornall, Brychan Thomas and Lucy Sweetman
Leadership for Sustainability in Higher Education,
Janet Haddock-Fraser, Peter Rands and Stephen Scoffham

Also available in the Perspectives on Leadership in Higher Education series

Cosmopolitan Perspectives on Academic Leadership in Higher Education,
edited by Feng Su and Margaret Wood
Mass Intellectuality and Democratic Leadership in Higher Education,
edited by Richard Hall and Joss Winn

Leadership in Higher Education from a Transrelational Perspective

Christopher M. Branson, Maureen Marra,
Margaret Franken and Dawn Penney

BLOOMSBURY ACADEMIC
LONDON • NEW YORK • OXFORD • NEW DELHI • SYDNEY

BLOOMSBURY ACADEMIC
Bloomsbury Publishing Plc
50 Bedford Square, London, WC1B 3DP, UK

BLOOMSBURY, BLOOMSBURY ACADEMIC and the Diana logo are trademarks
of Bloomsbury Publishing Plc

First published in Great Britain 2018

A catalogue record for this book is available from the British Library.

A catalog record for this book is available from the Library of Congress.

ISBN: HB: 978-1-3500-4238-4
ePDF: 978-1-3500-4239-1
ePub: 978-1-3500-4240-7

Series: Perspectives on Leadership in Higher Education

Typeset by Deanta Global Publishing Services, Chennai, India
Printed and bound in Great Britain

To find out more about our authors and books visit www.bloomsbury.com and
sign up for our newsletters.

Contents

Series Editors' Foreword

What are universities for in the twenty-first century? This is a question that is now debated not only within universities themselves but within wider society and across the political spectrum: we can no longer assume a consensus regarding the ends and purposes of higher education or the role of universities in fulfilling those ends and purposes. Consequently, leadership within higher education cannot simply be a matter of managing the status quo: leadership necessarily involves an understanding as well as analysis of the twenty-first-century world and of how the university might contribute to the economic, social, cultural and political challenges that we face. In short, it requires leadership that is both visionary and programmatic: visionary in its understanding of the past as well as present and future impacts of globalization, and programmatic in its grasp of how universities might respond to that impact.

What might such leadership look like? This series aims to address that question with reference to academic practice and development, institutional management and governance, the remapping of knowledge and sector-wide policy development. Central to each of these areas of concern is the importance of interconnectivity in a context of increasing institutional and global complexity: interconnectivity within and across institutions, regions and cognate fields. The gathering of agreement is one of the prerequisites of leadership at every level, and that requires an understanding of different viewpoints and opinions, some of which may be in direct conflict with others. The capacity to balance, respect and contain these differences is what constitutes leadership. This inevitably raises important ethical questions regarding leadership in a more complex and subtle setting, where leadership goes beyond the 'command' model of telling others what to do and expecting them to do it. The twin themes of interconnectivity and ethics cut across the series as a whole.

Leadership in Higher Education from a Transrelational Perspective offers a unique contribution to this series. The authors, Christopher M. Branson, Maureen Marra, Margaret Franken and Dawn Penney, have presented a work that establishes a renewed agenda for thinking about leadership, management and administration in higher education. They propose that leadership is deeply relational and that these connections are what render leadership purposeful and productive. Leaders, leadership and leading is a complex web of connections and interrelationships and thus, argue the authors, should be untangled from orthodoxies of management and administration. Across the chapters of this book, the importance of leadership in higher education is emphasized to further underscore the need to conceptualize and practise leadership *differently*. The core purpose of this text is to interrogate leadership practices and to offer a new theoretical foundation for transrelational leadership. There is a subtle and insistent plea for leadership in higher education to not mimic corporate models. The real potential that exists is for institutions of higher education to define and develop their own ways of enacting leadership. The challenge then is for leaders in higher education to demonstrate leadership knowledge and awareness that is mindful, collaborate and collegial. The first step, the authors suggest, is to move away from universalizing discourses and to consider how leadership is a connected set of activities in which all are engaged.

This book calls for us to rethink the nature and importance of leadership in higher education and the arguments put forward by the authors are of vital importance for universities and their leaders in the twenty-first century.

Introduction: What is Universal about Leadership in Higher Education?

There is not a more certain pathway to failure than to be following a faulty map. The pivotal message of this book is that, by and large, the maps that are currently guiding much of leadership knowledge and action in higher education are faulty in many ways. Key features are missing or misrepresented, connections between various elements are not always clear, and many prospective leaders may either struggle to see direction or only see a path that appears treacherous rather than rewarding. The inherent flaws are clearly evident not only in how individuals become leaders in higher education but, more importantly, the sustained perception among many higher education leadership authors and practitioners that leadership is an unproblematic phenomenon.

Mostly, staff in higher education progress through the various levels of leadership based more on the perceived quality of their discipline knowledge or practical achievements than on any formal leadership preparation. Importantly, there is abundant research literature highlighting the managerial, as distinct from leadership, aspect of middle leadership positions in higher education. In other words, these positions are often deficient for developing future effective leaders. Furthermore, many formal leadership development programmes are aligned with business administration skills and knowledge, which again address managerial rather than leadership responsibilities. People want to be led, not managed. They want to be inspired, not restrained; encouraged, not restricted; affirmed, not impugned; involved, not appeased. Furthermore, many individuals holding middle leadership positions in higher education want a similar shift in orientation and are attracted to leadership because of the opportunity that they hope (or expect) it will offer to enable others to thrive. Leadership seeks to maximize participation of all, whereas management seeks to unify the participation of all. As higher education institutions universally face new operational and sustainability challenges of an economic, demographic, curriculum and pedagogical nature, it is leadership rather than management that is required.

The significance of this emphasis on the need for leadership, as distinct from management, to be guiding higher education in the face of this plethora of challenges really comes to the fore when it is acknowledged that this shift mandates cultural change. On the one hand, higher education institutions will continue to struggle to meet these challenges if they remain entrenched in past cultural norms and practices. On the other hand, how institutions are able to meet these challenges through some form of effective cultural change is equally important to acknowledge and learn more about. According to Schein (2004: 11), if one wishes to distinguish leadership from management or administration, 'leadership creates and changes cultures, while management and administration act within a culture'.

Schein's (2004) comments reflect the worldwide acceptance that leadership and organizational culture are inextricably entwined and that their relationship is fundamentally important for organizations. Leadership influences the culture while, simultaneously, the culture influences the leadership. Moreover, you cannot change the culture without changing the leadership (approaches and practices) and vice versa. In the opinion of the doyen of organizational culture research literature, Edgar Schein (2004), the only really important task that leaders must do is to create and manage culture. Moreover, in his later edition (2010) of the *Organizational Culture and Leadership* book he adds substance to this view by arguing that leaders are the main architects of culture, that well-established cultures influence what kind of leadership is possible, and that if elements of the culture become obsolete, unhelpful or dysfunctional, leadership can and must do something to bring about cultural change.

In this era of rapid, constant, diverse and complex change within the higher education environment and in society as a whole, it is arguably imperative that those who hold formal leadership positions need to be leaders, and not managers or administrators, and focus their attention on culture. They must know and understand the difference between leadership and management, the ways in which their position is aligned and entwined within the institution's existing culture and, therefore, with opportunities and constraints in relation to both prospective leadership and cultural change.

Two essential points for further clarification come from this introductory discussion. First, there is a need to be more explicit in presenting our understandings of, and concerns about, the distinctions between leadership and management/administration in higher education. Secondly, it is important to explicate more clearly that which is universal in the practice of higher education leadership, given that these institutions exist in most nations around the world and that each national culture does, to some degree, influence the practice of leadership. Despite the possibility that there are aspects or forms of national distinctiveness in the practice of higher education leadership, there are well-researched and published common beliefs, perceptions and practices. It is these common beliefs, perceptions and practices that will be described and that are the focus of attention for the remainder of this book's leadership exploration.

The nature of leadership, management and administration

There is no general consensus regarding the similarities or differences among the use of the terms leadership, management and administration. They are variously viewed as entirely separate actions, different responsibilities within a single role, or as different words that describe the same thing. This later view gains some support when one considers the etymological foundations of each. Here it can be found that 'manage' has its mid-sixteenth-century roots in the Latin noun '*manus*', meaning 'hand', that became '*maneggiare*', meaning 'to handle or restrain', especially 'to control a horse', which parallels with the French word, '*manège*', for 'horsemanship'. This led to the introduction of the word 'management', meaning 'the act of managing', in the late sixteenth century, which was then applied to the actions of governing bodies in the mid-eighteenth century. In a very similar way, and during a similar time, the use of the word 'administration' comes from the two Latin words of '*ad*', meaning 'to', and '*ministrare*', meaning 'serve', so that administration came to mean 'to help, assist, manage, control, rule, or direct'. However, in early sixteenth century the term came to mean 'the management of a deceased person's estate under a commission from authority' from which came the word 'administrator', which later became aligned with 'a manager of public affairs' and, by the middle of the seventeenth century, 'one who holds executive power'. Thus, by this time the action of administration became aligned with executive, or publicly accountable, management as distinct from the management of the daily and routine logistical responsibilities. Quite differently, 'lead', as the root word for leadership, has its origins in very old English and Germanic words that were associated with meaning 'to guide', initially implying more about guiding oneself but then later to be guiding others or 'showing others the way'. By the fifteenth century this understanding of 'showing others the way' resulted in the word being applied to the person 'at the front of others' or 'someone in the first place'. This person was thus referred to as the 'leader'. Ultimately by the early nineteenth century, people who occupied positions quite literally at the front of others, particularly for those who played lead roles in theatre productions, were considered to be enacting 'leadership' whereby they were displaying the characteristics of a leader or they had the capacity to lead. However, it was not until the turn of the twentieth century that 'leadership' was applied to the perceived actions of those controlling businesses and industries, but essentially in the English-speaking Western societies.

These brief etymological insights also uncover some further insights into potential problems with our current confusion or misunderstandings about what is leadership compared to management and administration. Essentially, the etymological discussion provides the distinction that leadership is about 'guiding' and 'being at the front (or top)', management is about 'controlling or directing', and administration is about 'publicly accountable management'. At the turn of the twentieth century when the industrial revolution was coming to its zenith in the United States, Britain and some European countries, many different industries and businesses were seeking ways to enhance workplace efficiencies and worker effectiveness. In other words, the industrial magnates and business tycoons were striving to find new ways to better manage their workers in order to not only consolidate their factory or business but also to increase its profitability and, thereby, their personal wealth. Herein lies the potential confusion – largely individuals at the top of an organization, who were seemingly fulfilling a position aligned with what was called 'leadership', were acting in a way that was essentially management. But, in the early 1900s, as academic research into the concept of leadership rapidly gained widespread appeal and influence, the confused entanglement between leadership and management was not acknowledged. Consequently, much of the early leadership research was focused not on leadership but rather on magnate or tycoon-type management. Moreover, the incredible success of the Industrial Revolution's magnates and tycoons resulted in the almost universal acceptance of this alignment in leadership research and theorizing. In other words, the beginning of leadership research was more to do with describing management than it was about uncovering the nature and practice of leadership. Regrettably, by and large, our subsequent leadership theorizing has failed to escape from these initial, and from our perspective, seriously misguided roots.

If it is leadership and not management that is best suited to guide people and organizations through today's complex, unpredictable and ever-changing world, then it is incumbent upon us to know and understand conceptual and functional differences. Not surprisingly, many people see far less of a distinction between management and administration than they do with management and leadership. Often administration is taken to be the very formalized mandatory governance and accountability components within the management role. Simply stated, administration is an explicitly distinguishable component of management. Administration is not necessarily differentiated from management but rather it is accepted as an integral but prominent aspect of effective management. In contrast, leadership and management are seen as distinctively different in nature and practice. A common but simple descriptive distinction is the view that managers do things right whereas leaders do what is right. This suggests that managers are more concerned with ensuring that rules, policies, prescribed procedures, organizational protocols and performance expectations are closely followed, carefully monitored and largely achieved. Whereas, leaders are concerned with not only decision-making and direction setting but, more importantly, with being able to ensure that the right decisions are made and the best direction is chosen. Critically, the notion that decisions and direction are 'right' or 'best' varies distinctly with the adoption of a leadership rather than a management/administrative perspective. Other idioms that capture the distinctions include the understanding that a manager maintains while a leader develops, a manager measures while a leader explores, a manager focuses on processes while a leader focuses on people, a manager deals in details while a leader deals in possibilities, and, finally, followers look to managers for tasks while they look to leaders for purpose. Hamel (2007: 4) echoes similar views when he writes, 'Perhaps the problem with leadership is that we have reached the end of management. Perhaps we have more or less mastered the sciences of organizing human beings, allocating resources, defining objectives, laying out plans, and minimizing deviations from best practice.' What is also apparent in Hamel's view is an implied qualitative differentiation between leadership and management whereby leadership is conceptually elevated to a more important and prestigious level. This understanding is also captured in the thoughts of Margaret Wheatley (2006: 131) where she argues, 'In this chaotic world, we need leaders. But we do not need bosses. We need leaders to help us develop a clear identity that lights the dark moments of confusion. We need leaders to understand that we are best controlled by concepts that invite participation, not policies and procedures that curtail our contribution.' Within this differentiated perspective, management is associated with the practical responsibilities such as scheduling, timetabling, organizing, budgeting, meeting accountabilities, resourcing and overseeing quality control, whereas, leadership is associated with the more abstract responsibilities such as visioning, goal setting, planning, motivating, communicating and culture building.

The differentiations between leadership and management illustrated above can also be clearly heard in the words of line managers when they say something like, 'I need to step up and show some leadership,' when they are confronted with some form of unusual and/or complex task. Implicit in such a phrase is that leadership is not integral to their everyday work as a manager but, rather, is something that they recognize as required in particular circumstances and, often, when the going is getting tough. A similar differentiated distinction between leadership and management is echoed in a line manager's comments when encouraged to update their leadership knowledge and practice, 'Oh no, we've done leadership. We don't need to know anything more about leadership.' A further illustration comes with the declaration by a senior leader when talking to some middle leaders about organizational best practice that 'we tried leadership but it didn't work so we've gone back to management'. In all of these views is the implication that leadership is a static, predetermined prescription for how to act in certain circumstances. It is seen as a standardized way of acting rather than a dynamic, evolving, contextually influenced phenomenon. Furthermore, the preferred approach is that of management.

This raises the possibility that for many in formal leadership positions in higher education, externally imposed pressure to adopt managerialist practices has helped to justify a personal bias. For these higher education leaders there is no pressure, no apparent reason, to adopt actual leadership practices. An aim of this book is to overcome this misguided self-justification for avoiding leadership and either intentionally or inadvertently adopting management as a default and/or openly preferred basis for professional practice. The intent is to establish pressure upon higher education leaders to do what they must do, that is, to show leadership and be genuine leaders for their colleagues, institutions and fields.

Leadership in the context of this book

This somewhat simplified discussion of what constitutes leadership, management and administration creates the impression of what we call the 'Differentiated Perspective' whereby administration is an essential and distinguishable yet integral component of management while leadership is something quite separate

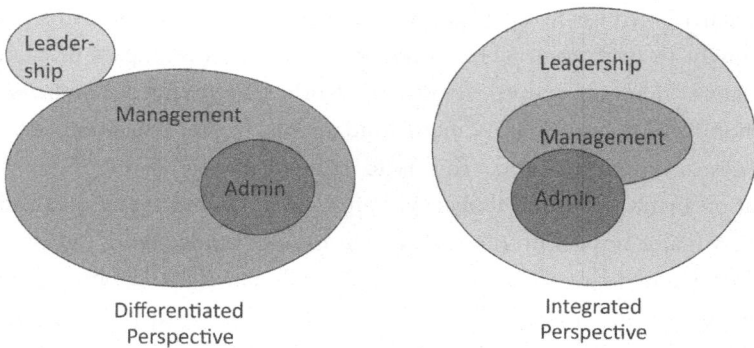

Figure 1.1 An illustration of the two competing perspectives of the relationship among leadership, management and administration

from management and administration. This understanding is illustrated in Figure 1.1. As claimed here, but described in far more detail throughout this book, we argue that this is the most common, but deficient, view held across the higher education institutional environment. Instead, the argument present in this book is for a far more 'Integrated Perspective' (see Figure 1.1) in which leadership is the fundamental activity but where and when necessary, management and administration are practised as well. The leader at times employs management or administration because that is what is required.

This elevation of leadership to be recognized as the primary practice of leaders in higher education echoes the sentiments of Gayle Avery (2006) who argues that much of our current organizational failures can be attributed to too much management and too little leadership. Trying to influence, control and organize in complex, fast-paced, changing conditions using traditional managerial paradigms will not work in her opinion. Instead, Avery calls for leaders who 'provide a clear vision of the future, develop a road map for the journey ahead, and motivate followers to realize the vision' (2006: 24). More particularly, she emphasizes that these leaders take into consideration the emotional commitment of followers. In other words, leadership is primarily people centred and not performance centred.

What is universal in higher education leadership?

As previously acknowledged, although a common understanding of the nature of leadership is arguably apparent, its universal application is far more disputable, particularly given the array of national, cultural and historical norms that can be brought to bear upon it. However, we argue that the impact of economic imperatives inherent within a globalized world has provided a sufficient and common force to largely unify many fundamental higher education leadership practices around the world. This is to argue that the world of the higher education institution is no longer what it used to be and that globalization is having a major impact on how leadership is being understood and practised. As described by many (see, for example, Churchman 2006; Dobbins, Knill and Vögtle 2011; Hamlin and Patel 2015; Lafferty and Flemming 2000; Ramsden 1998; Randle and Brady 1997; van Ameijde, Nelson, Billsberry and van Meurs 2009), the traditional higher education leadership practices are being rapidly replaced by management principles adopted from the business world. Increasingly, government policies around the world are requiring higher education institutions to account for the expenditure of public funds and provide evidence of 'value for money'. Such policies have been generically termed 'New Public Management' (Chandler, Barry and Clark 2002) or 'New Managerialism' (Deem 1998) or 'Corporatization' (Giroux, Karmis and Rouillard 2015). It is these business-influenced managerial practices that will be shown to be not only common to higher education institutions worldwide but also potentially detrimental to higher education achieving the very outcomes that are its core business. Moreover, subsequent chapters illustrate how these managerial practices are now recognized as not working in the business world, yet are still being unquestionably applied to higher education.

To describe these trends in higher education leadership more specifically, 'New Public Management' is depicted as placing an emphasis on the pressures upon higher education leaders to become far more entrepreneurial and business-like in their practices whereby 'mission statements, quality, strategies, performance measures, key performance indicators, targets, profiles and market segments are but a few of the concepts that now seem commonplace in university discourse' (Bellamy, Morley and Watty 2003: 14). Somewhat similarly, Anderson (2006: 578) defines 'Managerialism' as involving 'incorporation of approaches, systems, and techniques commonly found in the private sector, to the management and conduct of the public sector'. She further argues that it involves 'more muscular management style, an emphasis on particular forms of accountability, the development of a market-orientation, a focus on securing non-government funding, and increased concern with issues of efficiency and economy', all of which are effected through 'performance management schemes, quality assurance mechanisms, the restructuring of academic departments, and the implementation of budgetary devolution' (Bellamy, Morley and Watty 2003: 251–2). Moreover, managerialism is also aligned with causing the strong focus on international growth and rankings, an increased reliance on private funding, massive investments in advertising campaigns, and the use of normative markers such as 'excellence' (Readings 1996) and 'best practices' (Ginsburg 2011) to describe goals and the means to achieve them. Finally, for Giroux et al. (2015), 'Corporatization' is described as being at the heart of today's conception of the higher education institution due to the centralization of decision-making, the hierarchical professionalization of administrative positions and relations, and an organizational culture of superficial consultations with faculty, staff and students about the direction of the university. Arguably, each term in its own way provides an insight into what is now commonplace and highly recognizable in higher education.

Moreover, the universality of a form of higher educational leadership that is underpinned and informed by managerialism and corporatization is supported in the following literary examples. It is not the intention here to support or critique these examples but, rather, to highlight the diversity of countries in which the influence of managerialism upon higher education leadership has been noted. Deem, Hillyard and Reed (2007) illustrate the changes in the cultural and ideological dimensions of higher education leadership that neo-liberal managerialism has imposed in the UK. Similarly, Shumar (1997) had previously written that higher education was increasingly seen as a commodity rather than as a public good serving the needs of society and argued that the 'market' of higher education had become endemic in the United States. In 2013, Mok's research found that a hierarchical line of command and a high concentration of power had become firmly imbedded into Hong Kong higher education as a means towards making them more highly efficient corporations. In a similar call, Li, Lai and Lo (2013) and Lai (2013) describe the plight of Chinese academics resulting from the changing higher education governance strategies under the influence of Western managerialist leadership. Fredman and Doughney (2012) describe their study as showing that the negative attitudes among Australian academics to the new managerial style of higher education leadership were the third worst in world behind only the UK and Hong Kong. Meanwhile, Pick, Teo and Yeung (2012) expand this concern to include the adverse effect of such leadership upon the administrative, clerical and technical personnel working in higher education as well.

On a slightly different note, there are numerous research studies that focus more explicitly on the impact of managerialism on particular dimensions of the culture within higher education. For instance, Shore's New Zealand study (2010) proposes that managerialism not only greatly adds to the range and complexity of required tasks but, also, often creates contradictory missions and, thus, priorities. Santiago and Carvalho (2012) explored the influence of managerialism upon Portuguese academics and raised deep concern for the loss of autonomy and collegiality within the higher education workplace environment. Somewhat similarly, Sporn's (2010) Austrian higher education research recommended that managerialism needs to be very carefully introduced in order to ensure it does not reduce the level of trust and respect within the culture. Weinberg and Graham-Smith (2012) criticize the corporatization of South African higher education and claim that this has resulted in the loss of 'its soul and its autonomy'. To add detail to this concern, Tsheola and Nembambula (2014) posit that managerialism has triumphed over transformational leadership in South African higher education and this has decreased innovation, imagination, risk-taking, common sense and experimentation, all of which are considered essential to the future development of the country. Finally, and on a slightly more positive note, Smeenk and colleagues' research (2009) across the six European countries of Belgium, Finland, Germany, the Netherlands, Sweden and the UK provides data suggesting that the influence of managerialism in higher education leadership has a positive, albeit on the quality of employee performance.

This brief discussion about the perceptions garnered by researchers exploring the influence of managerialism upon the leadership of higher education institutions is presented here solely to support our claim that this form of leadership has become universal and, therefore, is the key form of leadership critiqued in this book. For the sake of simplicity, in the remainder of the book we refer to the form of leadership that arguably has become universal in higher education as simply 'managerialism'. But before commencing a critique of this form of leadership, it is important to note that the business world does not have a faultless leadership map. According to Deloitte's (2015) Global Human Capital Trends report, only 6 per cent of business executives around the world feel that they have been adequately prepared to meet their leadership responsibilities. Thus it is not surprising that 86 per cent of the human resource and business leaders who participated in the global research described in this report regarded the further development of leadership theory and practice as essential. These data are supported by the Corporate Executive Board's global research, with the indication that 63 per cent of today's business leaders lack the required abilities to achieve success for their organization. Furthermore, the business world does not offer a solution to the proper preparation of future leaders. A review conducted by PricewaterhouseCoopers found that 81 per cent of corporate executives rate leadership development programmes as less than highly effective. Further, the Institute for Corporate Productivity states that only 32 per cent of business middle leaders are able to exercise the type of leadership behaviour that is now seen as essential in today's highly competitive and globally influenced business world. Finally, and also in our view very pertinent to higher education, a survey by the Advance Learning Group found that 83 per cent of businesses do not have an adequate leadership development and succession plan.

Taken together, these data draw attention to three critically important insights. First, they provide a serious cautionary signal to those in higher education leadership positions to avoid the unexamined and superficially interpreted application of leadership practices that seek (or are presumed) to model those thought successful in the business world. Secondly, these data unequivocally highlight the need for explicit leadership development. The enactment of effective leadership should not be left to chance and cannot be expected to happen in the absence of planned, specific development work. Finally, these data promote the necessity for the development of a far more contemporary and thereby effective theory of leadership – a holistic theory that can guide successful higher educational leadership. Thus, the aim of this book is to comprehensively show how the theory of transrelational leadership is readily able to meet this requirement. As defined (Branson, Franken and Penney 2016: 155), the essence of transrelational leadership 'is to move others, the organisation and the leader to higher levels of functioning by means of relationships'. But such leadership knowledge and awareness needs to be explicitly learnt, as it can't be automatically and unquestionably modelled given that it does not exist in the world of business or elsewhere for that matter.

An overview of this book

The intention of this book is to not only provide a wide array of research literature to help explain why a form of leadership supposedly modelled on that used in the business/corporate world is deficient but also to draw on our research in higher education to construct and describe the proposed alternative transrelational approach to leadership. Importantly, the structure and sequencing of the theoretical and practical implications of this transrelational approach to higher education leadership closely follows that provided by a specific professional learning programme to a group of aspiring academic leaders in a New Zealand university. This structure and sequencing is captured in the following chapter outlines.

Chapter 1   Organizational culture – Recognizing its invisible force

This chapter elaborates upon the understanding raised in the Introduction that leadership and organizational culture are inextricably entwined. As previously stated, leadership influences the culture while, simultaneously, the culture influences the leadership. The aim of this chapter is to clearly show how this is so very true for higher education institutions. Thus, while the Introduction described the universally well-documented concerns about the nature and practice of leadership in higher education, this chapter presents and discusses research literature, which highlights more specifically the impact of managerialism upon higher education's organizational culture.

The chapter begins with a discussion of the nature and function of organizational culture, which then leads onto the presentation of literature that acknowledges the importance of considering the organizational culture of higher education and, in some, presenting arguments for it to change and become more relevant to the twenty-first century. However, little attention is given within this literature to the meaning of these changes for leadership both in bringing about the changes and in how leadership is best enacted in the new culture. In other words, the call is for the culture to change but for the practice of leadership to remain the same. Hence, current business research is referenced to emphasize the serious inadequacy of this oversight.

Finally, the chapter moves to specific research literature detailing the constraining issues in the organizational culture of higher education deemed to be directly resulting from the application of managerialism. This literature credits the extensive adoption of managerialism for producing numerous unsatisfactory cultural norms and expectations. Thus, the point is made that higher education needs to establish its own best leadership practice rather than uncritically adopting those practices that are not only thought to be greatly unsuccessful in the very field in which they were established but are also producing outcomes that are, at best, conflicting with or, worse, perverting the core business of higher education institutions.

Chapter 2   The theoretical foundations of transrelational leadership

Picking up on pragmatic concerns about ineffective leadership theory and practice established in Chapter 1, this chapter constructs a new theoretical foundation for leadership, which is referred to as 'transrelational' leadership. To this end, the basic leadership practices professed by Haslam, Reicher and Platow (2011) are used to describe leadership as essentially a transrelational phenomenon, along with a detailed illustration of how this understanding has been applied to higher education in a particular research context. Here the leader's focus is on the four fundamental leadership practices: being an authentic member of the group they are leading; championing the group; changing the groups' identity; and bringing the external relevant influences to the attention of the group. It is argued that it is these four practices that enable the group to accept and endorse the person as their leader, which then allows this person to eclectically choose how best to lead from the various principles presented by each of the previous leadership theories.

Chapter 3   Leadership as transrelational practice

This chapter addresses two extremely important implications that result from a commitment to a transrelational approach to leadership – pragmatics and credibility. Pragmatics addresses the need for the leader to be able to successfully work with others to achieve mutually desired outcomes whereas credibility addresses the need for the leader to be a role model. The leader must 'walk their talk', which means that they must be a transrelational person in every endeavour. From a pragmatic view, a theoretical perspective is of little benefit if it is unable to be translated into practical realities. But from a credibility view, achieving the practical reality must also comply with acting transrelationally. Transrelational practices must provide effective ways for the leader to achieve the essential responsibilities of being both an effective and credible leader. Hence, this chapter will describe and illustrate what a transrelational approach to leadership looks like in practice.

Chapter 4   Real power and influence

If it is essential for the transrelational leader to be able to change a group's identity, and to effectively bring any external relevant influences to the attention of the group so that they can successfully adapt, the implication is that the leader has some form of authority, power or influence that can get the group to consider change/ing. In support of maintaining coherence with the transrelational approach to leadership, this chapter describes the extensive research-based literature from such fields as sociology, cultural studies, behavioural studies and philosophy that counters some common assumptions about a leader's sources of power and influence. Instead, this literature promotes the acceptance of alternative sources of power and influence – based upon relationships rather than coercion or control. Essentially, such power and influence is identified as being founded upon the search for organizational truth by means of inclusive, cooperative and transparent means. This research supports the view that the true source of power and influence is more closely aligned with being a transrelational leader than with any previously described form of leadership. Transrelational leadership is therefore positioned as fundamentally influential because it is inherently grounded in relations and relational practice. The chapter concludes by describing in detail three pragmatic concerns that a commitment by a leader to pursue relational power may raise–employee duty, commitment and responsibility. Each of these concerns is described both from the traditional, managerial point of view and from a transrelational leadership perspective. In each case the relational approach is shown as presenting far greater prospects for leaders to achieve what they are truly looking for.

Chapter 5   The challenge of organizational change

The focus of this chapter is the suitability of transrelational leadership, in comparison to previous leadership theories, to leading successful organizational change. While change is now considered to be endemic within organizations, including higher education institutions, diverse large-scale research supports the view that only approximately 30 per cent of organizational change actually achieves its desired outcomes. Moreover, it is proposed that this unacceptable level of unsuccessful change is to a great degree due to a failure by organizational leaders to suitably attend to modifying the organization's culture so that it can support the desired changes in performance and 'ways of working'. This chapter argues that the fundamental principles of transrelational leadership, of being in the group, of championing the group and enhancing the group's identity automatically weaves leadership practice and organizational culture together. An authentic member of a group is automatically influenced by its culture since the simple definition of culture is 'the way we do things around here'. Thus, if a leader and the group want to change the way that things are to be done in the group, then this immediately implies that the supporting culture needs to be reviewed and, perhaps, adjusted. To this end, this chapter, supported by Snowden's (2005) organizational change framework, describes how a transrelational leader is more able to suitably work with their group through the four types of change – routine, complicated, complex and chaotic – while remaining ever mindful of attending to the necessary cultural adjustments that would be required to support any desired change.

Chapter 6 Seeking high performance

In today's highly competitive world, those organizations that are not striving to achieve high employee performance are most likely the ones that are disappearing. Hence, the capacity of the leader to ensure that their organization's culture is enabling high performance among its employees has become essential. Importantly, however, it is now acknowledged that enhanced organizational sustainability is aligned with high employee performance in the areas of creativity, ingenuity, inventiveness and risk-taking. Thus, the importance of this chapter is its use of research literature from a variety of fields to illustrate how transrelational leaders are far more able to nurture creativity, ingenuity and inventiveness. This is about encouraging risk-taking by accepting unsuccessful outcomes as opportunities to learn rather than actions to be avoided. Moreover, it is about favouring a growth mindset in which the open sharing of alternative opinions and perspectives is actively encouraged and embraced by all. Hence, trust between the leader and employee is absolutely fundamental, but trust is also an integral component of transrelational leadership. If there is no trust, there is no transrelational leadership.

Chapter 7 Reinventing Human Resource Management

The focus of this chapter is on highlighting the challenge that organizations, including higher education institutions, face in bringing about foundational change if transrelational leadership is to be embraced. Most large organizations seek to reproduce the status quo via a Human Resource Management (HRM) department. Simply defined, human resource management refers to the policies, practices and systems that influence employees' behaviour, attitudes and performance. Invariably, these outcomes are overseen by an HRM department charged with the responsibility to ensure that not only the implementation of the desired policies, practices and systems but also the required employee commitment to these is maintained. Hence, this chapter argues that a change to transformational leadership in higher education requires a simultaneous refinement in the focus of HRM. To this end, the growing awareness within HRM of the concept of 'corporate socially responsible' (CSR) organizations is described and aligned with the nature and practices of transformational leadership.

Chapter 8   Learning for future leadership

This chapter provides description and data from a research project that sought to develop a transrelational way of understanding the nature and practice of leadership to a group of aspiring leaders in a New Zealand university. Undoubtedly higher education institutions are concerned about leadership and are inclined towards improving its practice. However, most promotion within higher education is more aligned to professional outputs and outcomes in one's field of study. Hence, academics often come to be appointed to a formal leadership role without any specific knowledge and understanding of leadership theory and practice. Thus, this chapter describes some of the experiences of a number of prospective future higher education leaders, following the conclusion of their comprehensive transrelational leadership-learning programme. In this way, this chapter provides a critique of the challenges associated with trying to change approaches to leadership in higher education.

Conclusion   What might tomorrow bring?

This final chapter provides not only a summative review of the nature and practice of transrelational leadership within the context of higher education but also a critique of its possible adoption. As such, this chapter highlights the perceived benefits, as well as the likely challenges, for higher education institutions that might seek to introduce this new form of leadership. In conclusion, the chapter raises concerns about whether or not higher education actually has a choice in this regard. It emphasizes the need for not only the essential place of leadership-learning programmes for aspiring leaders in higher education but also that such programmes must be founded upon the conceptualization of leadership as fundamentally transrelational.

1

Organizational Culture: Recognizing its Invisible Force

Abstract

This chapter elaborates on the understanding raised in the Introduction that leadership and organizational culture are inextricably entwined. As previously stated, leadership influences the culture while, simultaneously, the culture influences leadership. The aim of this chapter is to clearly show how this is so very true in higher education institutions. Thus, while the Introduction described the universally well-documented concerns about the nature and practice of leadership in higher education, this chapter presents and discusses research literature that highlights more specifically the impact of managerialism on organizational culture/s of higher education, as experienced by middle leaders.

The chapter begins with a discussion of the nature and function of organizational culture. This provides the backdrop to the presentation of literature that acknowledges the importance of considering the organizational culture of higher education and, in some instances, recognizes the need to articulate arguments for it to change and become more relevant to the twenty-first century. It is notable that little attention is given within this literature to what changes in organizational culture mean for leadership, in terms of the role of leadership in facilitating changes and how leadership is best enacted in the new culture. In other words, the call is for the culture to change but for that change to occur amid an unchanged conceptualization of leadership and 'status quo' in leadership practices. Hence, current business research is referenced to emphasize the serious inadequacy of this oversight.

Finally, the chapter moves to specific research literature detailing the constraining issues in the organizational culture of higher education, deemed to arise directly from the application of managerialism. This literature credits the extensive adoption of managerialism for producing numerous unsatisfactory cultural norms and expectations. Thus, the point is made that higher education needs to establish its own best leadership practice rather than uncritically adopt practices that are recognized as unsuccessful in the very field in which they were established and furthermore, are producing outcomes that are, at best, conflicting with or, worse, perverting the core business of higher education institutions.

Introduction

Sadly, too many managerially inclined 'leaders' in higher education mistakenly adopt the simplistic understanding of organizational culture where it is thought of as 'how we do things around here'. Not only is such a simplistic view misleading, it is also misguiding. First, it is misleading because it suggests that organizational culture is only about behaviours and how people come to act in some uniform way within an organization. If organizational culture is only about behaviours then it is simple to manage, control and manipulate. A 'leader' with this simple understanding of organizational culture would hold the erroneous view that they can readily adapt the organizational culture to suit their own needs by simply mandating behavioural and performance expectations and institute aligned policies in the belief that the desired practical outcomes will be readily achieved. For persons holding a leadership position in higher education, this simplistic understanding of organizational culture is a sure recipe for failure both for their own leadership practice and for the success of the organization.

In addition, this view of organizational culture implies that culture can be described by a single characteristic; for example, 'We have a culture of bullying'. However, the reality is that an organization is a conglomerate of multiple sub-cultures that may or may not be aligned. Sub-cultures exist wherever a group of people interact regularly around a common purpose, and hence, sub-cultures exist across an organization. Schein (2010: 58–63) further identifies that every organizational culture has three competing functional sub-cultures that need to be in balance: (1) operator sub-culture with a basic assumption of 'we are the critical resource; we run the place'; (2) engineering sub-culture with a basic assumption 'that an ideal world is one of elegant machines and processes working in perfect precision and harmony without human intervention'; and (3) executive sub-culture with a basic assumption that 'financial survival is equivalent to perpetual war with competitors, and the economic environment is perpetually competitive and potentially hostile'.

A far more insightful understanding of organizational culture is that provided by Dr Linda Ford (2008: n.p.), where she described it as 'the invisible force that gently nudges you into compliance with how we do things around here'. Specifically, this description of organizational culture provides three initial important insights. First, the use of 'nudge' indicates a subtle influence and signals that the person has a choice about whether or not to adopt particular cultural norms and behaviours. There is no suggestion that culture mandates a person's behaviour or has the potential to do so. This awareness is reflected in our everyday experiences where we are regularly in touch with individuals, whose character, personality, dress sense or lifestyle is idiosyncratically distinctive, if not countercultural. However, by and large most people choose to comply with many cultural norms because it helps them to know how to 'fit in', to be accepted and to suitably contribute, and, thereby, to feel (more) safe and secure. Culture provides a person with the patterns of thinking and behaving that are widely accepted and practised within a particular group of people and which they are implicitly and explicitly encouraged to adopt and apply, if they wish to become, and be recognized and accepted as, a member of the group. Ford also described the organizational culture as 'invisible', which clearly distinguishes that its foundations extend beyond visible behaviours. From this perspective, culture promotes and effectively legitimates particular behaviours. This means that if we wish to understand a culture then it is essential to know what lies behind, generates and encourages observable behaviours and, simultaneously, discourages and does not legitimate other behaviours.

Finally, Ford describes this influence as a 'force', which again can be related to our everyday experiences, in which our lives are influenced by physical forces (such as strong winds or flowing water), and social and cultural forces, including parental expectations, peer pressure and notions of 'professional responsibility'. Variously these forces mean that we do things even if we would prefer not to. Experiences have also taught us that at times different forces can be in competition with each other and present us with challenges and dilemmas. Furthermore, competing forces are likely to arise or be accentuated during times of organizational, social, political and/or technological change, where an individual member of the group might challenge the group's 'norms' and thereby, generate tension within the group (see Chapter 5). In addition, these experiences have also shown that we can pretend to conform to a force while in reality resisting it. Employees can, for example, publicly say that they will adopt performance changes, but privately superficially engage with or avoid such changes whenever possible.

The position reflected in our work is that leaders must fully understand the nature and workings of the multiple sub-cultures 'at play', within organizations and prospectively impacting on them, including the sub-cultures leaders belong to themselves. Further, leaders need to be continually monitoring and adjusting the alignment of various sub-cultures to the organization's strategic intentions and priorities. To do this a leader must be able to identify the visible indicators of culture, ascertain if the antecedents are those that are desired and be prepared to respond to tensions arising. Leaders must acknowledge that there are many potential cultural forces at play besides those that they personally endeavour to create. Hence, we reiterate Schein's (2004) claim that the only really important task for leaders is to create and manage culture. This means that if the leader does not understand the nature and foundations of their organization's culture, other internal or external forces will create a culture that may well be organizationally unhelpful or even destructive. In addition, if the leader does not attend to the key foundational elements of sub-cultures in a suitable manner, then their influence upon them will be negligible. In this situation, instead of supporting the achievement of the strategic plan, these sub-cultures may nurture resistance to its achievement. Work to actively foster and sustain the alignment of sub-cultures with the organizational values and behaviours that reflect the desired strategic intent and priorities, therefore, needs to be at the core of leadership. Leaders cannot effectively embark on such work if they do not understand the foundations of culture.

The foundations of organizational culture

According to Schein (2004: 17), the culture of an organization, or more explicitly, as noted, its collection of sub-cultures (referred to hereafter simply as organizational culture), can be defined as 'a pattern of shared basic assumptions that was learned by [the] group as it solved its problems of external adaptation and internal integration, that has worked well enough to be considered valid and, therefore, to be taught to new members as the correct way to perceive, think, and feel in relation to those problems'. Moreover, these assumptions are formed out of a system of values and ways of thinking that permeate across the organization and through interactions among the people, the structures and the organizational systems, and ultimately shape what come to be recognized and accepted as behavioural norms (Abbasi and Zamani-Miandashti 2013). Culture spreads via norms formed from these assumptions, and the approval or disapproval attached to these expectations. Norms provide order and meaning to ambiguous or uncertain organizational situations, thereby providing standards of performance against which individuals can evaluate the appropriateness of behaviour (Hogan and Coote 2014).

More explicitly, Daft (2010) explains how culture exists at two levels. At the visible level are artefacts and observable behaviours – the degree to which people are engaged in their work, the processes by which people are affirmed and promoted, the opportunities people have to contribute to meeting agendas and discussions, the ways people dress and act, the type of control systems and power structures used by the organization, and the symbols, stories and ceremonies that organization members share. As O'Mahoney, Barnett and Matthews (2006) explain, verbal symbols are comprised of myths, legends, stories, slogans, creeds, jokes, rumours and names. Action symbols include ceremonies, rituals, celebrations and rites of passage. Such action symbols reveal what is considered to be important in the organization, and can symbolically convey desired organizational values and norms. Rituals celebrating successful events, such as an award ceremony or the success of a new strategy, reinforce the importance of expected behaviours and performance standards (Hogan and Coote 2014). Rituals have the potential to affirm and communicate to each organizational member in a more tangible and visible way an organization's underlying values and norms. Material symbols can be vision and mission statements, mottoes, logos, administrative hierarchy, role status, branding, awards, pins or flags. Together these symbols function in descriptive, purpose-controlling and system maintenance capacities. Symbols as descriptors provide an expression of the organization. In their purpose-controlling capacity, they either inspire or demotivate people within an organization.

However, as Daft (2010) goes on to add, these visible elements of culture are a reflection of deeper non-visible antecedents, which reside in the minds of each organization member. These are the underlying values, assumptions, beliefs and thought processes that operate unconsciously to define the true culture. Although not directly observable, values provide a powerful influence on beliefs, assumptions and resultant observable behaviours (Branson 2009). Thus the importance of values is to act as social principles or philosophies that guide behaviours and set standards and expectations for organizational routines and practices. For example, espoused values successfully communicated and modelled by senior leaders can greatly assist a proposed innovation by encouraging the take up of expected behaviours within the organization's culture. In this way, values can provide a subtle mechanism through which the leader can exercise influence. By emphasizing certain values, and by building corresponding norms for expected behaviours, leaders can begin to build an organizational culture that has a powerful and compelling influence on each employee's behaviour.

However, because values reside in people and not in the organization, desired organizational values mean nothing unless a majority of the people working in the organization willingly adopt and live by each and every one of the desired values. The 'critical mass' of adopters is crucial in efforts to foster cultural change. 'Take up' or 'buy in', however, depends on personal values. The personal choices humans make in life are dependent upon their personal values and not, necessarily, on the values promoted by others (Branson 2010). Personal values are seen as the importance or worth we attach to particular activities, objects or outcomes. They are principles and standards that we consider worthwhile and intrinsically desirable. They are, therefore, conceptions of what is ultimately good, proper or desirable in our life. Personal values are our individually selected preferences for achieving success, and influence our behaviour in every aspect of our daily activities. More particularly, Heifetz and Linsky (2002: 27) provide the insight that 'habits, values, and attitudes, even dysfunctional ones, are part of one's identity. To change the way people see and do things is to challenge how they define themselves.' It is not surprising then for these authors to add that 'you appear dangerous to people when you question their values, beliefs, or habits of a lifetime. You place yourself on the line when you tell people what they need to hear rather than what they want to hear. Although you may see with clarity and passion a promising future of progress and gain, people will see with equal passion the losses you are asking them to sustain' (Heifetz and Linsky 2002: 12).

Hence, where there is dissonance between an individual's personal values and those promoted in the organization by its leader, cultural fragmentation can occur. As described by Kujala, Lehtimäki and Pučetaite (2016), this form of cultural fragmentation can be defined as a lack of congruence or divergence in the values and goals between leadership and employees that can ultimately result in low commitment to the organization, low work ethics and/or alienation to work, scepticism towards the organizational vision and strategy, verbal conflicts, distrust and absenteeism. Moreover, studies have shown that this fragmentation may follow from, for instance, an economic reform and demographic diversity of employees (Liu 2003), organizational growth and decentralization (McPeak 2001) and privatization (Tyrall 2005). The downside of fragmentation is that it can prevent organizational learning (Senge and Kim 2012), retard timely decision-making and stall the taking of appropriate action in response to perceived deficiencies. Thus, academic researchers and writers have coined the term 'toxic cultures' for organizations in which the cultural fragmentation is so endemic that the people sense there is a lack of a clear purpose, the accepted norms are reinforcing ineffective performances, individuals are being singularly blamed for organizational underperformance, collegiality and collaboration are discouraged, and hostile interpersonal relationships are ignored. These are outcomes that no leader would ever deliberately set out to achieve but these are, nevertheless, realistic outcomes, albeit the worst-case scenario. If the leader overlooks or avoids considering how their leadership is influencing, and being influenced by, the culture then it is quite likely that the culture is heading somewhere along the path towards some or all of these outcomes.

Exploring higher education culture

In 1998, at a time when many influential political and corporate figures around the world were urging higher education institutions to adopt managerial practices, Jean Lipman-blumen, professor of public policy at the Peter F. Drucker Graduate School of Management, advanced her view that 'the time has come for business organizations to take a few lessons from universities, rather than the other way round' (1998: 49). While recognizing the importance of consolidating fiscal responsible processes under ever-increasing national economic constraints, Professor Lipman-blumen expressed concern that the call to operate more like 'for-profit' businesses was being taken far too seriously in higher education and that 'no organization lives by finances alone. Without effective leadership, all organizations eventually flounder' (1998: 49). Indeed, she raised the very important question of, 'Beyond financial considerations, why should universities try to follow the command-and-control model of traditional business leadership, especially when such leaders are faltering seriously?' (1998: 49). Regrettably, these insightful and prophetic words have not had the telling effect that they deserved.

The remainder of this chapter provides research literature in support of Professor Lipman-blumen's key points from her article, 'Connective Leadership: What business needs to learn from Academe'. Below, literature associated with research into the effects of managerialism upon the culture of higher education is explored. Then attention turns to corporate literature that highlights the growing chorus urging businesses to jettison managerialism due to its ineffectiveness in creating an organizational culture that can sustain success in today's highly competitive and complex corporate world. The final section of this chapter returns to Professor Lipman-blumen's article to briefly explore her reason for defending the culture of higher education against that offered by business managerialism. Here the view offered in this text is that the significantly distinctive cultural characteristics, she claimed to be widely existing in higher education in the form of *connective leadership*, now either only tenuously exist or only sparsely exist because they have since been universally overwhelmed by managerialism. The chapter concludes with the argument that Professor Lipman-blumen's stance was absolutely correct, but because the concept of *connective leadership* was not widely understood, its power to counter the theoretical and practical pressures from managerialism was weakened. This text's comprehensive description of the nature and practice of transrelational leadership embraces and extends connective leadership and, thereby, makes Professor Lipman-blumen's precepts and principles far more defensible, achievable and resistant.

The cultural effects of managerialism on higher education

According to Schein (2010), leadership and culture are two sides of the same coin, because authority relationships are a primary dimension of culture. Therefore, the effect of managerialism on the culture of departments or faculties has the potential to disrupt productivity if the culture is at odds with a managerialist approach. The functionality of a culture depends on the culture but also on the relationship of the culture to the environment in which it exists (Schein 2010). Hence, Vincent's (2011: 332) deepest concern with the inculcation of managerialism into higher education is its unchallenged ideological suitability and acceptability whereby it 'forms an unquestioned backdrop to policy'. As argued by Vincent, this application of managerialism has two highly questionable ideological characteristics. First, it invokes the assumption among its proponents that it provides a 'better' form of all-encompassing leadership and not just for the aspect of leadership. Thereby, it moves from the pragmatic to the zealous – from having a specific practical benefit in a given application to being the source of all truth and reality in every context. At the same time, it has gained the reputation of being more the 'common sense' approach to leadership in an economically influenced globalized world. Furthermore, as Vincent (2011: 332) adds, 'Such ideologically driven "common sense" usually invokes obfuscatory binaries,' whereby an alternative view to the realistic 'common sense' view is deemed to be an ideology that is treated with derision because it ignores the needs of the hard economic realities of our time. The notion of 'the hard economic realities' itself reflects an ideology that has been subsumed into an unquestioned world view espoused in many organizational contexts. Thus, this 'common sense' view of managerialism of higher education leadership promotes an organizational-cultural fable that it is the only proper form of leadership appropriate for our economic environment while, simultaneously, implicitly condemning any other form of leadership as being ineffective, if not irresponsible. In this way, managerialism moves from being an ideology to a hegemony because 'it masquerades as the only acceptable reality and pervades deeply into human lives, being largely unquestioned' (Vincent 2011: 333). Indeed, this concern is compounded by the application of managerialism outside of the specific environment in which it originated – the corporate world – because those applying it in higher education are seemingly unaware of the growing chorus of corporate literature, describing disillusionment with its incapacity to provide adequate leadership in today's complex and highly competitive business world.

Middlehurst, Kennie and Woodfield (2010) extend this ideological discussion of the application of managerialism to question its very foundational assumption in which the higher education institution is conceived as an organization. For these authors, it was far too simplistic and convenient to first assume that the higher education institution could be seen as a singular, unified whole and, thus, homogenized into being an organization like a car-making factory or a banking firm. Once such a false assumption was made, it then became a mere but misguided step to argue that the higher education institution can be run via managerialism just like every other organization. But, as described by Middlehurst and colleagues, higher education institutions were traditionally a community of scholars working towards diverse and varied personal and professional goals rather than a united body of people working to produce a common product. In this sense, higher education institutions are sites of 'organized anarchy' and not, unlike that of true organizations, places of varied but aligned work practices that come together to produce a particular tangible product. Producing knowledge is not the same as making a car. No one would wish to buy a car from a factory in which each person on the assembly line in a car-making factory made their part and assembled it in their own personalized way. Here, the application of some form of organization makes complete sense. But in a knowledge-creating institution, how, when and why knowledge is created is a very personally and disciplinarily idiosyncratic process, and one that defies prescriptive expectations and accountabilities.

More specifically, this practice of homogenizing the higher education culture in order to treat it like any other corporate organization is widely condemned for how it impacts upon the basic professional identity of the academic worker so as to undermine the core business of the institution (Brown and Humphreys 2006; Foreman and Whetten 2002; Shore 2010; Winter 2009). As Nixon (2006: 7) profoundly writes, 'A consequence of the changing conditions is that the occupation of the [higher education] teacher no longer automatically offers autonomy and status. Since autonomy and status have been defining characteristics of occupations that lay claim to being professions, these changes have occasioned a serious debate as to what kind of occupational group, or groups, [higher education] teachers now constitute.' Traditionally, the higher education teacher's sense of professional identity has arisen out of their personal commitment to their discipline rather than to their particular institution. Moreover, the institution nurtured their commitment to their discipline by providing an environment and certain resources that encouraged and supported but not, to any great degree, controlled or manipulated the way that they chose to work. In this way, the higher education teacher had the autonomy to pursue commitment to their chosen discipline in their own preferred way and, as a result, they gained professional status in accordance with their level of contribution, as did their particular employing institution.

In this era of managerialism, in which the business model of leadership predominates, the 'market' competitiveness and income-generating mechanisms of the university take precedence and re-frame academic work. Hence, the institution's strategy, policy and performance processes are singularly directed towards striving to meet these economic outcomes (Villa 2012). In this way, teaching loads are increased to generate more income, research priorities are predetermined around external grant sources, publication outputs are controlled according to relative contribution to international rankings, discipline reputations are hierarchically categorized according to public opinion and political preferences, and faculties are run like factories. The academic now feels like a cog in a machine that is expected to be continually churning out repetitive, predictable, largely mundane professional outputs for a seemingly predetermined, distant world. This is a far cry from research and scholarship being regarded as a unique, individualistic source of new knowledge, which produces a personal sense of meaning and purpose through a tangible sense of helping to create a better world. The shift in both the expected outcomes and the systems that they relate to also highlights the emotional response of higher education academics sensing the loss of a highly valued cultural characteristic – academic freedom. As Ayers (2014: 99) explains, 'Today's [higher education institution] is a unique conjuncture in which discourses of strategy, efficiency, and managerial control meet a deeply sedimented culture of professional autonomy, academic freedom, and deliberative decision-making.' While managerialism strives to create a more unified, distinctive, coalesced, whole institution that can be then considered a single organization under centralized control, these very same practices have been the instrument of fragmentation, disunity and derision because these have brought conflicting values and contrasting philosophical beliefs about what constitutes best practice (Giroux, Karmis and Rouillard 2015; Henkel 2005; Mok 2013) to the fore. When the balance between the designated leader's desired managerialist beliefs and principles and a particular group's way of behaving/working within an organization is out of kilter, the result is the total undermining of people's ability to do their work in an engaged and purposeful way. The organization's culture comes to feel like a war-zone as the designated leader and the group feel as though they are essentially under attack. The array of causes for this unwanted outcome is summarized in Table 1.1. Here it can be seen how a designated leader's managerialist beliefs and principles are largely devoid of any consideration for the personal needs of those they are meant to be leading. They are managing and not leading, which is resented by those being led.

Consequently, fewer academics, particularly the more experienced who occupy higher levels of academic appointments, feel any strong sense of attachment to the institution or even their faculty of department. The influence of institution-wide policies and processes are minimized or ignored where possible, attendance at formal meetings is irregular, willingness to assume additional administrative roles and responsibilities is dwindling, and interpersonal respect for those in formal leadership positions is drastically

Table 1.1 Beliefs and principles of a managerialist leader

Financial focus	• Without financial survival and growth, there are no returns to shareholders or to society. • Financial survival is equivalent to perpetual war with competitors.
Self-image: the embattled lone hero	• The economic environment is perpetually competitive and potentially hostile. • In a war, you cannot trust anyone. Therefore, the CEO must be 'the lone hero', isolated and alone, yet appearing to be omniscient, in total control, and feeling indispensable. • You cannot get reliable data from your subordinates as they will tell you what they think you want to hear; therefore, the CEO must trust his or her own judgement more and more (i.e., lack of accurate feedback increases the leader's sense of rightness and omniscience). • Organization and management are intrinsically hierarchical; the hierarchy is the measure of status and success and the primary means of maintaining control. • Though people are necessary, they are a necessary evil not an intrinsic value; people are a resource like other resources to be acquired and managed, not ends in themselves. • The well-oiled machine organization does not need whole people, only the activities they are contracted for.

Source: (Schein 2010: 63)

diminished. Rather than uniting the institution, managerialism is dividing and nullifying the organizational culture of higher education. As claimed by Weinberg and Graham-Smith (2012: 74), what has now become endemic in the culture of higher education 'is the critical loss of agency experienced by the teachers and researchers themselves. Formerly self-empowered as a practitioner of knowledge and an authority in the discipline, and in the running of the [institution], the practising academic has been relegated to the role of a mere functionary in a system whose core principles are essentially uncollegial.'

Within such a perceived misaligned cultural reality, it is highly likely that other issues are 'tarnished with the same brush'. That is to say, managerialism is rightly or wrongly associated with causing a number of other important cultural concerns as well. For example, there is research (see, for example, Chandler, Barry and Clark 2002; Fredman and Doughney 2012; Smeenk et al. 2009; Szekeres 2007) that managerialism greatly increases the wear and tear of higher education researchers, teachers and professional assistants because of its attention on increasing workloads. Others researchers (see, for example, Lafferty and Fleming 2000; Madsen, Longman and Daniels 2011; Nixon 2012) argue that the loss of the collegial form of higher education administration with the advent of managerialism has undermined the effective implementation of equal employment opportunity initiatives, such that women continue to remain in the lowest paid and least secure positions within these institutions. Finally, Nixon (2012) and Lynch (2014) describe how the manner by which managerialism prioritizes mechanisms within the culture that aid the institution's international ranking not only abrogates the importance of other roles and responsibilities of equal or greater value, but can also encourage unethical assumptions and practices. This later concern acknowledges that some academics can feel the pressure to lower academic standards in order to increase pass rates, or to self-plagiarize across multiple journal articles in order to increase publication outputs, or to ignore cheating among students to ensure higher student satis-faction ratings.

As noted earlier in this chapter, the justification for the adoption of managerialism to guide leadership practice in higher education institutions is the fundamental assumption that managerialism has proven success in the corporate world. Moreover, the explicit inherent ideology is that it is the best form of leadership because it is more closely aligned with the economic imperatives of today's globalized world. The implicit ideology is that any other form of leadership in such an economically dominated world is inherently deficient and should be immediately condemned. By presenting corporate literature that unequivocally challenges the effectiveness of managerialism in today's complex and highly competitive business world, the following section challenges these assumptions and ideologies, and therefore the unquestioned devotion to managerialism and the simultaneous discounting of any alternative form of leadership.

Corporate concerns with managerialism

A dire warning from within the corporate world that highlights the importance of recognizing the unequivocal link between organizational leadership and culture is found in Katzenbach et al. (2010: 113) research, which found that 'too often a company's strategy, imposed from above, is at odds with the ingrained practices and attitudes of its culture. Executives may underestimate how much a strategy's effectiveness depends on cultural alignment. **Culture trumps strategy every time.**' The previous discussion of concerns in higher education caused by the application of managerialism points to a serious mismatch between leadership strategies and organizational culture. This being so, Katzenbach and colleagues suggest that a managerialist model of leadership will never succeed in achieving its aims because it will be trumped by the culture; a significant number of people within the institution will continually strive to nullify its full effect. In other words, regardless of the beliefs of those who support and apply it, managerialism in higher education will never live up to its presumed promise. It is doomed to fail.

Be that as it may, there is also a growing body of corporate literature undermining the very foundations of managerialism. For example, in their Harvard Business Review article (2016: 48), Reeves, Levin and Ueda posit that while most companies are now operating in far more complex, competitive, diverse, dynamic and interconnected environments than ever before, 'many firms still pursue classic approaches to strategy that were designed for more stable times, emphasizing analysis and planning focused on maximizing short-term performance rather than long-term robustness'. Similarly, Hamel (2007: 6) poignantly illustrates how outdated, and thus ineffective, much of managerialism is when he describes its origins by saying that most of the essential tools and techniques of modern management were invented by individuals born in the nineteenth century, not long after the end of the American Civil War. Those intrepid pioneers developed standardized job descriptions and work methods. They invented protocols for production planning and scheduling. They mastered the intricacies of cost accounting and profits analysis. They instituted exception-based reporting and developed detailed financial controls. They devised incentive-based compensation schemes and set up personnel departments. They created sophisticated tools for capital budgeting and, by 1930, had also designed a basic architecture of the multi-divisional organization and enumerated the principles of brand management. Certainly these strategies, in company with the scientific management techniques of Frederick Winslow Taylor, brought much corporate success in the first half of last century, but this was a very different business world. As Einstein claimed, 'You cannot solve tomorrow's problems with yesterday's solutions'.

Hence, it is far from surprising that data from Gallup's worldwide employee engagement research indicates that only 13 per cent of employees are actively engaged in their workplace (see Chapter 6 for a more in-depth discussion), while over 50 per cent merely go through the motions of being fully engaged, and the rest are actively disengaged whereby they act out their discontent in counterproductive ways. For Kim and Mauborgne (2014), the solution to this unsustainable worldwide issue of employee non-engagement is what they refer to as 'Blue Ocean Leadership', with its underlying insight that leadership, in essence, must be thought of as a service. More specifically, they argue that the business leader should treat those they lead in the very same way that they would treat their customers. The leader should create the organizational conditions in which those they are leading want to 'buy' their leadership. 'When people value your leadership practices, they in effect buy your leadership. They're inspired to excel and act with commitment. But when employees don't buy your leadership, they disengage, becoming noncustomers of your leadership' (Kim and Mauborgne 2014: 62). Clearly, many who work in higher education today aren't 'buying' managerialism. According to Rigby, Sutherland and Takeuchi (2016: 42), today's organizational employees are looking for leaders who are far more flexible, inclusive, transparent and strategically agile. They want leaders whose methodologies 'involve new values, principles, practices, and benefits and are a radical alternative to command-and-control-style management'.

Thus in the corporate world it is recognized that organizational culture can be both an asset and an encumbrance for a business and that the actions of the leader play a large part in which of these outcomes are realized. Indeed, incorrectly led or totally ignored organizational culture will generate dysfunction or, as described in many research articles, 'toxic' organizational culture (Frost 2003; Goldman 2008; Kellerman 2004; Padilla, Hogan and Kaiser 2007; Riley 2015). Riley (2015: 3) defines a toxic organizational culture as 'one that creates an environment that can damage the emotional, physical or financial well-being of employees, customers and those associated with that organisation'. Although it is true that employees can become strong contributors to the formation of a toxic culture, given the focus of this text on leadership, our attention is on the way in which a leader can contribute to the formation of a dysfunctional or toxic culture. To this end, the summary from research provided by Riley (2015) of the common symptoms of a toxic organizational culture is insightful:

1. **Ineffective leadership** – many in the organization do not support strategy, direction or policies.
2. **Double standards by leaders** – those in formal leadership roles do not model expected behaviours.
3. **Transactional, authoritarian or bullying leadership** – performance compliance underpinned by a culture of obedience, subservience or fear.

4. **Closed mindset** – presumption that those in leadership roles have all the answers.

5. **Lack of transparency** – descriptions by leaders of the organization's reality does not match that in the minds of the followers.

6. **Dishonesty and unethical behaviour** – decisions by leaders appear to be more to do with self-interest rather than common good.

7. **Inflexible change strategies** – repetitive ineffective change strategies that stifle localized innovation and creativity.

8. **Us/them mentality** – little authentic interpersonal interaction between leaders and followers.

9. **Exclusivity** – input into strategic planning is devoid of grass-root experiences and perceptions.

10. **Security and support** – position disestablishment seems an ever-present reality and there is little organizational support for up-skilling and workplace knowledge enhancement.

Arguably, some or all of these symptoms are presumed to have surfaced in the culture of higher education as outcomes of managerialism, which has prompted a number of authors to promote alternative forms of leadership. Some of these are now presented and a common feature of them is highlighted for future elaboration.

Cultural insights for a better form of higher education leadership

This chapter began with reference to the views of Professor Jean Lipman-blumen who argues that the business world needs to learn how to use a better form of leadership, which she referred to as *connective leadership*. More specifically, she posits the presence of two fundamental requirements to be at the heart of such leadership. First, a connective leader must share decision-making with their colleagues. Higher education leaders 'must engage faculty [members] in the governance of their institutions, primarily through plenary faculty groups, committees, and task forces' (Lipman-blumen 1998: 50). These must be opportunities for the making of authentic contributions to the decision-making processes and not, as is currently commonly experienced, menial rubber-stamping invocations. Where there is true dialogue, open conversations, acceptance of divergent opinions and a common commitment to respectful and honest discussion is also 'where the culture, values, and norms of the institution are forcefully articulated, debated, and honed', without any need for edicts, policies or accountabilities to be mentioned. The second fundamental requirement of a connective leader is to reach out to those they are leading, to treat them as co-leaders, and entrust them to share burdens and enhance the leader's vision. This involves the leader being inclusive and flexible, acknowledging their own limitations, seeing strength and wisdom in others, and being willing to be guided by those who know more or can do things better. It is about providing a way in which everyone can feel a tangible commitment towards ensuring the success and sustainability of the institution. According to Lipman-blumen, connective leaders understand the connections between individual creativity and initiative, each person's desire for meaningful employment, and the potential barriers that can be created by organizational structures and procedures, and they strive to promote the most beneficial balance for all across each of these.

Rather than seeking connectivity, Burnes, Wend and By (2014) urge today's higher education leaders to reinvent collegiality in order to redress the suppressive outcomes generated by managerialism. As described by these authors, it is a form of collegiality 'which seeks to marry the need for central decision-making with local involvement in and control over the change process' (Burnes, Wend and By 2014: 920). This view acknowledges the fluidity of life in today's higher education institutions in which something very significant within the culture is changing. Thus, the experience of change is the constant cultural ingredient, along with the experience of change leadership, and it is this latter characteristic that is raised as the critical determinant of how the culture and its leadership is seen and respected. Too often, according to Burnes et al. the poor leadership of change is experienced, which means that respect for the leadership, generally, is greatly diminished. Hence, they urge higher education leaders to become more flexible and less top–down in their approach to change leadership. A more collegial approach would require the senior leaders to work with staff to develop a 'commonly understood strategic intent' (2014: 920), thereby enabling a more effective way of implementing decisions while, simultaneously, helping all staff to feel far more meaningfully involved in the running and development of their departments and the institution.

Shattock (2010) and Gray (2008) share this same belief that it is by enhancing collegiality and collaboration within the culture of higher education institutions that the ills of managerialism can be overcome. In our current era of complex, unpredictable and incomparable organizational challenges, it is creativity and imagination that is desperately required. Creativity and imagination is suppressed in a culture overseen by managerialism. Burgan (2006: 108) writes that

> sophisticated, independent minded and highly trained workers require modes of participation within organisations if the benefits of their initiative and imagination are to be realised. Further, the complexity of the organisation requires more rather than less discussion from within. It is via collegiality and collaboration that creativity and imagination can blossom within the culture of higher education and, in this way, be used to the best advantage of individuals and the institution.

The role of the leader is to not only provide and model the vision that instils a commitment to collegiality and collaboration, but also to build connectivity across the institution by bringing together the right people with the necessary knowledge, skills and disposition to solve a problem or to create a new pathway, regardless of their relative levels or areas of employment.

Clearly, there is a very common element across all of this literature – the need for a much closer relationship between those in formal leadership positions in higher education and those they are leading – whether it is described as being connective, collegial or collaborative. The following chapter builds upon this foundation in order to describe and discuss the phenomenon of transrelational leadership. The remainder of the text then critiques the application of this form of leadership to the key challenges facing all organizations today, and particularly, those providing higher education service.

The Theoretical Foundations of Transrelational Leadership

Abstract

Picking up on the concerns raised in Chapter 1 relating to inadequate and ineffective leadership theory and practice, this chapter constructs a new theoretical foundation for leadership, which is referred to as 'transrelational' leadership. The basic leadership practices professed by Haslam, Reicher and Platow (2011) are used to describe leadership as essentially a transrelational phenomenon, and a detailed illustration is provided of how this understanding has been applied to higher education in a particular research context. Within the frame of transrelational leadership, the leader's focus is on the four fundamental leadership practices: being an authentic member of the group they are leading; championing the group; changing the groups' identity; and bringing the external relevant influences to the attention of the group. It is argued that these four practices enable the group to accept and endorse the person as their leader, which then allows this person to eclectically choose how best to lead from the various principles presented by each of the previous leadership theories.

Introduction

Before you can fix a problem you first must be able to see the problem for what it truly is. Then you must know how to fix the actual problem, and have the capacity and confidence to be able to move ahead with applying the solutions identified to effectively respond to and fix the problem. Despite the abundance of research and academic writing highlighting the issues, it seems that many higher education leaders either don't wish to see the problems now confronting their institutions, or simply don't know how to fix these problems, or don't feel they are able to fix them. This book removes the excuse that either the most serious problems facing higher education can't be seen for what they truly are, and/or that there is no known way to fix them even if the problems can be identified. To this end, the previous two chapters sought to identify and describe the most fundamental problems facing today's higher education institutions. Thus, these problems can now be seen for what they truly are. This chapter turns attention to the solutions. It comprehensively describes the form of leadership that can fix the problems that our experience and extensive literature indicate are undermining the essential core business of higher education institutions. More specifically, this chapter comprehensively describes why today's organizations (and in particular higher education institutions) require transrelational leadership, and explores in depth the nature and practice of transrelational leadership.

Making leadership the first priority

In his book, *The Seven Habits of Highly Effective People*, Steven Covey (1989) describes how our habits can be our undoing. If we think we are very good at doing something, then we try to apply this wherever we can, even when its effect is questionable if not unhelpful. Maslow (1966: 15) says, 'I suppose it is tempting, if the only tool you have is a hammer, to treat everything as if it were a nail.' Similarly, if you are a higher education leader but you see your strengths are in managing tasks, then you are very likely to try and apply managerial actions to every problem facing your institution. But managerial actions cannot fix the problems described in the previous chapters. Tightening performance review procedures won't fix staff disengagement. Decreasing staff numbers won't increase student enrolments. Increasing levels of bureaucracy won't improve organizational communication. Mandating staff on-campus attendance won't increase professional outputs. Applying stringent fiscal constraints won't make departments more professionally productive. Building modern facilities won't improve organizational morale. It is leadership, and not management, that is required.

A leader's devotion to enact managerial responses to perceived leadership problems is explained by Dr Carol Dweck (2006) in her book, *Mindset: The New Psychology of Success*, which is based on her research and teachings over the course of twenty years. Dweck describes how individuals can develop one of two mindsets – fixed or growth. Fundamentally, she has found that people with fixed mindsets believe qualities are 'set in stone' (2006: 6), whereas those with growth mindsets believe 'basic qualities are things you can cultivate through your efforts' (2006: 7). 'In one world – the world of fixed traits – success is about proving you're smart or talented. ... In the other – the world of changing qualities – it's about stretching yourself to learn something new' (2006: 15). Based on Dweck's extensive research, the nature of thinking and analysis that people with a fixed mindset engage in is characterized as 'static'. This leads them to have a desire to be in control and look smart. They therefore have a tendency to discount alternative views and avoid challenges, to quickly discount doing things differently because they see the effort as fruitless or impracticable. Hence, they ignore prospectively useful feedback, respond aggressively to dissent and feel threatened by the success of others. Essentially, people with a fixed mindset have a deterministic view of their world and seek technical solutions to problems. A fixed mindset is most suited to managerial roles. In contrast, Dweck describes how people with a growth mindset firmly believe that their thinking and analysing can be developed and hence, they have a keen desire to understand and learn. These people embrace new challenges despite any personal sense of uncertainty or lack of full understanding. Indeed, these individuals see the effort it might take to overcome their own limitations when dealing with a new challenge as a path to growth and mastery. As they are keen to overcome their personal limitations, growth mindset individuals seek to learn from alternative points of view, even criticism, and find lessons and inspiration from the success of others.

The contrasts in a leader's mindset that Dweck identifies play out in the nature of the organizational culture that the leader will foster. A leader's growth mindset generates an organizational culture that encourages creativity, ingenuity, initiative, divergent thinking and strategic risk-taking among employees, whereas a leader's fixed mindset generates a culture of repetitive, safe, predictable and career-harm minimization among employees. Hence, we argue that in today's complex, unpredictable, highly competitive and ever-changing higher education environment, it is a growth mindset that is required in leaders. Further, we propose that it is incumbent upon each and every higher education leader to work towards developing a growth mindset. Importantly, although Dweck presents her research in this dichotomous manner, she strongly argues that these are not naturalistic characteristics. Hence, there is the potential for each and every person to develop a preferred mindset. One of the things that our research has also highlighted, however, is that having the conditions to support and sustain a growth mindset is critical. This again directs us back to the key role of culture.

Overcoming past habits and convictions

One of the difficult challenges for a higher education leader wishing to break away from a fixed mindset habit of applying managerial solutions to leadership responsibilities is overcoming leadership convictions formed from certain past experiences. These leadership convictions are prospectively very misleading, yet likely to be powerful and embedded. They stem from past experiences of apparently successful leaders, of personally gaining high academic credibility, of managing a department and/or faculty, and of supposed leadership development programmes, among others. Trying to reproduce the leadership actions of another person, despite how successful these may have appeared to be, is, however, fraught with danger. We cannot presume that another person at a different site under different circumstances and at a later time can clone leadership actions previously employed at another particular site under different circumstances. Although we can observe, judge and interpret the leadership behaviours of another person, it is impossible to know everything that informed their behaviours, including the personal and professional facts, values, principles, attitudes, preferences and motives that influenced the person's choice of leadership behaviour. Trying to copy the leadership behaviour of another person can also easily cause confusion, uncertainty and self-doubt because the intended behaviour does not align with one's own values, principles, attitudes, preferences and motives. Even the essential objective facts necessitating the leadership behaviour are unlikely to be identical to those previously present when the leadership behaviour was first observed. Thus, it is essential to note that leadership is influenced both contextually and personally. Past experiences of apparently successful leadership performed by others provide limited guidance for being a successful leader in today's very different higher education world and with a prospectively very different group of people.

The second challenge for a leader wishing to break away from a fixed mindset habit of applying managerial solutions to leadership responsibilities is in being able to overcome certain personal beliefs formed from gaining high academic credibility. This is a very individualistic achievement that is founded upon some essential character traits, including self-direction, personal responsibility, self-interest, self-motivation, determination, self-satisfaction and single-mindedness. Invariably, a successful, highly credible academic would have learnt how to develop a point of view and then to stridently defend it if necessary. Largely, this is about firmly believing that your point of view is right and strongly resisting criticism. Also, the journey to achieving high credibility often involves essentially working and communicating with like-minded individuals or groups and on tasks that are relatively short-term focused. One's work mostly revolves around teaching, researching, publishing and presenting within a particular field of a given discipline. It is therefore natural that one's close colleagues and confidants are similarly placed. However, while this provides immense disciplinary confidence and capacity, whereby the person becomes highly regarded and recognized within the discipline, it is not explicitly leadership development. Regrettably, it is wrongly assumed that highly credible academics will automatically be successful higher education leaders. This assumption is based on a false understanding of leadership. Just because an academic might appear to be at the top, or ahead of others, in their academic field, this is a different interpretation of 'leading'. Indeed, many highly credible academics become very poor leaders because they are uncomfortable working with others from outside their field and discipline, and/or struggle to comprehend the influence of their actions on others. Regardless of their level of academic success, each and every person appointed to a leadership position in higher education should be provided with an opportunity to formally learn how to become a leader so that they can successfully lead others confidently and capably. In our experience, many leaders in higher education are denied this opportunity.

The third challenge for a leader wishing to break away from a fixed mindset habit of applying managerial solutions to leadership responsibilities is in being able to overcome convictions that are associated with a structural hierarchy and that are often developed while managing a department, school or faculty. It is easy for the faculty dean or the department head to assume that they are only a 'link in the administrative chain' and that they have little or no flexibility to do things differently. They assume they need to show reliability, responsibility, loyalty and compliance to their line managers and those in leadership positions above them. Such a view automatically induces management behaviours whereby they pursue controlling strategies that seek to produce predictability, stability and conflict avoidance. They strive to implement policies and procedures as smoothly and efficiently as possible. They endeavour to retell the institution's vision but in a somewhat matter-of-fact way, lacking personal passion and conviction, because it is a vision they have inherited rather than created. Interaction with those they are leading tends to be largely planned around formal meetings and transactional in nature, because they are ever mindful of being bound by imposed budgetary constraints, performance expectations and feel answerable to those above them who may not share their personal views. These higher education middle leaders are continually second guessing their actions and decisions – they want to be seen to be running their faculty or department efficiently and effectively in the eyes of their line manager and senior leaders. So their attention is more attuned to what those above them want than what those below them would wish for. Hence, they are managers, and not leaders, and yet they are the ones most likely to become future higher education 'leaders'. Sadly, many also think that they are leaders and struggle when things don't go as planned. Because they are managing and not leading, when things do go wrong the tendency is to revert to micromanagement and thus, implement the plans, policy, processes with an added level of detail and more strictly, without realizing that this usually only inflames the situation. The most common outcome from this managerial approach to being a dean or department head is a lack of authentic employee engagement and, thereby, diminished performance (see Chapter 6 for more specific details). To counter this probability, as previously noted, formal opportunities to learn to become a leader are essential to enable those appointed to middle leadership positions to have a chance of success and in order to go some way towards ensuring that all that is desired at an organizational level will be achieved.

The final challenge for a leader wishing to break away from a fixed mindset habit of applying managerial solutions to leadership responsibilities is in being able to overcome certain views gained from participating in certain formal leadership development programmes. Often, because there is no deep appreciation of what constitutes leadership and knowledge of how it is possible for a person to become the leader rather than simply being appointed as a leader, those who come to a higher education leadership role seek formal learning through masters of business administration (MBA) and similar courses. More concerning are those higher education institutions that provide this type of course but re-label it as a masters in higher education leadership. The intention of those higher education leaders who commit to these courses is laudable but misguided. Largely, these courses instil knowledge and skills more aligned to management and administration and much less to leadership. These courses focus more on financial, resourcing, legal and planning responsibilities, which are beneficial but limited. Without first knowing how to properly lead, a person who gains the knowledge and skills from these courses can prioritize these above those of working with the people they are leading, of shaping the culture, of affirming and inspiring others, of championing the vision, of listening to criticism and different points of view in order to gain a deeper awareness and understanding, and of gaining the trust and confidence of all those they are leading. These are the required leadership qualities for today's higher education institutions and these are the qualities that those who are appointed to leadership positions in higher education need to learn and apply. Today, completing an MBA-type course is not sufficient leadership development and will not address essential leadership learning.

Acknowledging the inherent limitations of management

In order to further appreciate why an MBA-type or management-based course is insufficient, it is necessary to recognize the historical limitations of management practices. Just as we would not want to be treated by doctors whose medical knowledge is almost 100 years out of date, or to be guided by lawyers whose legal knowledge is confined to early-twentieth-century law, why would we allow today's higher education institutions to be led by practices that were developed in the first half of last century? As indicated in Chapter 1, historical understandings have had and continue to have a profound influence on management practices. In his 1986 article, 'The Decline and Fall of Science in Educational Administration', Thomas Greenfield assigned responsibility for transforming the field of management to that which is still present today to the work of Herbert Simon and, in particular, the understandings, rules and guidelines he first published in his 1947 book, *Administrative Behavior*. In Greenfield's opinion, the essence of Simon's work was that 'it brought the force of science to buttress any claims that might be made about the nature of administration or about the best means for improving organizations and life within them' (1947: 58). As a result, organizational management practice became founded upon the presumed 'power, objectivity, and utility of science' whereby the only things of concern were those that could be objectified, measured and controlled. Organizational management became technical, clinical and objectively rational. Unfortunately, although science has moved a long way from its Newtonian fundamentals, which influenced Simon's premises, in order to embrace a far more abstract, non-measurable, connected and interdependent world as described by complexity theory, modern management theory and practice have not kept pace with it.

Margaret Wheatley (2006: 7) extends this understanding of the detrimental division of management theory from a contemporary scientific influence when she laments that

> each of us lives and works in organizations design from Newtonian images of the universe. We manage by separating things into parts, we believe that influence

occurs as a direct result of forces exerted from one person to another, we engage in complex planning for a world that we keep expecting to be predictable, and research continually for better methods of objectively measuring and perceiving that world.

Instead of the highly technical, clinical, objectively rationalistic world of outdated management, which treats people like 'cogs' in an organizational 'machine', Wheatley argues for the application of leadership as informed by our 'new science' of complexity theory and its associated understanding of complex adaptive systems. Instead of trying to explicitly define in order to control the functioning of the institution, today's higher education leader needs to realize that there is no objective reality of their institution waiting to reveal its secrets based on some historically founded managerial formula. 'There are no recipes or formulas, no checklists or expert advice that describes reality. If context is as crucial as the science explains, then nothing merely transfers; everything is always new and different and unique to each of us' (Wheatley 2006: 9). Rather, 'connectivity' becomes the most important organizational feature. For the leader, this means prioritizing relationships. In the subatomic world, things only exist in relationship to something else; interdependence is the fundamental key to continued existence. In the complex higher education world of today, successful leadership will only come from those who know how to create and sustain positive and mutually rewarding relationships.

The foundation of leadership for today's organizations

More and more leadership researchers and writers are embracing the view that leadership of today's organizations needs to be informed by the scientific principles associated with complexity theory, instead of Newtonian physics. For example, Avolio, Walumbwa and Weber (2009: 430) state that 'simply viewing the leader and follower in a simple exchange process won't fly in terms of explaining the full dynamics of leadership'. For Hazy, Goldstein and Lichtenstein (2007: 2), the application of complexity theory to the practice of leadership implies that 'leadership [is] enacted through any interaction in an organization ... leadership is an emergent phenomenon within complex systems'. More particularly, as described by Uhl-Bien et al. (2007), leadership is an interactive system of dynamic, unpredictable persons who interact with each other in complex feedback networks, which can then produce unexpected beneficial outcomes.

From this perspective, the key problems now facing higher education are not technical problems, but rather, adaptive challenges. While technical problems can be solved by previously prescribed knowledge and procedures, adaptive challenges are problems that require new learning, innovation, creative thinking and new patterns of behaviour. Adaptive challenges require exploration, new discoveries and cultural adjustments. Technical problems can be managed whereas adaptive challenges need leadership.

Given these observations, it is not surprising that contemporary leadership writers are beginning to emphasize relationships as the fundamental ingredient of authentic leadership. The previous chapter described how a number of higher education-focused writers, including Lipman-blumen (1998), Burnes, Wend and By (2014), Shattock (2010) and Gray (2008), have emphasized the importance of growing the relational capacity of today's higher education leaders for institutional sustainability and success. However, this view is shared far more universally than simply in the context of higher education. Although not widely acknowledged, this relational perspective of leadership does have a somewhat historical, yet very compelling, theoretical foundation. Burns' (1978: 11) seminal leadership theory encompassed the argument that the authentic authority of any leader is made manifest through relationships. According to Burns, 'The most powerful influences consist of deeply human relationships in which two or more persons *engage* with one another' and, thus, for a leader, the 'arena of power is no longer the exclusive preserve of a power elite or an establishment or persons clothed with legitimacy. Power is ubiquitous; it permeates human relationships' (Burns 1978: 15).

Sadly, Burns' dichotomous categorization of leadership as being either transactional or transformational attracted worldwide attention while his *a priori* view of the leader's relationships with those they are leading gained little attention. For the next thirty years or so leadership theorists strove to describe how leaders could transform those they were leading so as to be acknowledged as a transformational leader. Following the release of his 1978 text, the search for greater clarity and certainty about what constituted transformational leadership continued. Hence there has been a plethora of subsequent theories (e.g. servant, stewardship, moral, ethical, distributed, shared, instructional, authentic, to name but a few) that have sought to explain the nature and function of leadership. Importantly, each of these theories features a wish to ensure that the leader is more transformational by being less concerned with control and self-interest. Burns argued that once an employee felt more capable in doing work that is more meaningful to them, they will naturally perform their work more efficiently and effectively, and so do not require to be closely managed via the more controlling and directive transactional approach. In response, each subsequent theory endeavoured to show, in its particular way, how the leader was able to meet Burns' description of transformational leadership whereby the leader would not only concentrate on making the employees more knowledgeable and skilful about their work, but also to meet their need to be involved in personally meaningful work.

Despite the largely universal acceptance of the principle of transformational leadership, and the intended worthiness of each of its various incarnations (some of which are identified above), research data shows that few leaders feel able to confidently claim to be transformational. Although there are countless descriptions of its constituent characteristics, the theory does not appear to relate to the lived reality of leaders. Arguably, transformational leadership is best experienced in its written description than in any experience of practice. There are too many moments in the daily life of a leader where they feel compelled to act in a way that does not seem transformational and this undermines their confidence to categorize their leadership practice as such. Simply, the theory does not describe or fully guide the reality. Given this tangible disjunction between the theory and practice of leadership it is not surprising to see the popularity of management. Where leadership theory failed to provide coherent and comprehensive guidance to the person in a leadership role, management practices seemed to provide some practical and achievable ways forward. But, as previously explained, management practices, as the name indicates, only deal with those objective parts of reality that can be managed because these are able to be seen, isolated, measured and controlled. As a result, in those situations where leadership is most wanted, it is most likely that management is being applied. For Alvesson (1996), Alvesson and Sveningsson (2003), Avolio (2007), Avolio, Walumbwa and Weber (2009), Day et al. (2014), Dinh et al. (2014), Eacott (2015), Plowman et al. (2007), van Knippenberg and Sitkin (2013), Yukl (2012) and others, this seemingly incoherent and conflicted experience of leadership practice highlights the deficiency of our current leadership theory to adequately explain its true nature. According to Haslam, Reicher and Platow (2011), this deficiency arises from it being far too much about the leader, and what they should do, and not focusing enough on how to become and be a leader. Similarly, for quite some time Evers and Lakomski (2001, 2012) have argued that our leadership theory has been over influenced by an outdated view of scientific reasoning, one based upon logical, sequential and empirical rationalization and devoid of the ever-present and natural subjective and affective influences and, as a result, our theories of leadership do not match the experience of it. As indicated in our Introduction to this book, the challenges of leadership invariably occur in emotionally charged situations where feelings, beliefs and values – the foundations of subjectivity – play a powerful role. Hence, to ignore these ever-present and natural subjective and affective influences is to deny the reality of leadership. Furthermore, to suggest that these subjective and affective influences are only present during emotionally charged events is also to deny our human nature (Branson 2009). All behaviour is influenced, to a greater or lesser degree, by our subjective and affective inducements. This is particularly so in social situations where consideration of the impact of our behaviour upon others plays a critically important, and highly desirable, role. By definition, leadership is a social activity – you cannot be a leader without someone, or some others, to lead. Thus, subjectivity and affectivity are an undeniable integral aspect of leadership and, therefore, this must be reflected in our leadership theory.

What all this means is that leadership must be seen as being formed in, and resulting from, human relationships. Complexity science now acknowledges interrelationships as being the fundamental component of living organisms and leadership theory now acknowledges its erroneous oversight of the interrelational reality of leadership practice. Unequivocally, leadership is intrinsically a relational phenomenon. Logically then, the most important knowledge a leader can gain is in knowing how to become and be a leader in a relational sense. Knowing how to act as a leader, which has been the focus of much of our theorizing to date, is secondary. If you have not meaningfully become the leader of the group, then no amount of knowing how to act as a leader will turn you into the leader. As has been pointed out previously, being appointed to a position does not mean that you automatically become the leader. To think otherwise is the first step towards leadership failure. The next section describes what a person must know in order to be accepted and, thereby, become a leader.

Embracing the essential relational aspect of leadership

This section has two aims. First it describes in detail the characteristics of a relational leader as promoted by both complexity theory and relational theory. Secondly, it describes how it is possible for a person to authentically become a leader so that these characteristics are natural, and not spurious personal qualities and outcomes.

Complexity theory urges us to acknowledge the daily presence of surprise and emergence. Not only do unanticipated things regularly happen but also new ways of successfully dealing with these happenings can unexpectedly emerge. Moreover, no matter how determined we are to control our environment in order to maintain predictability and security, surprise and predicaments invariably arise. Hence, it is argued that today's leaders cannot totally prevail over an organization's internal environment or control future outcomes as traditional leadership research suggested. If leaders cannot control the organization's internal environment or predict and manipulate the future state of the external environment, they need to acknowledge and accept that this emerges from the interactions among people throughout the organization. Much more than what the leader might choose to do, it is the people in the organization who bring about what will happen in the organization. It is through the willing involvement of the people that the leader is able to enact their leadership. This is a contrary view to the common taken-for-granted, but misguided, belief that a person can immediately enact leadership in whatever way they wish once they are appointed to a leadership role. The formal acknowledgement of a person's public designation as a leader is also usually encapsulated in the belief that this person occupies a particularly important and essential role, which is distinguishable and discrete from that of those they are to lead. Moreover, the desired outcomes and expected actions of the role holder are often captured in a role statement to which the leader can be held accountable. Thus, both the establishment of the role and the description of the role promote a detached, line management view of the affiliation between the leader and those they are to lead.

Recent advances in sociology call into question these common assumptions associated with 'roles' and prefer to label these as 'positions' (Davies and Harré 1999; Harré and Moghaddam 2003; Harré and Slocum 2003). Seeing the responsibility of leadership as a role gives the impression that the nature of its enactment, and how others experience it, is the prerogative of the role holder and their line managers. In this sense, a role has the potential to be imposed. However, the reality of imposed roles rarely equates with the ideal. The natural tendency of those being led is to use whatever subtle or explicit means they can to cause the leader to modify their style of leadership to that of a more acceptable form. Hence, there are no real leadership roles, but rather, only negotiated leadership positions. In other words, in order to become a leader, the person must realize that the genesis of their leadership is in the everyday human interactions they have with each and every person they have the responsibility to be leading (Crevani, Lindgren and Packendorff 2010).

Leadership as a 'position' acknowledges that the practice and outcomes of leadership evolves largely in response to the effects generated by their interactions with those they are leading (Harré and Van Langenhove 1999). Thus, the leader is enacting a 'position' rather than performing a 'role'. Positions are socially shaped behaviours around patterns of mutually accepted beliefs, needs and expectations. Roles, on the other hand, are prescribed behaviours that are more explicit, precise, individualistic, and practical in formation and nature, and often reflect an ideal rather than the reality. To become a leader, the person needs to first negotiate with those they are leading, to build a mutually understood and accepted view of what the inherent responsibilities of the leadership position are, and how it is best to be performed (Harré and Moghaddam 2003). As a negotiated position, the ultimate image of leadership is co-constructed through the realization and consolidation of mutually accepted values, beliefs and expectations. Furthermore, Davies and Harré (1999: 32) posit that the concept of position readily embraces the dynamic aspects of externally structured and imposed human engagements 'in contrast to the way in which the use of "role" serves to highlight static, formal and ritualistic aspects'.

Essentially, leadership is constructed in the common daily social inter-actions among the nominated leader and those they are tasked with leading. This implies that the commonly held view of the individualism on leadership needs to be challenged. Rather, leadership is co-constructed such that the effectiveness of a leader cannot be measured by their achievement of certain practical competencies but more on how well they are able to establish mutually beneficial relational processes with those they are leading. These processes are authentically human in nature and cannot be reduced to mechanical, technical or clinical intentions designed to achieve the self-interests of the supposed leader. They 'are characterized by a social flow of interacting and connecting whereby organizations, groups, leaders, leadership and so forth are constantly under construction and re-construction' (Crevani, Lindgren and Packendorff 2010: 79). Thus, leadership is not formed from key or significant or prescribed actions initiated in particular circumstances in certain ways or at given times by a person appointed to a leadership role. Declaring a vision or implementing a policy or publicizing a new development or presenting an annual budget and so forth have little to do with the person's leadership reputation. Quite the opposite – the acceptance of a person as a leader and judgements about them as a leader are things that are incrementally formed as they move around the organization and interact with individuals and groups (Lichtenstein and Plowman 2009). Those being led are slow to judge the leadership capacity of the formal leader. They need to trust that what they first see is not only acceptable, but also authentic and typical. They need to firmly believe that the formal leader can be trusted and is reliable in their leadership behaviours. The person can only enact true leadership when, and only when, they are accepted as the leader. This means that 'leadership is not a one-way influence process but rather a reciprocal influence relationship. ... As in any other relationship, both sides contribute to its formation, nature and consequences' (Shamir 2011: 310). Essentially, the relational cornerstone of leadership is the reciprocal and dynamic interaction process between the formal leaders and those to be led.

How then does leadership practice become a tangible experience? Leaders who are attuned to the pivotal relational dimension underpinning their leadership allow multiple futures and are open in terms of what these might be. Rather than controlling futures they cultivate conditions where others can produce innovations that lead to somewhat unpredictable yet largely productive future states (Plowman et al. 2007). Their influence derives from their ability to allow rather than to direct and is grounded in people in the organization remaining engaged and connected (for a more detailed explanation, see Chapter 6). Through recognizing the importance of interactions as the ideal source of employee engagement, high performance and innovation, these leaders build 'correlation': the emergence of a common or shared organizational vision and a recognizable widespread pattern of positive organizational behaviour. Through this focus everyone in the organization can find meaning and purpose in whatever is unfolding.

In addition, these leaders enable the emergence of new ideas and behaviours that sustain and grow the organization by directing attention to what is important to note from contrasting the internal and external organizational environments. From this perspective, building collegiality, cooperation and teamwork should not be seen as only part of leadership but, rather, be understood as its very essence. Leadership is contextual and not generic because it emerges out of a sincere interpersonal engagement of the leader with those they are leading. In short, leadership is first and foremost relational, which implies that it is specifically suited to the unique context. Furthermore, its essence is a relationship that seeks to create a culture based upon the shared values of trust, openness, transparency, honesty, integrity, collegiality and ethicalness (Branson 2009, 2014c). This is a culture in which all feel a sense of safety and security because they each feel that they can rely on each other in order to achieve their best. Through facilitating and supporting mutually beneficial relationships, the leader enables the organizational conditions to be created whereby those they are leading willingly and readily perform at their best. This, in turn, allows the leader to actually become the leader, and to continue to enact true leadership, which ensures the growth and sustainability of the organization. This is 'transrelational' leadership, because leadership 'is best understood as a transrelational phenomenon as its essence is to move others, the organisation and the leader to another level of functioning by means of relationships' (Branson, Franken and Penney 2016: 155). What this means in practice will now be described in detail.

Embodying transrelational leadership

Positioning the genesis of leadership within the phenomenon of a human relationship might seem to imply that it can be easily achieved. Except for hermits and certain religious orders, humans are a very relationally oriented species. We readily seek the company of others. Indeed, our lives are enriched through our relationships with family, friends, relatives, work colleagues, club members, social groups, educational colleagues and religious membership, to name but a few sources. Forming relationships is a natural and automatic outcome that we all seek. But there is a very significant difference in the case of a leader. While it is true that we each seek to form relationships, we do this in a very selective way. We choose to form a relationship with some people but not with others. A leader does not have this luxury. If the essence of leadership is relational, the leader needs to have the capacity to form a positive relationship with each person they are leading. This essential requirement for becoming a leader may well be the prime reason why not everyone can be a leader. If it is beyond the capacity of a person to form a positive relationship with every person that they have a responsibility to be leading, then they are incapable of leadership. People appointed to a leadership position who do not have the capacity to build sincere and authentic relationships with those they are leading are most likely to revert to management actions. Consciously or subconsciously they will sense that they cannot sufficiently influence others without using such things as diverse policies, prescribed processes, accountability regimes and performance management measures as a crutch.

The second delimiting factor in becoming a leader is being able to ensure that the relationships established are sincere and authentic, and not dishonest and opportunistic. Hence the call is for the leader to 'embody' transrelational leadership. Here, leaders are seen as 'embodied subjects – as subjective objects of feeling matter' (de Quincey 2002: 48). Within this understanding, the leader's actions and consciousness are not separated entities but rather co-eternal, mutually complementary, realities. When striving for transrelational leadership, consciousness is seen as the process of the leader informing their self in regard to the perceived level of their relational sincerity and authenticity. In this sense, the leader's relational consciousness is their ability to feel, to know and to direct their relationship-building self. Moreover, the leader's relational consciousness is informed by the impressions of others. How we think we are relating to someone is not always the same as how it is being experienced by the other person. For example, a person might believe they are showing enthusiasm but this may be interpreted by someone else as being loud or brash. Another might believe they are being imaginative, but this could be seen as unpredictability. Or the person could be acting cautiously but be seen by others as being resistant or inflexible. We all 'read' people and their contextualized behaviours in different ways. Transrelational leadership requires that the leader is not merely open to these different interpretations, but actively seeks to explore them. Moreover, a potential leader who, on occasions or under certain circumstances, displays personal characteristics such as aloofness, unfriendliness, disaffection, unsociability, unapproachability, moodiness, ingratitude or discourtesy will invariably find that they are not able to nurture the quality of interpersonal relationships that will elevate them to be accepted as the leader. Others will not sufficiently trust them in order to accept them as their leader. Instead, they will suspect that this potential leader will ignore their workplace security at some time in the future because they do not sufficiently know and understand them. It is therefore essential for the leader to be continually seeking signs, symbols, views and interpretations from many different sources in regard to the quality of their relationships with all of those they are leading.

Essentially, what we have described is a specifically focused process of self-reflection or mindfulness. Senge et al. (2007: 50) describe mindfulness as a deliberate action to raise a person's own conscious awareness. Moreover, these authors describe the process for increasing mindfulness as: 'If you bring a certain kind of open, moment-to-moment, non-judgemental awareness to what you're attending to, you'll begin to develop a more penetrative awareness that sees beyond the surface of what's going on in your field of awareness. This is mindfulness. Mindfulness makes it possible to see connections that may not have been visible before.' Mindfulness around the quality of the leader's interpersonal relationships is more than simply knowing what is happening, who is involved, what is the array of possibilities for improving the relationship, and how the other person might be affected by the situation and/or by the way in which the relationship is being nurtured. Rather, the concept of mindfulness builds on our traditional dependency on such knowledge and judgement by adding the requirement that the leader must also 'be able to suspend their thoughts so that they can become aware of and inspect their everyday thoughts and, thereby, reduce their influence on what they see' (Senge et al. 2007: 29). In other words, increased relational mindfulness is about being able to make informed and astute judgements about the interpersonal situation at hand. Moreover, increased relational mindfulness is about the leader having a more enriched, proactive and aware consciousness about the effect and affect of their presence and communication on others, which provides the groundwork for continual growth and development as a relational leader.

Such relational mindfulness can occur through two perspectives – the entity perspective and the relational perspective (see, for example, Uhl-Bien 2006). The far more commonly operationalized perspective is that of the entity level because its focus is on how the individual experiences, interprets and comes to know how a particular relational interaction with another appears to their self. Here the relationship is understood as 'a particular type of connection existing between people related to or having dealings with each other' (Uhl-Bien 2006: 656). Each person is seen as an entity with the capacity 'to reason, to learn, to invent, to produce, and to manage' (Hosking, Dachler and Gergen 1995) all that is required when choosing to form or not form a relationship. Hence, this choosing person is 'understood as the architect and controller of an internal and external order' (Uhl-Bien 2006: 655), which is the tangible experience of the relationship upon their self. The entity perspective draws attention to the perceptions, intentions, behaviours, personalities, expectations and evaluations that the leader and those they are leading bring to bear upon the relationship development processes.

In the case of a person wishing to advance their leadership acceptance and capacity, theoretical insights from the fields of psychology, sociology and behavioural studies readily provide avenues for self-reflection and mindfulness. For example, the complex self-concept theory (see Aronson 1995) proposes that part of a person's difficulty in being able to create relationships with some people arises from their own limited life experiences. The consistency theory (see Krauss and Critchfield 1975) suggests that we judge others based upon how we judge ourselves. Yet our self-evaluations are not always accurate and so we can easily misjudge others when developing relationships. Adult attachment theory (see Richards and Hackett 2012) posits that people right from a very young age develop relationship scripts for how and when they choose to develop a relationship and these same scripts can endure into their adult years, thereby influencing not only how and when relationships are formed but also how the person tends to act when involved in group activity. The leader–member exchange theory (see Graen and Uhl-Bien 1995) describes how the perceived levels of mutual trust, respect, liking and obligation provides an impression of relative psychological benefit to be gained from the relationship between a leader and someone they are leading, which then determines the quality of the relationship. The social network theory (see Balkundi and Kilduff 2005) describes the principles upon which people determine how they will interact with others when placed in some formalized network with a common purpose. These are only a sample of possible theoretical insights that can be considered by a leader as they strive to reflect and critique how they are thinking about forming or not forming relationships with each of those they are leading. Essentially, this is about being ever mindful that one's natural cautiousness or resistance towards forming a relationship may well be based upon false, misleading or inappropriate personal perceptions and thoughts.

The relational perspective acknowledges the limitations of these entity insights where these only provide knowledge and understanding predominantly from an individual's understanding. Rather, the relational perspective 'assumes that any formulations of thoughts and assumptions have to be understood in the context of ongoing conversations and relations' (Uhl-Bien 2006: 661, our emphasis). In this sense, the forming of a relationship is not a moment-in-time event, but rather evolves over time based not only on the entity of thoughts and assumptions but also, and perhaps even more importantly, as a product of the interplay of ongoing conversations, social connections and professional networking. This understanding sees relationships as co-constructed and co-evolving, such that they are continually growing out of the myriad of frequent ways in which two or more people interact. Moreover, what is important is not so much the beliefs and assumptions the person has about the other, as in the case of the entity perspective, but rather, what they think about their self in relation to the other as a result of a given context and how, in turn, this makes them feel about the other at that particular time (Hosking 2007). Based upon these mutually evolving considerations at this particular time, and in conjunction with those previously and similarly created, each person will form a sense of what the relationship means for their self. Flowing out of this sense of the relationship are consequential behaviours along such continuums as loyalty and unwillingness, responsibility and carelessness, engagement and disinterest, respect and disapproval, appreciation and indifference, enthusiasm and disillusionment and so on.

The implication of this relational perspective for leadership is that nothing can be taken for granted. A person appointed to a leadership position must realize that they are always on show; each person they encounter directly (individually) or indirectly (as a member of a group) each day will be judging their leadership capacity based upon what they see, experience and feel about what this contact might mean for them in their work. The leadership capacity of the person appointed to a leadership role is neither a universally agreed outcome across everyone in the group or organization nor is it a constant outcome in the opinion of an individual, a group or the organization. It may eventually become more universal and constant after a period of time during which those being led come to draw the same opinion and conclusions about the quality of their relationships with the person appointed to the role of the leader. When a new leader is appointed, some may immediately discount their leadership capacity based upon some initial contacts and observations of this leader. Others might have a 'wait and see' view, whereby they neither accept nor deny that the person has leadership potential. Others might immediately accept the person as their leader and hope that he or she will live up to their expectation. Essentially, as will be described in far more detail in the ensuing chapters, what those being led are subconsciously monitoring is the level of trust that they can place in the person appointed to the leadership position. The more trust that is engendered through the relationship the more likely the person will be accepted as the leader. But this also means that any action or communication by the person in the leadership position that undermines this trust will likely result in their losing leadership support. With the passing of time providing far more occasions for contact, observations and communications, these initial views will be confirmed, modified or revised essentially based upon each person's judgements about what the newly appointed leader might mean for them as they go about their daily work responsibilities.

The possible outcomes from these personal interactions and judgements with the leader include accepting them as the leader, not accepting them as the leader, or accepting that they have partial leadership capacity where they show leadership in some areas but not in others. Importantly, if a person in a leadership role realizes the fundamental relational role of being accepted as the leader, then they are able to see how they can redress any negative opinions of their leadership capacity. Rebuilding a relationship, or achieving outcomes via a far more relational and inclusive means, can change a person's or group's opinion. Maintaining a commitment to management procedures is far more likely to confirm, entrench and strengthen leadership capacity opinions. This implies that every important action by the leader must be continually reinforcing their commitment to a relational approach to their leadership. This imperative is explained in far more detail in later chapters.

The four fundamental qualities of a transrelational leader

What the preceding discussion highlights about the fundamental role of relationships in leadership is that 'acceptance' and not 'appointment' creates leadership. Being accepted as the leader is the bedrock for becoming a leader. Simply stated, the person must first be accepted as the leader before they can begin to behave as the leader so as to have the influence commonly associated with successful leadership. Furthermore, being accepted as the leader is solely dependent upon the establishment of widespread, socially positive, mutually beneficial, interpersonal relationships with those to be lead. To this end, Haslam, Reicher and Platow (2011) argue that the very first step in becoming a leader is to become an 'in group' member.

When first appointed, the potential leader must continually strive to be seen in words and deeds as a fully active member of the group to be led. The leader must be seen to be one-of-the-group, whereby they appear relaxed and at ease in the group, show ongoing interest and enthusiasm about what is happening in the group, are able to readily and openly talk with all in the group, and show that they have the best interests of the group continually in mind. Each of these required outcomes are crucially dependent upon the quality of the leader's relational capacity with each member of the group. Simply, to become the leader the person must be seen to be sincerely involved in the joys and celebrations, the hopes and dreams, the challenges and difficulties, and the doubts and uncertainties of the group.

For the leader to be an 'in-group' member it is not solely about establishing the right relationship with those they are to lead. Once established, the actions of the leader must be seen as maintaining this relationship. Trust is at the heart of all relationships and trust is built upon predictability, consistency and authenticity (Branson 2014b). Being trustworthy is about the leader willingly acting openly, honestly and consistently. It is more than simply telling the truth. Trustworthiness in a leader means that they consistently display total congruence between who they say they are and what they do. In other words, how a leader is able to influence their group members must support and not undermine the relationship that binds them to the group. The leader's influence is by means of, and consistent with, the relationship and not distinct from it. It is in this way that we argue that leadership is transrelational. The essence of leadership understood as a transrelational phenomenon is moving the group members, the organization and the leader to another level of functioning by means of the relationship between the leader and each member of the group. One of the exceptional qualities of Martin Luther King's leadership was how deeply he was accepted. His thousands and thousands of followers trusted his passionate words and convictions unquestionably because they knew that he and his family suffered the same racially motivated obstacles, fears, limitations and restrictions as they did. Martin Luther King's dream was their dream. The new world order that he longed for, they longed for. He could describe their reality in a way that they couldn't but in the way that they could readily relate to. His voice speaking out loud and clear to the rest of America, and to the world, was their voice. He was one of them; he was in their 'group' well and truly. But being 'in the group', is only the first step towards leadership. In itself, it is deficient.

The second step towards leadership is to 'champion' the group and its members (Haslam, Reicher and Platow 2011). Perhaps one of the most telling examples of leadership championing was Winston Churchill's classic speech to the British people as they thought the country was about to be invaded by the German armed forces during the Second World War in which he said, 'We shall defend our island, whatever the cost may be, we shall fight on the beaches, we shall fight on the landing grounds, we shall fight in the fields and in the streets, we shall fight in the hills; we shall never surrender.' Churchill's words captured and re-instilled the British people's self-belief in their dogged fighting spirit and dour resistance capacities, which they may have been overlooking under the duress from a pending invasion. He 'championed' a particular quality of the British people that they not only recognized as authentically true to their character but also something that they were proud of and which could provide them with inner strength at a time of immense anxiety and fear.

Simply, championing is about affirming, praising and celebrating the achievements and successes of individuals and the group both in formal and informal ways, on stage or in corridors. This is about being able to see and appreciate all of the good things that are happening no matter how large or small the outcome. Importantly, it is about seeing how such achievements are slowly but surely achieving the vision and mission of the group. A leader's influence thus does not come into play until after they are authentically established as a member of the group and, as a consequence, can readily and willingly champion, affirm and promote the activities of the group, and its individual members, in various forums. To be able to truly champion the group, or its members, a leader must first be able to deeply understand and appreciate what is happening, which requires the leader to be one with the group. But, it is also about filtering and protecting the group from unnecessary or unsuitable demands. This is about acknowledging and appreciating the current levels of commitment and engagement, and thereby understanding the incapacity of the group to fully or partially take on any additional responsibilities. Or it is realizing just how distracting an externally proposed change would be to the group's commitments. Fundamentally, this form of championing is about the leader being willing to defend the group's right to accept, amend or reject additional commitments or responsibilities. This form of championing provides those being led with the greatest sense of trust in their leader. Where such championing does not exist, the perceived leadership capacity is minimized and any proposed change is far more likely to be resisted. Thus, the change has to be managed, which magnifies the likelihood of resistance (see Chapter 5 for further discussion).

Importantly, a leader also needs to have developed widespread mutually beneficial interpersonal relationships with each and every member of their 'group' in order to be seen as a sincere and equitable champion of the group. One of the most serious ways to damage trust is for a possible leader to be seen to be selectively choosing who, what and when to champion. If a leader only relates to some of the group, or only shows interest in some of the group's activities, then they can only champion some of the group and are limited in describing what is being achieved. Such constrained championing creates suspicion, division and frustration within the group, which not only undermines the confidence and acceptance of the leader but also creates tension and disunity within the group.

Once a potential leader has established themselves within the group, and has built relational trust through championing the group, Haslam, Reicher and Platow (2011) posit that they are then able to initiate the third step towards being the group's leader, which is about 'shaping the group's identity'. Shaping the group's identity is about building on the group's strengths and achievements in order to help the group work better as individuals and teams. This involves implementing appreciative enquiry processes to nurture a group that is able to learn about how it achieves its goals and how this might be done more effectively. The group members are being encouraged to learn from each other and to network better together in order to improve current practices. In this way, the leadership is evolving as the group is becoming more and more open to having its organizational culture being more finely tuned to meeting its strategic vision. A prime example of a leader shaping their group's identity in this way was that of Mahatma Gandhi, who led India to independence from the British Empire, essentially through peaceful resistance. Gandhi not only accepted the seemingly peaceful and somewhat compliant nature of his people but also used this as the foundation of the resistance movement. He did not try to change the character of the Indian people but rather inspired them to see how this could be used in an extremely powerful yet non-violent way to achieve independence and self-government. Instead of trying in vain to change the identity of the people of India so that they would rise up in anger against their British rulers, he chose to shape their identity whereby he was able to show how their natural passive way of being could be used strategically to show the very same stance.

The final step towards becoming totally accepted as the leader is in striving towards 'aligning the group's identity to its wider reality' (Haslam, Reicher and Platow 2011). Once the group is working better together, and showing that it is determined to work better as individuals and in teams, the designated leader is then in a position to draw the attention of the group to the changing nature and demands of the external environment. This involves the group being supported in looking to the future in order to determine what is necessary to be initiated in the present. Rather than telling the group what needs to happen, the accepted leader draws attention to the future possible challenges for the group in an open, honest and inclusive manner, and seeks feedback from the group members as to what this might mean for the group, what individually and collectively the members of the group now need to do in order to meet these challenges, and how it would be best to initiate these required developments. As will be explained in Chapter 5, this is about engaging the people in creating, rather than simply completing, the necessary change strategies. It is about allowing the group to be involved in designing its future rather than having it thrust upon them with little understanding of why things need to change. People resist change when they cannot see and fully understand the purpose for the change. By aligning the group's identity to its wider reality, the leader is beginning any change process by clearly establishing its purpose in the minds and hearts of each and every group member. Nelson Mandela is a perfect example of a leader aligning their group's identity to the wider reality. After countless years of physical, emotional and social oppression, discrimination and segregation caused by apartheid in South Africa, it would have been completely understandable if the black South African peoples had sought to reverse the situation so that the white South Africans would experience what they had previously experienced. But, by and large, Nelson Mandela drew their attention to what this might mean in the eyes of the rest of the world. He encouraged his people to look beyond just their own country in order to see South Africa as a global success, a country that could take its unique place in the world with pride and confidence. Mandela was able to move the majority of the black South African peoples away from seeking revenge and towards national pride on the global stage. He was able to get them to raise the horizon of their national identity from that of an isolated, self-interested country to one that was internationally connected and globally oriented.

An example of a transrelational leader

When seamlessly drawn together, the four sequential steps of being an 'in-group' member, championing the group, shaping the group's identity and aligning the group's identity to its wider reality form the manner by which a person appointed to a leadership position is able to gain acceptance from the group in order to actually become its leader. Indeed, leaders who follow this path can become very influential and successful leaders. For example, we argue that Christina Noble is an exemplary model of a transrelational leader whose leadership in improving the lives of abused and orphaned Vietnamese children epitomizes a commitment to these four steps.

Christina Noble was not Vietnamese but Irish, yet her own very troubled childhood that resulted in her being abused and orphaned enabled her to passionately align her life with that of the grossly disadvantaged Vietnamese children. As it is claimed, she responded with 'An Irish gutter is the same as a Vietnamese gutter,' to a challenge from Vietnamese officials about her suitability for working in the interests of the Vietnamese children. Indeed, she was so capable at championing the needs of these children that large sums of donations and sponsorships began to flow into her cause. So much so that Christina was soon able to provide numerous homes in which shelter, safety, security, sustenance and well-being became a priority for these children. Rather than being a sad, forgotten and neglected constraint on the country's recovery from the aftermath of the Vietnam War, Christina's efforts brought joy and happiness into the lives of the children, along with national pride and satisfaction in what was being achieved. She had changed the identity of not only the children she helped but also that of the country and how it viewed the children. Finally, Christina reached out beyond Vietnam to gain the support and resources to ensure that as many Vietnamese orphaned and abused children as possible could be helped. She was able to work closely and constructively with the Vietnamese government to ensure that it felt respected and fully able to support her international endeavours. Christina enabled the government to accept and embrace the wider reality. Through these incredible leadership efforts it is calculated that Christina Noble has dramatically improved the lives of over 700,000 Vietnamese children. Indeed, Christina Noble's leadership amid extremely challenging and unusual circumstances was so successful that she has been tasked with establishing a similar programme for the orphaned children of Mongolia. The life's work of Christina Noble clearly shows how transrelational leadership can change people and organizations in very powerful ways.

Conclusion

What has been argued in this chapter is that the genesis of leadership is the quality, the interdependency, the intimacy of the relationship between the leader and the people they are intending to lead; moreover, that the authentic formation of this relationship is achieved through the four sequential steps of becoming an 'in-group' member, championing the group, shaping the group's identity and aligning the group's identity to its wider reality. However, as explained in this chapter, becoming the leader does not necessarily result in remaining as the leader. To be the leader, the person must be accepted as the leader and such acceptance is an ongoing construction. Those being led are continually determining whether or not to accept the person as their leader. Specifically, those being led are determining whether or not they can continue to trust the person to lead them. If trust is lost, then acceptance of the leader as such is simultaneously lost. This means that each and every key action of the leader must reinforce and not undermine such trust. If this is so, there are four organizational implications that people in positions of leadership need to be ever mindful of to ensure that trust in their leadership is not undermined. These four implications relate to the issues of power, duty, commitment and responsibility. Power explores the nature and function of the influence that a leader has with those they are leading. Duty addresses the issue of how those being led come to understand what needs to be done. Commitment attends to the need for those being led accepting what needs to be done, while responsibility focuses on how those being led attend to the agreed tasks. Power is the focus of the next chapter. Duty, commitment and responsibility are explored together in Chapter 4.

3

Leadership as Transrelational Practice

Abstract

This chapter addresses two extremely important implications that arise from a commitment to a transrelational approach to leadership – pragmatics and credibility. Pragmatics addresses the need for the leader to be able to successfully work with others to achieve mutually desired outcomes. Credibility addresses the need for the leader to be a role model. The leader must 'walk their talk', which means that they must be a transrelational person in every endeavour. From a pragmatic viewpoint, a theoretical perspective is of little benefit if it is unable to be translated into practical realities. From a credibility view, achieving the practical reality must also comply with acting transrelationally. Transrelational practices must provide effective ways for the leader to achieve the essential responsibilities of being both an effective and credible leader. Hence, this chapter will describe and illustrate what a transrelational approach to leadership looks like in practice.

Introduction

Before proceeding to describe and illustrate what a transrelational approach to leadership looks like in practice, we wish to make our view very clear – *leadership is leadership is leadership*! Here we share the growing chorus of concern about the proliferation of 'adjectival' leadership theories, whereby particular interpretations of how leaders should act are presented as new leadership theories and distinguished from other such theories by a preceding adjectival descriptor. This includes interpretations of leadership such as servant leadership, ethical leadership, moral leadership, distributed leadership, shared leadership, instructional leadership and authentic leadership, among countless others. This is not meant to discount the important insights about leadership practice that these and other leadership descriptors provide. Rather, we argue that these are bounded practices that an accepted leader can enact when the context necessitates the application of the particular practice. We also add, however, that a leader committed to a transrelational approach to their leadership practice will be far more attuned to their context at any given time. As a consequence, they will be far more intuitive in eclectically selecting the most beneficial of these practices for attending to their leadership responsibilities in the particular situation.

So, why 'transrelational'? There are three important reasons for the prefix 'trans' being added. First, it draws attention to the significant scope and variation in the everyday relational activities of the leader. The leader's relationships must be far broader, deeper and sincere than group members' relationships. As explained in the previous chapter, the leader must build an open, inclusive and mutually beneficial relationship with each person they are directly leading. They cannot be selective in who they relate to, nor can they communicate superficially with either some individuals or the group. A leader's relationships with those they are striving to lead are the bedrock, and not the topsoil, of their leadership because it forms the basis of their acceptance as the leader, and in turn, allows them to lead. Secondly, the addition of 'trans' highlights that the relationship itself is what causes the leader, those being led and the organization to 'move' or 'change' for the better. The relationships between the leader and those being led are the conduit for individual and organizational learning and growth.

Finally, the inclusion of the 'trans' prefix continues the leadership theory development work of James Macgregor Burns (1978, 2010) in which he introduced the terms 'transactional' and 'transformational' into our understanding of leadership practice. The re-publication in 2010 of Burns' 1978 book, *Leadership*, acknowledges the significance and importance of his seminal leadership understandings. For Burns, *transactional* leadership implies that leadership is about the action of the leader to get those being led to do what the leader requires. The leader controls and directs others usually through physical or psychological, formal or informal, rewards or coercions. Rightly or wrongly, this type of leadership has often been aligned with what is understood as management – 'getting others to do what is considered to be right'. *Transformational leadership* is associated with people who are being led to become better at what they do, and being 'transformed' through the transformational leaders' leadership actions. Ideally, the attention of the transformational leader is on looking after the needs and interests of the employee, whereas the attention of the transactional leader is on looking after the quality of the work that is produced. As indicated in Chapter 2, although Burns' dichotomous description of alternative ways to lead has gained universal acknowledgement and acceptance, regrettably there has been much less attention and acceptance of his emphasis on the fundamental role of relationships in leadership practice. To reiterate (see Chapter 2), according to Burns, for a truly accepted and effective leader the 'arena of power is no longer the exclusive preserve of a power elite or an establishment or persons clothed with legitimacy. Power is ubiquitous; it permeates human relationships' (1978: 15). The leader's most effective source of influence upon those they are leading, their 'power' to unite all in the achievement of a common vision, is the relationships that the leader creates with each and every person they are leading. Thus, the addition of 'trans' to form 'transrelational' recognizes Burns' prioritization of the crucially important 'relational' aspect of leadership. In addition it acknowledges the essential need to consider the relational role in leadership alongside that of transactional and transformational practices in understanding the nature and function of leadership.

As illustrated in Figure 3.1, we contend that the transrelational aspect of leadership is the foundation upon which both transformational and transactional leadership practices rest and rely in order to be successful. Figure 3.1 also reflects our understanding that a leader requires relevant knowledge and skills in leadership as well as in that which pertains to the functioning and output of the group they are leading. Once a leader has developed sufficient levels of such knowledge and skills and commenced a leadership position, they then need, first, to grow the transrelational aspects of their leadership as described in the previous chapter. They need to take every opportunity to build mutually beneficial relationships with those they are leading, and particularly with all those who directly report to them. By concentrating on becoming a member of the 'group' and championing the group when and wherever possible, their acceptance as the leader among the group will broaden and strengthen. In this initial phase there will certainly be times when decisions have to be made and actions taken. But this will be accepted as necessary and acceptable provided those being led can see that, whenever possible, their new leader appears to be a part of the group and is fully supportive of the group.

Only after adequate time has been devoted to properly developing the transrelational aspects of their leadership can the leader begin to shape the group's identity and align this identity to its wider reality, to transform the group

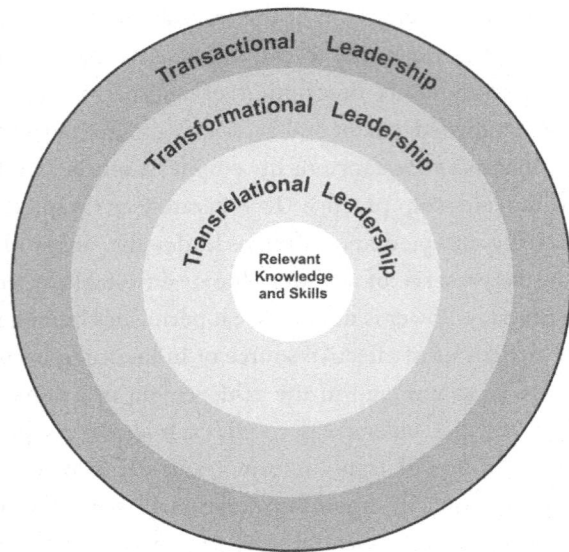

Figure 3.1 An illustration of the integrated aspects of leadership

and individuals within the group. Without the transrelational foundations, any action to transform individuals, teams or the whole group is likely to be met with scepticism or suspicion. Trust is fundamental to secure support for a proposed change. Without this, no matter how small or well intentioned the change, people will struggle to see the personal benefit it is meant to afford and are likely to instead concentrate on the current personal benefits that they believe they will lose if the change proceeds. As a consequence they may well think that the change is unnecessary and/or is designed more for the benefit of the leader and/ or organization than for themselves, and so become reluctant or resistant group members. In contrast, where very positive relationships exist between the leader and those being led, the reasons for any proposed change will be far more widely understood and accepted, so that the prospects of resistance are greatly reduced. In these circumstances, transformational leadership will be far more effective and influential.

While emphasizing this positive potential, we nevertheless also highlight the important responsibility of leading organizational change, and discuss this in far more detail in Chapter 5. Furthermore, despite the best intentions of the leader to create a highly conducive, engaging and purposeful working environment by means of a commitment to leadership, that is, transrelational and transformational, it is likely that some individuals will act in a way that is not in the best interests of their self, others or the group. When an individual steps outside the bounds of mutual respect and integrity, or acts contrary to legally binding norms or codes, or brings potential harm to their self or others, or consistently ignores understandable and commonly accepted workplace practices, or frequently produces work of a recognizably unacceptable standard, then transactional leadership actions are the most appropriate. Where a leader has sincerely attended to developing their transrelational approach to their leadership practice, it is far more likely that this application of a transactional approach will be more effective and influential. When a person realizes that they are usually treated justly and fairly by a leader, who knows and communicates openly and invitingly with them on a somewhat regular basis, it is far more difficult for them to discount or ignore a strong directive they are then given by this same leader. However, if there is a very impoverished relationship between the leader and the individual, then it is very easy for the individual to become defensive and to interpret the leader's transactional directive as a form of bullying. What may well arise is an emotional outburst from a person who has limited understanding about what is happening.

Essentially, then, what is being presented in this book, and illustrated in Figure 3.1, is that leadership begins with the transrelational aspect and this orientation becomes more explicit through the eclectic application of the transformational and transactional aspects. The transrelational aspect of leadership is thus universal and constant and the leader must be ever mindful of attending to it in order to maintain trust and constantly build positive relations. From this basis the leader can grow the transformational aspect of their leadership by helping the group to become better at what they do and supporting them as they prepare to confidently and capably meet future challenges in their work. Transactional leadership practices can be introduced into the milieu of transrelational and transformational leadership practices, but only when deemed necessary and essential.

The remainder of this chapter will do two things. First, a far more specific description of transactional, transformational and transrelational aspects of leadership will be provided and discussed. By comparing and contrasting each of these three aspects of leadership this chapter will provide a far more insightful guide to their respective practice. Secondly, the chapter will provide a research-informed discussion of leadership that is not underpinned by a transrelational approach but rather a more managerial, transactional approach and what this means for leadership in higher education.

Contrasting leadership characteristics

Given that the inherent characteristics of the transactional and transformational approaches to leadership have been discussed, described and promoted in books and research articles for the past forty years, people are generally familiar with their distinctive differences. But how do these two approaches differ from that of the transrelational approach? Table 3.1 is provided as an illustration of the differences among these three approaches and a brief discussion of the table elements will follow.

Leaders who lean towards a transactional approach are firm in their opinion that it is possible for them to control and direct employee performance and thereby produce the desired quality of the organization's output. They are of the opinion that they largely know what is best for the organization and so institute a predominantly exclusive, top–down, controlled and inflexible working

Table 3.1 A comparison of the different leadership characteristics across the transactional, transformational and transrelational approaches to leadership

Leadership focus	Transactional	Transformational	Transrelational
Leadership style	Authoritative	Shared	Interactive
Mode of cooperation	Exclusive	Inclusive	Engaging
Workplace culture	Controlled	Meaningful	Purposeful
Power source	Coercion	Involvement	Truth
Key attention	Product	People	Future
Decision-making	Top–down control	Bottom–up influence	Emergent influence
Problem solving	Inflexible	Flexible	Discovery
Formation of teams	Rationalized groupings	Task-defined teams	Strategic networks
Organizational development	Technical–rational learning	Organizational learning	Holistic learning
Organizational success	Skill	Capacity	Functional connectedness
Goal setting	Performance standards	Review/reflection	Imagination/ creativity
Organizational sustainability	Productivity	Adaptability	Innovative risk-taking
Desired employee quality	Accountability	Responsibility	Growth
Organizational structure	Hierarchical	Diffused	Flat

environment. Those they are leading see them as being very managerial, authoritative and single-minded. Few get to influence the important decisions that are made or to influence how such decisions are to be enacted. Hence the organization structure is very hierarchical which distances the leader both physically and socially from most in the organization. In order to reinforce this very aloof and impersonal environment, the transactional leader largely depends on coercive measures to try and achieve employee compliance to their directives, which are most often couched in terms of policies and expected processes. Such measures vary along a coercion continuum from the lesser end of annual goal-setting processes around meeting performance standards to the more coercive contractualization of employment and to the extreme measure of position disestablishment. The belief is that employees will be motivated to comply and perform for fear of losing their position or being overlooked for career advancement opportunities. Accountability is the key feature used to determine the worth of the employee, with a skill-based focus and assessments addressing how well the employee's skills are producing what is required. Determining how to maintain the sustainability of the organization is a technical–rational decision, which regularly implies improving what is already happening. Similarly, where it is thought necessary to form a team of employees to produce a desired output, those who form the team are chosen by the leader based upon the leader's opinion of who is best suited to be a team member. Often when such teams are formed they endure because the leader has a high opinion of the team members and so keeps giving the team more tasks to complete even when the required skills, knowledge and experience to complete a particular task do not sufficiently reside in any of the team members.

In contrast, a leader with a far more transformational approach with a sincere commitment to 'forming' those they are leading will readily seek to share or distribute leadership by providing opportunities, where possible and practical, for others to assume some leadership responsibilities. In this way, the organizational structure is more diffused and flexible, as various individuals form part of the leadership structure for particular reasons at different times. Hence such leadership practice is founded upon a more inclusive, people-centred and flexible approach to decision-making and workplace performance. The leader seeks to influence processes and outputs by being willing to involve others in defining, analysing and solving organizational problems and thereby creating a meaningful workplace culture. Essentially, the transformational leader allows for a 'bottom-up' influence upon their personal organizational thoughts and actions in order to boost employee responsibility to the organization. This leader also seeks to help the employee to develop their skills, knowledge and capacity, and this is informed by an annual goal-setting process that is far more employee centred. Employees are afforded the freedom to reflect and learn from what has or has not been achieved in the past year as a guide for determining ways to build personal capacity and attain desirable goals beneficial to both their self and the organization in the coming year. The presumed indirect benefit is a far more adaptable employee and, thereby, organization. As each employee adapts to sustain their desired workplace capacity, so the organization maintains its overall capacity and sustainability. Moreover, organizational success and sustainability is enhanced through a commitment to organizational learning and task-defined teamwork. This is a workplace environment in which individuals and teams explore ways to better understand the fundamental components of their workplace practices in order to create new ways of improving them and solving any new organizational problems.

Finally, a leader committed to embracing a fundamentally transrelational approach to their leadership practice, will be striving to create as flat an organizational structure as practicable, particularly in terms of communication and decision-making. Given that the genesis of their leadership is founded upon extensive and mutually beneficial relationships, this leader will be seen as highly interactive and engaging with others, regardless of their personality, background or positional level within the organization. Their source of power or influence is more aligned with persuasion than compulsion. It is formed out of a search for truth (see Chapter 4 for further explanation) in which all, including the leader, have the opportunity to describe the organizational reality and to present divergent, imaginative and creative ways towards producing a successful and sustainable future. Furthermore, inherent within this commitment to allowing new ideas and new practices to emerge from anywhere within the organization is the encouragement of innovative risk-taking, where failure is accepted provided it engenders learning. Through the sharing of divergent views, truth is discovered and new ideas for the organization's growth are revealed. In this way, all employees can feel more purposeful because they are able to contribute to the building of a far more secure future for the organization. Moreover, what is being encouraged is a holistic understanding of the organization in which all are committed to learning not only about how the organization functions and how this can be improved, but also about how they are contributing to the organization and how they can do so even more in the future. This is about providing a means by which each employee can come to know their strengths and can build upon them in imaginative and creative ways. The annual goal-setting process is therefore replaced with a far more regular and intimate dialogue between the employee and their line manager about how the employee feels they might be better prepared and positioned to contribute towards the strategic direction of the organization. The organization's strategic direction is also further supported by the formation of strategic networks whereby employees with the required skills, knowledge and expertise are brought together specifically and solely to solve particular challenging organizational problems. This involves the process of functional connectedness whereby problems are solved by those with the capacity to solve them, regardless of their positional status within the organization. It is through connectedness, that is, relationships, that the future of the organization is assured under the leadership of a transrelational leader.

Two serious future implications for higher education leadership

While it is true that the transactional approach to leadership still has an important place in certain circumstances, as previously described, the problem within the higher education context is that it dominates as the preferred mode of practice. Rather than being selectively applied to address specific issues, it is frequently the sole mode of leadership. Simply, the transactional approach is more akin to management than leadership. Moreover, in higher education, with its growing commitment to the new managerialism, new public management, corporatization method of leadership, which is progressively reverting to micromanagement practices as a futile attempt to redress its inherent failures, a far more extreme and perverse form of transactional leadership is emerging in many institutions. As a consequence, this misuse of the transactional leadership approach will be confronted with two extremely serious implications in the near future – destructive leadership and millennial opposition.

Destructive leadership

From a desire to seek new ways to improve organizational culture and productivity, research has turned its attention to the study of how to overcome negative organizational behaviours, which more recently has led to a focus on the concept of destructive leadership (see, for example, Goldman 2008; Lu et al. 2012; Schyns and Schilling 2013; Shaw, Erickson and Harvey 2011; Thoroughgood et al. 2012). As defined (Krasikova, Green and LeBreton 2013: 1310), destructive leadership is 'volitional behavior by a leader that can harm or intends to harm a leader's organization and/or followers by (1) encouraging followers to pursue goals that contravene the legitimate interests of the organization and/or (2) employing a leadership style that involves the use of harmful methods of influence with followers, regardless of justifications for such behaviour'. It is true that few, if any, serious leaders would set out to deliberately become a destructive leader, but this aligns more to part (1) of this definition. It is part (2) that mainly concerns our discussion where we are arguing that a leader's preferred practice can become destructive. Specifically, an emphasis upon a transactional, managerial approach to leadership will eventually become a form of destructive leadership.

As described by Padilla and colleagues (2007), leadership research has surfaced two alternative perspectives on destructive leadership – as a process and as an outcome. Those researchers who see destructive leadership as a process emphasize syndromes, such as narcissism and psychopathy. They associate destructive leadership with producing employee alienation and betrayal, or with leadership behaviours like manipulation, intimidation, coercion and one-way communication. Such leadership evolves from the practices of those leaders who assume that they have a complete and accurate view of the organization's reality. They tend to overestimate their own personal leadership capabilities, and they disregard the views of others. From this perspective, destructive leadership is something that leaders do, independent of the outcomes from these behaviours.

Other writers see destructive leadership from an outcomes' perspective and thus posit that deciding whether leadership is constructive or destructive is a matter of long-term group performance (Padilla, Hogan and Kaiser 2007). For these writers, the test of destructive leadership is a matter of the outcomes it eventually generates. From this perspective destructive leadership involves the leader imposing goals and performance expectations on those they are leading without their agreement, and without consideration of the long-term impact that these goals and performance standards will have upon continuing employment and/or future careers options. Such a process is ultimately alienating because it fails to make goals and performance expectations personally meaningful to those being led and, hence, there is little commitment to the achievement of these expectations.

Importantly, from either perspective – process or outcomes – it is those being led who decide whether or not the leadership is destructive. The greatest mistake a leader can make is to avoid considering whether or not their leadership practice is destructive. As has already been clearly stated, once a leader loses the trust of those they are leading, employee commitment, engagement, performance and productivity diminish. Being judged to be a destructive leader destroys employee trust. Undesirable outcomes result from progressive evolution and/or impact avoidance whereby a leader's initially well-intentioned actions ultimately become destructive, but the leader deliberately or involuntarily ignores the impact of their leadership style.

One of the important lessons here is that a leader cannot assume that actions that seemed to work effectively in the past will continue to do so in the present and the future. As people and society change, so does the organizational culture. What once was acceptable leadership behaviour can eventually become unacceptable and, thus, destructive leadership behaviour. A past leader's highly authoritarian and assertive directives might now be viewed as unacceptable bullying behaviour. Today's employee wants to be treated with respect and dignity and as an adult and not like a naughty, thoughtless child. They want to be seen and acknowledged for what they are and can contribute, rather than being largely ignored until blame is applied when something goes awry. Those being led today are less indulgent and compliant, and far more judgemental and critical of their leader's behaviours. Where a leader's behaviour falls short of that which is expected by those they are leading, then destructive leadership outcomes will progressively evolve. The impact of destructive leadership can have detrimental effects not only on employee engagement (see Chapter 6) but also, and of far more concern, on employee 'social, psychological and psychosomatic' well-being thereby reducing the organization's 'productivity, financial bottom-line, and employee morale' (Shaw, Erickson and Harvey 2011: 575).

Destructive leadership that results from an overdependence upon a transactional, managerial approach to leadership is based upon the leader's grossly outdated understanding of today's organizational reality. Whether they are willing to accept it or not, the outdated understanding is described by Wheatley (2006: 169) as reflecting 'a mechanistic world managed by bureaucracy, governed by policies and laws, filled with people who did what they were told, who surrendered their freedom to leaders and sat passively waiting for actions'. She adds that this flawed view craves efficiency and obedience and relies on the unattainable belief that a standard operating procedure can be devised for every situation; an assumption that organizational life is universal and predictable, where every section and individual in the organization thinks and acts the same. For Wheatley, this organizational reality 'is a man-made, dangerous fiction that destroys any capacity to deal well with what's really going on. The real world, not this fake one, demands that we learn to cope with chaos, that we understand what motivates humans, and that we adopt strategies and behaviours that lead to order, not more chaos' (2006: 169).

However, the greatest challenge is not so much in describing the nature and impact of destructive leadership but rather to realize that its remedy lies in the very hands of those who are responsible for its existence. Only those leaders in higher education, who are committed to an overdependence upon managerialism in their leadership practice, can prevent it from happening. These leaders must accept its potential existence, acknowledge their role in its formation and change their leadership so that it becomes founded upon transrelational principles. As captured by Wheatley (2006: 169), this is a challenge for these higher education leaders because they are 'caught between a worldview that no longer works and a new one that seems too bizarre to contemplate'. Choosing not to change will be ultimately disastrous for their leadership, the people they are leading and the organization, particularly given the workplace outlook of the millennial employees, as will now be discussed.

Millennial opposition

Every leader, regardless of their preferred form of leadership practice, knows that they must keep an eye on the future as an essential source of data in developing their strategic organizational plans. Hence, for each and every leader there is no escaping from the likely consequences of having to employ millennials, those born approximately from 1980 to 1999. Workplaces around the world, including higher education institutions, are now experiencing a large demographic change as millions of the baby boomer generation enter the retirement phase and the younger millennials take their places (Bodenhausen and Curtis 2016; Twenge et al. 2010). With this transition, these younger generation employees will have very different expectations of their organization's leadership and what influence it will have upon their careers and lifestyles. This generation is said to be optimistic, idealistic and goal driven (Chen and Choi 2008), possibly over-indulgent (Chou 2012), and needing constant guidance (Ferri-Reed 2014). With so many of the millennial generation entering the workforce, researchers have advocated the idea of having millennial employees more involved in the workplace to prevent boredom and promote attachment (Myers and Oetzel 2003; Myers and Sadaghiani 2010).

More specifically, research shows that millennials, as employees, tend to believe in 'the more the merrier' and enjoy collective action (Maier et al. 2015: 387), and are optimistic about the future (Gursoy, Maier and Chi 2008). Mostly millennials show a strong will to get things done with great energy and enthusiasm. They are good collaborators in the workplace, favour teamwork and place a strong emphasis on work–life balance. But millennials are also 'very independent, self-confident, and self-expressive, and seek recognition, affirmation and respect because they believe in putting much of themselves into their work' (Maier et al. 2015: 387). They appear to be indifferent towards titles and positional status, and expect their supervisors and managers to, at least, know their names and acknowledge their good work. Millennials believe leaders should try to get to know everyone and give personal attention to each employee. Even though millennials believe in collective action, they have a tendency to question the status quo, because they believe rules are made to be broken. Millennials simply reject the notion that their generation has to stay within the rigid confines of a job description. Hence, millennials are likely to challenge workplace norms such as dress codes, inflexibility of the standard workday and employee/supervisor relations. They take electronic collaboration for granted and are highly adaptive to social media and emergent technology (Gursoy, Maier and Chi 2008).

The particularity of the millennial generational personality is also likely to determine what these individuals want from their work, what kind of workplace environment is valued, and how leaders within the organization are better able to satisfy those wants and desires. From their research, Myers and Sadaghiani (2010) point to the widespread idea that building a career is not the principal motivator for most millennials. They prefer flexible jobs, work–life balance and spending time developing close personal relationships (Altizer 2010). Their strong desire for meaningful relationships with peers and line managers suggests that open and inclusive organizational communications might be a way of promoting job stability for millennial workers. From Deloitte's (2016b) Millennial Survey, these employees want to see that the needs of employees take precedence over organizational policies and profits and that their organization is making a positive contribution to society at large. The belief that their personal values are not being compromised by what they are expected to be doing in their workplace is of great importance to the millennial employee. They also strive to achieve a sense of purpose in what they are doing and have innate leadership aspirations. Thus, they welcome the opportunity to be mentored by more experienced and capable co-employees in learning both how to perform better and contribute more and how to build their leadership capacities. This means that they are not put off from being held accountable provided that they are able to help determine their assigned accountabilities. Millennials look to find employment in organizations that provide performance flexibility as they wish to be personally involved in defining and developing their position description, performance practices and productive measurements. A key part of their openness to any co-constructed accountability is the expectation that they will be provided with professional development opportunities that will ensure they are able to maintain the required knowledge and skill levels.

Because of the characteristics described, most of the organizational outcomes generated by a managerial approach will cause value and behavioural conflicts with millennial employees. Moreover, perhaps unlike the outgoing baby boomer generation, who mostly sought the safety, predictability and security of continuous employment, millennials will willingly change employment and do so on a relatively frequent basis. If their organizational environment is less than satisfactory in their opinion, the millennial is very likely to quickly seek alternative employment. In today's higher education environment, leaders need to ensure that their practices are not turning current and potential millennial employees away.

In contemporary times, therefore, the continuation of a predominantly managerial approach to leadership in higher education is fraught with dangers. Where managerialism seeks uniformity and control, millennials want to experience flexibility and openness. Managerialism promotes exclusivity in decision-making and leadership opportunities, and measures productivity at the individual employee performance level. However, a millennial employee wishes to be able to contribute to the decision-making processes and to be offered leadership opportunities. They also value the work quality produced by collaboration, networking and teamwork far more than that of individual efforts. Hence, they are drawn to those organizations with a tangible employee-centred culture, which contrasts markedly from a product/profit-oriented culture proffered through managerialism. For the millennial, an organizational culture that is founded on equitable and ethical practices is far more enticing than one that is explicitly hierarchical and authoritative. Thus, while managerialism relies upon positional status and authority, in association with organizational rules couched in policies and prescriptive processes, millennial employees are far less influenced by such organizational artefacts and much more inclined to be positively affected by personal contact with their line managers, guidance from supportive and highly competent workplace mentors, and professional development opportunities.

If managerialism remains as the most dominant form of leadership, the future of higher education becomes significantly clouded. Constant employee turnover is a significant threat to any organization, but particularly higher education. Yet, constant employee turnover will become a natural part of the culture for managerialist-led organizations as the employment of millennials grows. If higher education institutions wish to maintain high-quality teaching, research and publication outputs, which are their core businesses, then it is essential that a non-managerialist approach to leadership becomes the preferred option. Indeed, we argue that the most suitable and applicable form of leadership that will not only engage but also advance the strengths and talents of the millennial employees is the transrelational approach to higher education leadership.

Conclusion

The aim of this chapter was to provide a far more detailed and pragmatic description of the nature and practice of transrelational leadership. Comparing and contrasting its essential tenets and practices with those of transactional leadership and transformational leadership achieved this. In this way, transrelational leadership can be seen to be a clearly distinguishable form of leadership. However, this chapter also supports the view that transactional, transformational and transrelational leadership, although individually distinguishable by their respective characteristics, should not be understood as unrelated, discrete types of leadership but, rather, as particular approaches to leadership that are applied as required. As was stated at the beginning of this chapter, we argue that 'leadership is leadership is leadership' and that any preceding adjective (e.g. transrelational or transformational or servant or distributed, etc.) only provides an insight into the underpinning values and principles guiding the practice of leadership at a given time in a given situation. In other words, an individual leader can be transrelational, transformational, servant, distributive or whatever, when necessary. But, we also argue that establishing transrelational capacity and credibility in the first instance is the essential foundation of effective and successful leadership.

This chapter has also described serious concerns associated with managerialism, identified as an exaggerated form of transactional leadership, because of its apparent dominant application in higher education. Here it was argued that the continued application of managerialism in higher education would most likely lead to destructive leadership and employee discontinuity with millennial employees. It is argued that core business sustainability must become the primary determinant of higher education leadership practice and that it is therefore essential that transrelational leadership replaces managerialism. But what would the application of a transrelational approach to higher education leadership mean in practice? The following chapters seek to provide a far more explicit description of some key leadership perspectives and practical responsibilities. In this way, they collectively provide strong support to the understanding that transrelational leadership is not simply ideology because it has very explicitly definable and achievable practical implications. Specifically, the chapters that follow will comprehensively describe these practical implications by discussing leadership matters associated with power and influence, duty, commitment, responsibility, change, performance and engagement.

4

Real Power and Influence

Abstract

If it is essential for the transrelational leader to be able to change a group's identity, and effectively bring external relevant influences to the attention of the group so that they can successfully adapt, then the implication is that the leader has some form of authority, power or influence. To maintain coherence with the transrelational approach to leadership, this chapter describes the extensive research-based literature from such fields as sociology, cultural studies, behavioural studies and philosophy that counters some common assumptions about a leader's sources of power and influence. This literature promotes a focus on an alternative source of power and influence – one based upon relationships rather than coercion or control. Essentially, such power and influence are described as being founded upon the search for organizational truth by means of inclusivity, cooperation and transparency. This research supports the view that the true source of power and influence is more closely aligned with being a transrelational leader than any previously described form of leadership. The chapter concludes by describing in detail three pragmatic concerns that such a commitment to relational power generate: employee duty, commitment and responsibility. Each of these concerns is described both from the managerial point of view and from a transrelational leadership perspective. In each case we illustrate how the relational approach is far more able to achieve what leaders are truly looking for.

Introduction

Our view is that every human organization requires the best possible leadership in order to unite those who work in the organization and to encourage everyone within the organization to maximize their contribution towards the organization's goals. To this end, leadership effectiveness is aligned with how well the organization is able to accomplish its purpose. In other words, leadership effectiveness is directly related to the leader's power to influence those they are leading to better accomplish the organization's goals and purpose. However, just as our understanding of the nature and function of leadership practice has varied greatly over the past century, so too have understandings about the nature of a leader's power. For example, Weber (1954) described the power of a leader in terms of their capacity to impose their will upon the behaviour of another. In a similar vein, Folger, Poole and Stutman (1993: 69) defined the power of the leader as simply 'the capacity to act effectively'. This perspective posits that those in leadership positions have the power to get others to do what they want them to do simply because they are the leader. However, this autocratic, transactional form of leadership power becomes more transformational when the nature of a leader's power is described as a form of influence or persuasion. For example, the views of McClelland and Burnham (1976), Etzioni (1975) and Rogers (1973) are aligned with that of Yukl and Becker (2006: 146) who state that 'power involves the capacity of one party (the agent) to influence another party (the target)'. Hersey, Blanchard and Johnson (2001: 204) concur by arguing that 'power is influential potential – the resource that enables a leader to gain compliance or commitment from others'. Krausz (1986: 69) argued that 'power is the ability to influence the actions of others, individuals or groups. It is understood as the leader's influence potential.' Hersey and Blanchard (1982) suggest that effective leadership action is the process of influencing the activities of an individual or group in efforts towards goal achievement in a given situation.

Subsequent to the acceptance of the leader's power being more aligned to that of influence than autocracy, writers have tried to expand upon the nature of such influence. Tannenbaum (1962) believed that effective leaders have the ability, through interpersonal influence, to cause their subordinates to attain specific personal as well as organizational goals. In taking this stance Tannenbaum highlighted a belief that the leader's power is an outcome of the interpersonal relationship they have developed with their followers. This is an understanding aligned with that of Verderber and Verderber (1992: 280) as they describe the leader's influence in terms of a social power and argue that this 'social power is a potential for changing attitudes, beliefs, and behaviors of others'. Cangemi (1992: 499) asserted that 'power is the individual's capacity to move others, to entice others, to persuade and encourage others to attain specific goals or to engage in specific behavior; it is the capacity to influence and motivate others'.

The common focus coming through in the above statements is the way in which leaders influence their followers to produce a desired outcome through the quality and characteristics of the relationships that they establish with their followers. Although there is no universally accepted definition of leadership, most tend to confirm this pivotal principle that leadership requires the power to influence others. For example, Yukl's (2006: 8) commonly applied definition states that leadership is 'the process of influencing others to understand and agree about what needs to be done and how to do it, and the process of facilitating individual and collective efforts to accomplish shared objectives'. This, then, raises questions about the nature of the leader's 'power' to influence. Indeed, how the leader sees the nature of their 'power' to influence determines their actual approach to leadership practice. The nature of this power in a transactional approach is very different to that in a transrelational approach. The first section of this chapter sets out to clearly describe this difference.

Possible sources of power

To more deeply understand the foundation of power within human relationships, the studies of Kreisberg (1992) may prove beneficial. Kreisberg's work, *Transforming power: Domination, empowerment, and education*, highlighted the distinction between two sources of power: 'power over' and 'power with'. He defined 'power over' as 'a conception of power as the ability to impose one's will on others as a means towards fulfilling one's desired goals. It is the ability to direct and control and to manipulate and coerce if need be, sometimes for the good of all, most often for the good of the few' (1992: 45). We experience this form of leadership power when trust is not openly shared in communication with others. Decisions are made, for example, about budgetary matters with limited information shared between key stakeholders. Recommendations provided during committee meetings later appear to be modified or superseded. Meetings are used to disseminate pieces of information. Professional valuations are designed as hoop-jumping activities rather than as formative professional growth. Another form of 'power over' occurs when the leader acts in a way that undermines trust because the actions cause an emotional disturbance in others such as actions that are viewed as unethical or discriminatory or present the leader as being moody or unpredictable. Power over is evident when the real purpose of a leader's action is to serve the needs of their self or selected individuals. For Pierro et al. (2013: 1124), they classify this source as 'harsh' power, which they classify as power that 'constrain individual's freedom to comply with the leader's demands' and add that it is based on the intentional manipulation of coercion, reward, position, equity and reciprocity.

'Power with' accepts that people must be free of domination to develop to their full capacity, and that it is only within the context of relationships with others that the individual can realize power. 'Power over' is exploitative power; 'power with' is integrative power. 'Power with' in leadership argues that the greater the leader is able to develop each individual, the more able both will become, the more effective will be the leadership, and less need there is for the leader to feel that they have to limit or restrict others. Similarly, Pierro et al. (2013: 1124) categorize such sources as 'soft power', which 'endower organizational members with more freedom and autonomy in accepting the demands from the influencing agent'. Importantly, contemporary research (see, for example, Barth-Farkas and Vera 2014; Koslowski, Schwarzwald and Ashuri 2001; Pierro, Kruglanski and Raven 2012; Reiley and Jacobs 2016) is clearly showing that the so-called 'soft power' sources are invariably having a far more productive impact as these are associated with more positive individual and organizational outcomes. Moreover, the 'hard' sources are more closely aligned with managerialism while the soft sources are aligned with leadership.

Expanding upon these dichotomous perspectives in order to better understand what constitutes hard or soft sources of power, the highly regarded (see Braynion 2004) research of French and Raven (1959) proposes five sources of a leader's power with the first three being hard sources and the latter two soft sources. The first source is that of 'coercive power', which is based on control over punishments including actions such as suspensions, warnings, exclusions, and is used to secure compliance. The degree of coercion usually falls between lenience and harshness and is at the leader's discretion. According to Segiovanni (1992), the assumed power base here is bureaucratic authority and it is underpinned by mandates, rules, regulations, job descriptions and performance expectations. When leaders base their power on bureaucratic authority, those being led are expected to respond appropriately or face the consequences. Shackleton (1995) observes that despite its negative connotations, coercive power is frequently explicitly used to try and ensure day-to-day compliance issues such as regularity of attendance, appropriate use of technology and the timely commitment to deadlines. It is also implicitly applied within many annual goal-setting and performance management processes. The fundamental ingredient in this source of power is its intention to induce some element of fear – of losing a job, of reduced income, of not receiving a bonus, of not being given work commensurate with knowledge and skills, of having certain workplace responsibilities given to others, of not being included on important committees, of losing career options, of not being affirmed or acknowledged for achievements gained, and so on.

French and Raven's (1959) second source is that of 'reward power', the ability to reward desired performances and outcomes. This source of power is based on the leader's ability to control valued organizational assets, for example, pay, promotion, affirmation and information. Here, the leader's influence is believed to depend on the amount of access to rewards: the greater the access the stronger the perceived influence. For Handy (1993), this is the least popular of the power bases, as people do not like to feel they are being bought. This powerbase is also strongly affected by the perception of those being led – they must believe that the leader can provide something useful. Furthermore, this source of power is often met with scepticism because any rewards are as easily removed as what they are given or what is rewarded today might not be rewarded tomorrow. The issuing of any reward appears to be at the whim of the leader such that the lack of any transparency in the reward allocation process immediately undermines trust in the leader. Hence the reward not only fails to be a source of motivation but also has the potential to reduce the leader's credibility and, thereby, their power to influence.

'Legitimate power' is the third of French and Raven's (1959) leadership power power sources. This stems from the view of those being led that the leader has the legitimate right and/or authority to influence them and that they are obliged to comply with the leader's wishes. Handy (1993) posits that this source of power is more prevalent where the leader is unable to utilize other sources, such as coercive and/or reward power, but has the backing of the organization's shareholders or directors. However, this source of power only influences the areas of behaviour where those being led believe the leader has the right to influence. Hersey, Blanchard and Johnson (2001) further argue that the effectiveness of legitimate power is often dependent upon the existing commitment of those being led. Those who have a less than positive view of the organization will be unlikely to afford the leader much in the way of legitimate power. Also, the latter part of last century, particularly in the Western world, witnessed the slow decay of this source of power. The Second World War war crimes, the anti-Vietnam War demonstrations, the anti-apartheid demonstrations, feminism, critical theory, the hippy and flower-power movements and so on all contributed to a general scepticism, if not distrust, of authority and blind loyalty. Leaders now have to earn trust in order to have the power to influence others. Such trust and power is rarely automatically given to a leader today.

The first of the soft sources of power is French and Raven's (1959) fourth source, 'referent power', which is based on the identification of those being led with the leader, and on how much they like, admire, respect and want to be like the leader. In this situation, 'the follower wants to be closely associated with the leader and what they do' (Braynion 2004: 449) because the leader is perceived as an attractive person who displays warmth, understanding, charisma and perhaps empathy. Hersey, Blanchard and Johnson (2001) point out that referent power is particularly important in being able to build others' trust and confidences.

Finally, the second soft source of power is what French and Raven refer to as 'expert power'. This is a source of power to influence that is based on an accepted belief that the leader possesses skills and/or abilities that those being led value and need. This power base constantly needs renewing, whereby the leader continues to acquire additional skills and knowledge.

While this discussion has highlighted that a leader's power to influence the thoughts and behaviours of others can potentially be achieved in a number of different ways, with variable beneficial outcomes depending on the source used, it has not isolated the universal ingredient that enables any of the means described to become a means for influencing others. To this end, the views of Sergiovanni (1992) provide a valuable insight. Sergiovanni posits that the hard sources of coercion, reward and legitimacy proffer a 'follow me' influence and adds that these cannot work without some external force to get free-thinking people to do what is desired. Thus these sources of power always require some type of formalized monitoring to ensure that the desired outcomes are continuously achieved. In other words, these sources of power are management intensive, which, in the short term can get people to cooperate but cannot inspire the kind of commitment that will make workplaces more productive because it tends to induce a state of subordination among those being led rather than a sincere commitment by them to their assigned responsibilities.

Sergiovanni (1992) argues that the soft sources of referent and expert power proffer a 'within' influence. Here the source of influence comes from within the person being led and is not externally imposed upon them. The most powerful source of influence is that which has its genesis within the person being led rather than from what the leader might do (coerce or reward) or the position the leader might hold (legitimate). But this is not to say that the role of the leader is independent to the development of this source of influence. Clearly this is not the case. Although the genesis of the influence is within the person, the catalyst is the nature of the relationship that the person has with their possible leader. Hard sources of power are most likely accompanied by distant, aloof, or strained interpersonal relationships between the leader and those to be led, and are the most ineffective. While the soft sources of power are more associated with sociable, friendly, inclusive and cooperative interpersonal relationships between the leader and those to be led, and are the most effective. In other words, the true essence of a leader's effective influential power is relational.

In this chapter and throughout the book, we contend that leadership that is founded on a transrelational approach will be far more effective in influencing those being led than any managerial form of leadership. To better understand how this might be so, our discussion explores the concept of power more deeply. The next section seeks to deconstruct relational power so that it can become more accessible in the daily practice of a transrelational leader.

Relational power deconstructed

In the words of the American broadcast journalist and noted social commentator, Edward Murrow, 'To be persuasive we must be believable, to be believable we must be credible, to be credible we must be truthful.' This is the challenge for any leader – to be persuasive, believable, credible and truthful – but especially for a transrelational leader. One could presume from Murrow's description that the attainment of each of these admirable and desirable qualities is at the discretionary prerogative of the individual person. However, as has just been argued, in our understanding of transrelational leadership, these qualities, and thus the capacity of the leader to be able to persuade, to have the power to influence others, are a relational and not an individual phenomenon. A Foucauldian conceptualization of power provides a means to develop a deeper awareness of how this can be so.

According to Foucault, the existence of influential interpersonal power needs to be understood as embedded in and expressed through relationships (see Lynch 1998; Verderber and Verderber 1992). Foucault's conceptualization of power posits that rather than the source of a leader's power emanating from their role, or from their capacity to reward or punish, or from their superior knowledge, it arises out of the outcomes generated by the interactions between the leader and those they lead. In other words, power emanates from the dynamics of the relationship between the leader and their group. Although we frequently assume that a leader's level of power is derived from their appointment to a particular role, or their inferred level of authority to reward or punish to some degree, or their perceived amount of relevant knowledge, their power is always and strictly relational (Lynch 1998).

Moreover, the essence of this relational power is said to be access to truth about the organization (Widder 2004). Where a leader is willing and able to create and support relationships with their group that encourages an open, transparent and shared discussion about the organization, relational power is generated (Abel 2005). What this means is that the power of a leader emanates from their willingness and capacity to generate knowledge and truth in a cooperative, relational manner. This is about the leader having a growth mindset, as described in Chapter 3, whereby they willingly acknowledge their own professional and experiential limitations and so seek to augment their knowledge, beliefs, experiences and perceptions with those from diverse fields. These leaders know that their view of the organization is only one of many and a more realistic view can only be formed when these different views are openly shared and critiqued. At the same time, those being led come to appreciate the opportunity not only to contribute but also to take decisions about the organization's success and sustainability, and thus their own job security, and are being informed by a truthful view of the organization. Hence, such knowledge and truth about the organization is co-constructed and not imposed, consistent and not arbitrary, shared and not withheld, and dynamic and not static. Moreover, it is through this co-constructed, relationally formed knowledge and truth about the organization that the leader gains the power to influence others. The approach and process binds all involved to a common purpose and with loyalty and responsibility. In contrast, when a leader tries to impose their own limited view of the organization's reality, and uses this to justify decisions, its perceived limitations become obvious to many of those being led. Hence, it is not accepted as the 'truth' about the organization, and suspicion and resistance is generated, resulting in the leader's loss of influential power. The approach encourages people to limit their involvement to that which is known to be required and easily achievable.

Simply, the transrelational leader's source of relational power emanates from having a growth mindset whereby they are willing to have an open and transparent discussion about how well the organization is achieving its goals and strategy. Through their interpretation of the myriad of discourses experienced within the organization, each person constructs a belief about the degree of comprehensiveness and completeness of the organizational knowledge presented by the leader and, thereby, the level of truth within the organization. It is upon this personal judgement that the leader's degree of power is assessed and the measure of required resistance is determined (Abel 2005). The more relationally constructed that the truthfulness of the leader's presentation is of what they believe to be the organization's current reality status, the more power they will possess to influence those they are leading.

The theoretical position developed and employed in our description of the need for higher education leadership to become fundamentally transrelational is informed by these understandings of power. This description of this transrelational approach to leadership with its dependence upon relational power would, however, remain incomplete if it did not include a description of the practical implications of adopting such a position. The following section therefore describes the organizational application of a fully transrelational approach to higher education leadership, focusing on the three key organizational features of employee duty, commitment and responsibility.

Three important applications of relational power

This description of the organizational application of relational power discusses how it is possible for the leader to influence others to not only accept an obligation to their employer to do their best work for the organization but also to understand and agree about what needs to be done and on how to do it through the transrelational rather than the more managerial approach. To this end, this discussion explores the issues of duty, commitment and responsibility. Duty addresses the issue of how those being led come to accept their obligation to provide the best work effort for their employer. Commitment attends to the need for those being led to accept what needs to be done. Responsibility focuses on how those being led attend to the agreed tasks.

Duty

From a managerial perspective, issues associated with employee duty, obligation and loyalty to the organization have been explored as the expected response from the employee as a result of being given employment. A form of implied contractual obligation – the leader provides an important benefit to the person with employment and a source of regular income, and the employee in response provides high-quality work output, which is an important benefit to the organization. Moreover, within a managerial perspective, it is the leader who determines the degree to which this implied duty to the organization is being met. It is the leader who decides whether or not the organization is getting value for money – whether or not the employee is doing sufficient work at an expected level. Furthermore, if, in the opinion of the leader, an employee is not meeting their employment duty then they feel well within their right to implement individual accountability and performance standard strategies in an attempt to rectify the perception of diminished performance.

From this perspective, the onus is completely upon the employee to change; there is no acknowledgement of other factors that might be at play including, but not limited to, a lack of full awareness by the leader of what the employee is actually doing, a lack of sufficient resources provided to the employee to do their work, a lack of opportunity for the full use of the employee's true strengths in their current role, a lack of acceptance that the workplace culture could be undermining the employee's workplace conditions, a lack of understanding by the employee of what is actually being expected of them, a lack of acceptance that recent workplace changes have undermined the role of the employee, or a lack of interest in the private life of the employee that could have become a serious workplace distraction. However, as a growing body of research explores the issue of employee workplace satisfaction, engagement and loyalty, (see, for example, Bordia, Restugbog and Tang 2008; Jensen, Opland and Ryan 2010; Paillé and Raineri 2016; Rayton and Yalabik 2014; Robinson and Morrison 2000) this understanding of employee duty is coming under increasing pressure. This expectation of an employee having a duty to the organization, although judged by its practical existence, is essentially a psychological phenomenon. At the heart of any sense of duty is the issue of motivation – what motivates the employee to do their very best for the leader and the organization.

Despite literature from the fields of psychology and sociology clearly indicating that intrinsic factors relating to an employee's wish for opportunities to grow in workplace knowledge and skills are more motivational than extrinsic factors associated with pay and conditions, the outdated employee duty expectation is underpinned by the false belief that the employee should be motivated to do their best because of their organizational pay and conditions. As distinguished social scientist Michael de Certeau (1984) argues, it is self-motivation, the enactment of personal agency in everyday practices that creates an employee's sense of duty. No matter what the leader might wish to be happening, any sense of employee duty, obligation or loyalty to the organization wholly resides in the mind of the employee. It is the employee who decides whether or not the leader, and thus the organization, deserves to have them respond with duty, obligation or loyalty. Moreover, since the global recession of the 1980s, when many businesses worldwide laid off workers in order to reduce organizational costs, it has been far more difficult for leaders to achieve such a response. During this period the long-held employee belief that they would have security of employment throughout their working life, provided that they worked hard and did what the organization required of them, was destroyed. Importantly, the psychological sense of duty was destroyed by business leaders and not by the employees. Once employees realized that their loyalty to the organization was not reciprocated, then there was no obligation for them to be duty bound to the organization.

Now, in a world viewed as globally interdependent, where the financial mistakes of individuals in one country can cause extreme hardships and the loss of personal property across many other countries, employees see that their organizational leaders possess much less control over employment security (Clarke and Hennig 2012). Today, the employee's sense of their own personal authority, which arises out of their skill and knowledge, is considered to be far more important than that of their leader. It is the employee's judgement of the level and effectiveness of their own personal skill and knowledge, which provides them with a sense of purpose and meaning rather than any sense of duty, obligation or loyalty to the organization. It is an employee's level of interest and fulfilment in completing a particular workplace task that provides the greatest sense of duty (Wheatley 2006). In other words, the leader who can engage with those they are leading in order to ensure that each employee is maximizing the use of their physical and mental strengths will automatically induce employee duty to them and to the organization. Furthermore, the ongoing economic rationalization processes regularly applied by managerialism have perpetuated this undermining of employee duty. In those organizations where common cost-cutting occurrences frequently reduce resources and opportunities, or where economic risk management is said to mandate high levels of part-time or fixed-term or contracted positions, or where position descriptions are significantly changed without consultation, employees feel no loyalty from their leaders or from the organization and so, understandably, respond with no sense of duty or obligation.

From a transrelational position, this understanding of duty, or self-forming motivation, calls for all in leadership positions across the whole organization to be able to create the conditions in which each employee has the freedom to reflect and question their workplace circumstances, to nurture a kind of curiosity about how to better their workplace skills and knowledge within these circumstances, and to seek ways to become more productive in these and future circumstances (May 2006). This view is shared by Foucault (1997: 225), who argued that the task of the leader is to help 'individuals to effect by their own means a certain number of operations on their own bodies and souls, thoughts, conduct, and way of being, so as to transform themselves'. Essentially, this requires the leader to have nurtured an interdependent relationship with each of the employees that they have responsibility for explicitly leading. Here, this relationally based form of leadership requires the leader to be in the group in order to learn about each group member and the affordances and constraints they are imposing upon themselves; and what each group member considers to be their personal strengths and aspirations (Haslam, Reicher and Platow 2011). Through this relationship, the leader is able to discover what is meaningful to each employee as they are engaged in their work. What issues and behaviours get their attention? What topics generate the most energy, positive and negative?

In order to answer such questions, the leader must be working *with* the employee, not sitting on the side observing behaviour or interviewing individuals. Secondly, the leader must assume that, in every group, there are as many different interpretations of the current situation as there are people in the group. Thus the leader must assume that they will discover multiple and divergent interpretations, perspectives and meanings for everything that is happening and that needs to occur. Hence it is important for the leader to 'try to put ideas and issues on the table as experiments to discover these different meanings, not as a particular person's recommendations for what should be meaningful. [The leader must] try to stay open to the different reactions [they] get, rather than instantly categorizing people as resistors or allies. [The leader must] expect diverse responses; and, gradually, even learn to welcome them' (Wheatley 2006: 148).

When employees feel that their experiences, opinions, views and suggestions are listened to, and seriously considered, they sense they are personally contributing to the future viability and success of the organization. They feel more productive; and their work becomes more meaningful. Under these conditions, the employee's sense of duty does not have to be externally maintained because it becomes natural and automatic.

Commitment

For much of last century the expectation was that a key responsibility of a leader was to implement principles and processes that foster employee discipline, punctuality, efficiency, rationality and order (Hamel 2007). This managerial perspective directed the leader's attention to administration and coordination activities. Hamel adds that such a managerial approach is 'very good at aggregating efforts, at coordinating the activities of many people with widely varying roles. But [it is] not very good at mobilizing effort, at inspiring people to go above and beyond' (2007: 62). In contrast, he advocates for a relational, 'community', form of leadership. In a managerial organization, the basis for exchange is contractual – you get paid for doing what is assigned to you. In a relationally rich organization, exchange is voluntary – you give your labour in return for the chance to make a difference, or exercise your talents. In a managerial organization, you are a factor of production. In a relationally rich organization, you are a partner in a cause. Dedication and commitment are based on the employee's affiliation with the organization's aims and goals. When it comes to supervision and control, managerial organizations rely on multiple layers of management and a web of policies and rules. Relationally rich organizations, by contrast, depend on norms, values and the gentle prodding of one's peers.

Contemporary sociologists (see, for example, Bauman 1992, 1999; Castells 2000) highlight the tendency of people to seek to network with particular others. As employees look to enhance their own skills and knowledge to increase their personal capacities and, thereby, sense of purpose and meaning, they strategically seek to work with others who are seen as being able to contribute towards this process of ongoing self-formation (Castells 2000). These workplace networks are created in such a way that individuals attempt to 'avoid those interactions where they will spend more benefit than they gain, and they will pursue those interactions where they have a good chance of increasing their level of benefit. They also tend to avoid those interactions where their lack of capacity will be apparent' (Allan 2011: 317). As a result, it is argued that employees now tend to want to separate themselves into symbolic or status groups or networks around other employees who are seen as having mutually beneficial knowledge, skills and expertise. Through a tangible sense of solidarity with others, whose knowledge, skills and expertise are seen to be mutually complementary and beneficial, the employee gains the deepest sense of workplace purpose and security.

With this awareness of a natural tendency towards networking through selective solidarity in mind, the leader's attention can be drawn towards gaining the benefits from enabling rather than constraining its occurrence. First, rather than seeing selective solidarity solely as an individualistic phenomenon, the transrelational leader must see it as a natural tendency that can work to the advantage of all. To this end, if left unimpeded or actually nurtured, selective solidarity will cause each employee to strive to do their best and to keep improving. Quality work emerges out of the individual's need to be seen as worthy by their co-employees. Under such circumstances, employees do not have to be explicitly organized so as to work well, they will do it 'naturally', provided that they are not limited, frustrated, suppressed or controlled by their leader.

More specifically, the leader's task in this process is to create *dynamic connectedness* (Dutton and Heaphy 2003). This calls upon the leader to proactively build relationships of worth and merit, to maximize opportunities for productive networks to form, and to ensure that each employee's perceived worth is growing (Holland 1995; Marion and Uhl-Bien 2001). Through the creation of dynamic connectedness, the leader is able to expand selective solidarity so that many more employees and groups within the particular organization are willing and able to interact collaboratively to better achieve not only their personal need for solidarity, but also the primary focus of the organization (Regine and Lewin 2000). In this way, the approach produces success and sustainability for the organization. Moreover, leaders wishing to utilize the selective solidarity tendency of group members through the creation of dynamic connectedness do not try to direct change or control future outcomes. Rather, they encourage connections, interrelationships, among all of those they are leading in unpredictable, dynamic, strategic, fluid, creative and emergent ways. They seek to create as many co-employee connections as possible and all based upon equality, respect, collegiality, support, encouragement and empathy.

Responsibility

The perceived quality of a person's performance in an organization has been the focus of leadership since Frederick Winslow Taylor introduced scientific management into organizational culture (Hamel 2007); simply stated, ever since the introduction of scientific management leadership has been consumed by the need to determine 'how well people are doing their jobs' (Luecke 2007: 116). In contemporary workplaces, this need is couched in terms of accountability – holding the employee accountable for the quality of their workplace performance. The employee is held accountable through an explicit performance review process, with the purpose 'to improve future work performance by examining how well the person is doing in carrying out their respective elements of the [organizational] plan and their specific tasks' (Macdonald, Burke and Stewart 2006: 152). From a managerial perspective it is the leader who takes responsibility for not only determining what is deemed to be an acceptable level of performance but also for establishing the means by which an employee's performance can be compared to this expected level.

In contrast to this view, Bauman (1992) argues that the contemporary employee's own desire for selective solidarity with others in the form of workplace networks means that they highly value self-determination. Under such workplace circumstances, employees do not want to be distracted or misdirected by externally and impersonally imposed rules, expectations and accountabilities, which are likely to have them working with others who appear to offer little benefit to the partnership. Similarly, they do not want to be completing responsibilities that do not seem to fully utilize or extend their knowledge and skills. In other words, not only does the employee look to be working with others who are committed to a mutually beneficial relationship, but, they are also fully aware that every other employee is doing the same. The employee is conscious of being both a judge of others and the focus of judgement by others. Thus, the employee is aware that they must be continually self-monitoring their performance to ensure that it presents well in the judgements of others. In this way personal responsibility, rather than leadership-imposed accountability, becomes the fundamental processes for maintaining performance standards.

In these conditions, the leader's task is not to make sure that each employee knows exactly what to do and how to do it. Instead, it is to ensure that there is strong and evolving clarity about what is happening in the organizational environment and what this is requiring of employees. Simply stated, it is important for the leader to ensure that the employees are not just looking at themselves and each other but that they are also able to fully comprehend what is happening around them. This is not about the leader imposing an image of the organizational environment upon each employee, but more that the leader is able to richly describe that environment and to draw the attention of the employees to the acknowledged purpose of that particular organization within that environment. This helps to create a discourse concerning what challenges lay ahead while not mandating how these are to be addressed. It is about trusting in the commitment, creativity, ingenuity, determination and personal responsibility of the employees to automatically begin to move towards meeting any new knowledge and skill requirements, and to start to invent ways to overcome the challenges.

When the emphasis is on transrelational leading, achieving performance expectations thus becomes the responsibility of the employee supported and guided by the leader. This contrasts to a managerial situation in which achieving performance expectations becomes mandated through formalized review and accountability procedures. Transrelational practices empower the employee; managerial practices dis-empower the employee. Transrelational leadership provides the employee with the opportunity to dwell on the meaning ascribed to their work so as to discover common issues and problems that are deemed significant and addressable. Responsibility becomes personal and spontaneous. Although we see responsibility at the material level, processes that are immaterial generate it. Thus, leadership must look for these invisible relational processes rather than the accountability regulations and policies that they seem to engender. Leaders must look for those processes that give rise to meaning for those whom they lead. They must look beyond the traditional ways of achieving performance expectations to utilize the processes that give them worth and value. As explained by Wheately (2006: 133), 'When leaders honour us with opportunities to know the truth of what is occurring and support us to explore the deeper meaning of the events, we instinctively reach out to them. Those who help us center our work in deeper purpose are leaders we cherish, and to whom we return love, gift for gift. With meaning as our centering place, we can journey through the realms of chaos and make sense of the world. With meaning as an attractor, we can re-create ourselves to carry forward what we value most.' With meaning and purpose as a motivator, employees do not need to be held accountable, they just need the freedom to become responsible.

Conclusion

The primary aim of this chapter has been to provide a very specific and detailed description of a commonly held, but not well understood, characteristic of leadership – the power to influence the thinking and actions of others – but from a transrelational approach to leadership perspective. If such power is presumed to reside in the position of leadership, or in the leader's superior knowledge or authority to reward or punish, then the concept of transrelational leadership flounders because the need for the leader to develop relationships in order to influence others becomes moot. This chapter has described the inherent fallacies and problems associated with this mistaken presumption. As described above, the real essence of a leader's power to influence others is their capacity to develop relational power. This understanding is illustrated more comprehensively in Figure 4.1. From this illustration it can be gleaned that the more dependent the leader is upon relational power the more likely they are able to enact transrelational leadership.

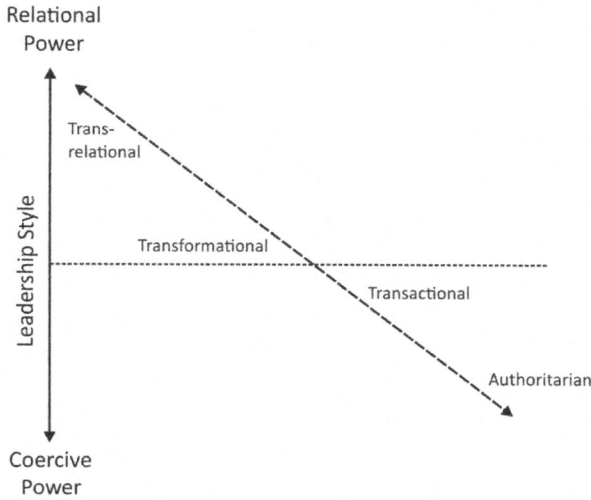

Figure 4.1 An illustration of the relationship between the degree of relational power and the likely preferred style of leadership

The latter section of this chapter reflected the pragmatic concerns that such a commitment by a leader to relational power might raise. Three key organizational issues were discussed – employee duty, commitment and responsibility – from both the managerial point of view and a transrelational approach to leadership perspective. In each case the merits of a relational approach have been highlighted.

It is acknowledged that the three issues have been presented from the employee's viewpoint and that the argument centres round what today's leader needs to do in order to achieve the desired outcome from the employee. There are also important practical outcomes that a contemporary leader is invariably concerned with. Hence the next two chapters will each discuss an important organizational outcome in today's corporate world. Chapter 6 will discuss the leadership of organizational change and Chapter 7 will discuss performance management and employee engagement.

The Challenge of Organizational Change

Abstract

The chapter sets out to show that transrelational leadership is inherently more suited to leading successful organizational change than other leadership theories. While change is now considered to be endemic within organizations, including higher education institutions, diverse large-scale research supports the view that only approximately 30 per cent of organizational change actually achieves its desired outcomes. Moreover, it is proposed that this unacceptable level of unsuccessful change is due to a failure on the part of organizational leaders to suitably attend to modifying the organization's culture. By necessity, if change is required then the organization's culture needs to be reviewed and, potentially, adjusted to enable and support change. This chapter argues that the fundamental principles of transrelational leadership weave leadership practice and organizational culture together, and that therefore, transrelational leadership is inherently more suited to achieving successful organizational change than other leadership approaches. To this end, this chapter describes how a transrelational leader is more able to suitably work with those they are leading through different types of change – routine, complicated, complex and chaotic – while remaining ever mindful of attending to the cultural adjustments that are required to support any desired change.

Introduction

The widely recognized catch phrase, 'the only constant is change' once aroused surprise and astonishment because it seemed to highlight something about our lives that was unexpected, abnormal and unwanted. Today, change is largely accepted as a part of life. Many would claim that, due to the impact of modern science, technology, transportation and the globalization and internationalization of communications, business and employment, change in today's world is both endemic and dramatic. Our lives are surrounded by, and enriched by, the impact of change. But this does not mean that everyone automatically accepts change, particularly when it appears to impact on them personally. Within an organizational context, the likelihood of employee resistance to change is ever present. Indeed, overcoming resistance to desired organizational change is a challenge that few leaders appear capable of effectively addressing. Since it is people, rather than any plan, that ultimately produce organizational change, where sufficient resistance exists, attempted change fails.

With this understanding it is perhaps not surprising to find that ongoing large-scale international research indicates that there is only a 30 per cent success rate for desired organizational change. Moreover, the McKinsey Comany's longitudinal research (see DeSmet et al. 2014) shows that this 30 per cent success rate has remained consistent since 1995, regardless of the nature of the organizational context. This view is also supported by internationally acclaimed business management and leadership researcher, Margaret Wheatley, who writes that 'senior corporate leaders report that up to 75% of their change projects do not yield the promised results' (2006: 138). Furthermore, these low success rates can be regarded as occurring across the higher education sector, in a similar way to the business sector, the health sector and the industrial sector. This appalling level of change failure has continued despite not only countless published views on how to successfully lead organizational change, but also billions of dollars being spent by organizations attempting to produce desired changes according to these published views.

Harvard Business College professor, Gary Hamel, suggests that 'perhaps the problem with [change] leadership is that we have reached the end of management. Perhaps we have more or less mastered the sciences of organizing human beings, allocating resources, defining objectives, laying out plans, and minimizing deviations from best practice' (2007: 4). What we argue is that the critical fault in the published views about successful leadership of organizational change was not so much the proposed plan, because every desired change needs a plan to guide the strategy, but rather the implied expectation that the plan would be managed – that a key person, the leader, would diligently and closely follow the plan to its ultimately successful conclusion. Managers follow and implement plans; leaders focus on and inspire people. Successful organizational change cannot be managed; it must be led. Furthermore, it requires the right sort of leadership, that draws people to the change and is then able to keep them engaged with the change regardless of their individual responses to the change.

This chapter describes why the transrelational approach to leadership is by far and away the best way to achieve successful organizational change. To this end, it begins by providing a brief, research-informed view of contemporary concerns about organizational change in higher education. This is followed by a comprehensive description of the different types of organizational change, and how each is best led. As employee resistance to change is widely recognized as an ever-present obstacle to the achievement of successful organizational change, the chapter then moves on to provide some important insights about how a leader can help to minimize the presence of resistance. The chapter concludes with the recommendation that the future of successful organizational change might be better achieved if leaders move away from a dependence on episodic change to instead focus on establishing and maintaining an ever-evolving change culture within their organization.

Organizational change in the higher education context

While the adoption of transrelational leadership mandates the implementation of organizational change, the need for such change is far more pervasive. Higher education institutions now face serious new challenges of an economic, demographic, curriculum and pedagogical nature. As described by Franken, Branson and Penney (2016), these include but are not limited to competition and ensuing marketization, a reduction in state funding, an increasingly non-tenured and part-time workforce, the massification of education, the diversification of the student body, and the incorporation of online pedagogies in course delivery. Those in formal leadership positions now have an essential responsibility to ensure the capacity to enable the institution to constructively and effectively attend to these new challenges. In other words, the capacity to successfully lead complex organizational change is now an integral leadership responsibility in higher education institutions.

However, as McRoy and Gibbs (2009) describe, the plurality and complexity of higher education institutions renders organizational change as an extremely difficult challenge. Higher education institutions are professional service organizations and the professionals and para-professionals within them vary in their training, interests and methods of working. Leading this diversity and complexity through some form of desired change exaggerates and adds complexity to the demands and responsibilities. Unfortunately, into this complex mix we must now add the impact of managerialism, which, as By, Diefenbach and Klarner (2008) have highlighted, brings in its own structural and procedural reform agendas that circle around prescribed changes to basic organizational principles and practices. Consequently, Baert and Shipman's (2005) research draws attention to the distractive influence of these managerialist reforms, because of the requisite audit trails taking academics, the producers of the core business of higher education, away from what they are actually being paid to do. It is then not surprising that Chaharbaghi (2007: 319–20) laments managerialism's impact on higher education, identifying it as having 'added a costly administrative burden that is undermining the morale, motivation and goodwill of [the] professionals … destroying accomplishment, satisfaction and motivation, and in the end, is destroying performance'. By, Diefenbach and Klarner posit that managerially imposed changes upon the higher education environment will 'ultimately lead to a less effective, less purposeful, unproductive and weaker HE where few will be left to actually perform those functions required by society' (2008: 32).

What this brief discussion highlights is that there are multiple reasons why contemporary leaders of higher education institutions need to be extremely adept at leading successful organizational change. The practical wisdom gained from being a highly credible professional academic does not typically lead to the highly specific leadership skills and knowledge that higher education leaders require. As Goleman (1999: 3) describes, much more is being required of today's leaders because they 'are being judged by a new yardstick: not just by their training or expertise, but also by how well they handle their self and others'. Wheatley (2006: 131) extends this view by arguing that, in organizations involved in complex change, the need is for leaders, 'not bosses', because the people actually making the change happen need leaders who help them develop a positive view of the future 'that lights the dark moments of confusion'. Furthermore, she suggests that effective leaders of complex organizational change need to understand that those they are leading 'are best controlled by concepts that invite participation, not policies and procedures that curtail [their] contribution'. More specifically, Bolman and Deal (2008: 435) claim that, in organizations like higher education institutions which are undergoing constant and complex change, the unequivocal need is for 'wise leaders' with 'high levels of personal artistry' so that they can confidently 'respond to today's challenges, ambiguities, and paradoxes'. They add that such leaders 'need versatility in thinking that fosters flexibility in action. They need capacity to act inconsistently when uniformity fails, diplomatically when emotions are raw, non-rationally when reason flags, politically in the face of vocal parochial self-interest, and playfully when fixating on task and purpose backfires' (Bolman and Deal 2008: 435). This form of leadership is as much about understanding people as it is about knowing what to do.

Being a leader of change in contemporary higher education thus requires learning how to be the person who can readily understand others in order to create the most effective workplace culture that maximizes people's engagement and output. Here, again, the business world does not necessarily provide a model of successful leadership of organizational change. Not only is the success rate of organizational change in the business world appalling, but also its dominant values and tenets are counterproductive for higher educational institutions. By, Diefenbach and Klarner (2008) argue that the rise of managerialism has ironically not made the leadership of higher education institutions more effective but has instead added a costly administrative burden that is undermining the morale, motivation and goodwill of the university personnel and has destroyed accomplishment, satisfaction and motivation, and performance. More speci-fically, the consequences of the accountability and audit culture inherent within the managerial processes means that far less time is now being spent on teaching and research because ever more time is being spent on form-filling and positional justification activities.

To better understand and appreciate the inherent demands and challenges of organizational change in order to see and accept how it is best led successfully, it is necessary first to develop a deeper appreciation of its inconsistencies. For much too long those describing how to manage successful organizational change have presented the view that there is only one form of change. This is not so and each different form requires a different approach to its leadership. Thus, the next section describes the different forms of organizational change and the type of leadership approach that is required for each of these.

An overview of developments in organizational change

As previously described elsewhere (Branson 2009), although organizational change is unfolding rather than explicit, the organizational change literature still acknowledges distinguishable trends in this ongoing process. Current organizational change practices are informed by transactional, transformational or complexity theory.

As discussed in Chapter 3, transactional changes within organizations are brought about by mandating or motivating the people to perform more effectively, or differently, according to prescribed parameters in exchange for specific rewards (Randall and Coakley 2007). The implementation of such changes is very much controlled by the formal leader and line managers, and is characterized by the expectation that everyone will commit to their respective clearly defined roles and responsibilities in order for the organization to successfully achieve its predictable and anticipated new outcome (Fairholm 2004). Furthermore, progress towards the successful achievement of this new outcome, and the degree to which the key people are committed to their assigned roles and responsibilities, is deemed to be measurable through audits, reviews and reports.

There are extensive sources of help for any leader seeking to enact a transactional change. First, most of the plethora of 'how to manage change' books provide relatively detailed descriptions of transactional change processes. The majority of the titles of such self-help texts actually use the word 'manage' and not 'lead', reflecting that the transactional process is essentially management and not leadership. Although these change management texts might each include a number of distinctive elements, they share the same theoretical foundation of transactional change. A second source of help is that regularly provided by the external organizational change and/or change management 'expert'. Such experts rarely take the time to gain a full understanding of the organization and its employees. Rather, they oversee the facilitation of a largely preconceived and pre-modelled logical–sequential process. Any organizational change process promoted or facilitated in this way cannot be anything other than transactional.

Many organizational change researchers (see, for example, De Smet, Lavoie and Hioe 2012; Ewenstein, Smith and Sologar 2015; Kezar 2013; Louvel 2013; Martin 2014; McRoy and Gibbs 2009) argue that this transactional approach to organizational change with its highly technical, controlled, impersonal and inflexible qualities is prone to failure because it develops too much resistance from those employees who are expected to make the change happen. However, the contemporary organizational change theory and practice of David Snowden (see Snowden and Boone 2007), as described by his *Cynefin Decision Making Framework*, which has gained international recognition and acclaim in the corporate world, provides a slightly more optimistic view. The transactional approach aligns well with two of Snowden's forms of organizational change – 'simple' and 'chaotic'. According to Snowden, the inherent characteristics of a 'simple' organizational change are that (1) the problem is occurring repeatedly and consistently, (2) there is a clear cause-and-effect relationship between the problem and the solution proposed by the leader, and (3) everyone can readily see the problem, and therefore, can also understand and accept the leader's proposed solution. Where these characteristics are evident, Snowden believes that a very closely managed, transactional approach will not only be widely supported by those involved with the change but, importantly, it should be successful. But any success with this approach can be its downfall. If it is applied to more complex problems it is destined to fail. Moreover, most of the important contemporary organizational problems (and certainly, in our experience, many problems faced in higher education) do not meet the aforementioned characteristics, meaning that most of these are not cases requiring simple change.

With respect to Snowden's 'chaotic' form of organizational change, its inherent characteristics, as its name suggests, are extremely high levels of turbulence, tension, indecision, disunity and immediacy. It appears that no one in the organization either knows what is happening or what should happen – there are multiple problems all with no apparent cause and effect. Everyone seems to be doing their own thing even if it appears to be providing little benefit. People are mainly looking after their own personal interests. When confronted with such a rare but potentially catastrophic organizational environment, Snowden argues that the leader needs, first, to make a decision about what is the most important problem to address then, secondly, decide on a likely solution and, finally, enforce the implementation of the chosen solution and see what happens. This is transactional change at its most fundamental level. If the solution works, repeat it with the problem deemed to be the next most important to address. There should be no concern about making a wrong decision because the environment is already chaotic. But Snowden warns that as soon as some semblance of order appears in the organization, the leader should cease the transactional approach and apply an approach directly suited to the type of problem requiring attention as described below.

According to Wilber (2000), organizational change that is transactional in nature only concentrates on changing the 'exterior' dimensions of the change process and ignores the equally important 'interior' dimensions. In the context of an organization, the exterior dimension of the individual is their role function and the exterior dimension of the organization is its operational structure. This means that changes to role function and operational structure are the key features of transactional organizational development. Change processes associated with role re-visioning, restructuring, downsizing, re-engineering and merging reflect a strong commitment to transactional organizational change. What these strategies overlook is the inherent interior dimensions of any form of change. The interior dimensions of change include the interior of the organization, which is its culture, and the interior dimension of the individual, which are the personal thinking and emotions of each person in the organization experiencing the change.

Wilber's philosophical arguments are supported by extensive international research. For example, the organizational change research of Blenkin, Edwards and Kelly (1997) plus Hopkins, Ainscow and West (1997) as well as House and McQuillan (1998) all highlight the need for any change process to pay equal attention to the sociopolitical perspective. This reflects the view that any form of change inevitably arouses ongoing political, social and cultural struggles as individuals and groups apply various strategies, and various sources of power and influence, to further their own interests. Furthermore, Hechanova and Cementina-Olpoc's (2013: 17) longitudinal and comprehensive organizational change in higher education research highlighted 'the importance of recognizing the role of culture' when leading successful change. Even more compelling is the research by De Smet, Schaninger and Smith (2014) on behalf of the large multinational research and professional development corporation of the McKinsey Company. This longitudinal research involving more than eight hundred organizations worldwide shows that far more successful organizational change is accomplished if the change process looks at both health and performances when seeking potential solutions to a perceived problem. By 'health' De Smet, Lavoie and Hioe (2014) are referring to the tangible outcomes of the culture including the proclaimed vision, the level of engagement, the stated values, the amount of cooperation and mentoring, the commitment to workplace learning, and the effectiveness of the style of leadership. These authors claim that 'when companies manage with an equal eye to performance and health, they more than double the probability of outperforming their competitors' (De Smet, Lavoie and Hioe 2014: 1). More specifically, this research data supports the view that 'healthy companies generated total returns to shareholders three times higher than those of unhealthy ones' (De Smet, Lavoie and Hioe 2014: 2). For these authors, successful leaders are not simply concerned with vision and strategy but also with the culture of their organization. Furthermore, invariably more can be gained from changing the culture of the organization to make it healthier than from simply attending to organizational norms, structure and performance.

From Chapter 1 you will recall the strident view of Katzenbach, Steffen and Kronley (2012: 113) who posit that 'culture trumps strategy every time' when it comes to organizational change. To this end, then, the key feature of transformational organizational change is said to be its attention to organizational culture, the interior dimension of the organization. Transformational changes within organizations are brought about primarily by including people in the process of implementing change. The leadership provides an opportunity for others to review 'why' change should be considered and 'what' needs to happen; the 'how' that happens needs to come from those who will be required to implement the changes. Otherwise the existing culture will indeed trump the change. As described in Chapter 1, organizational culture is comprised of multiple sub-cultures; it is at the sub-cultural level that implementation occurs and at the sub-cultural level where change is resisted because the existing 'norms' of the group are powerful enough to induce the resistance. Therefore in order to implement transformational change successfully the following conditions must be in place before people choose to become involved in the change. People will become more readily involved in an organizational change if the following characteristics (Table 5.1) are deemed to be present.

This is because within the organization itself, 'the primary change levers are considered to be the attitudes, beliefs and values' (Chapman 2002: 17) of those who work in the organization. Importantly, the employees' attitudes, beliefs and values are what maintain the organization's culture such that any process of

Table 5.1 Conditions that need to be met before people will engage in organizational change

1	A compelling story	People understand what is being asked of them and it makes sense
2	Localized involvement	People have been consulted about what should happen and how this should happen
3	Cultural fit	Collaboration, creativity and risk taking are encouraged
4	Supported transformation	Opportunities for professional development to meet new knowledge and skill requirements is readily available
5	Reinforcement mechanisms	Organizational structures, processes and systems are adjusted to support the required changes
6	Role modelling	The behaviour of leaders models the change

refinement to these is about the implementation of cultural change. Changing the culture is about refining attitudes, beliefs and values, which, in turn, has the potential to change behaviours and performances. Thus transformational change has also been described as 'gamma' change (Golembiewski, Billingsley and Yeager 1976), or 'second-order' change (Watzlawick, Weakland and Fisch 1974), because it indirectly changes behaviours and performances. Proponents argue that it is exactly because of the primary attention to cultural change that this approach results not only in a move to a different level of understanding across the organization, but also a positive shift in most employees' operational practices.

Snowden's 'complicated' category of organizational change aligns well with that of transformational change. Here, he proposes that there is no immediately knowable cause-and-effect relationship but, rather, it has to be discovered. Only through a far more comprehensive exploration of the problem through attention to both the explicit performance characteristics and the implicit cultural characteristics can the reasons for the problem become known. Snowden also adds that there is a likelihood of finding more than one right way to address the problem. The astute leader will work closely with those they are leading towards choosing the most beneficial and supportable solution. Importantly, from Snowden's perspective, transformational change will only be effective where the cause-and-effect relationship can be eventually determined and those being led see this process as being clearly transparent and inclusive. Importantly, those being led can both contribute towards clarifying the cause of the problem and can provide insight into how best to fix the problem.

Unlike transactional change where the leader, or an outside expert, can manage the actual change process, this is not so with transformational change. Any change process needs to begin with processes that are able to explore the problem from below its symptoms in order to unearth its actual cause. The difficulties for the leader, if they were to attempt to lead this exploration process, are threefold. First, they need to have a thorough understanding of how to conduct the process. Secondly, they need to have the capacity to overcome any personal unconscious biases that have the potential to compromise the process. Third, they need to accept that their leadership may be a significant part of the cause of the observed problem and this would create a potential conflict of interest. An external facilitator can avoid these difficulties not as someone who runs the change process, but rather a person who can ask the right questions so that the leader, along with those employed in the organization, is able to eventually see the cause of the problem. Such an external facilitator needs to be able to manage two key processes – a performance audit and a cultural audit. The performance audit explores the perceived problem through multiple lenses and through numerous iterations until an agreed cause–effect relationship is clearly established. Once the actual cause–effect relationship becomes known, then and only then can a plan be devised by a team formed from those in the organization with the most suitable and relevant knowledge, skill, experience and interest. In conjunction with this process is the cultural audit, which explores the elements of the organization's culture that maintain the problem, that underpin the cause, that can benefit or constrain the required changes to overcome the cause of the problem, and that need to be consolidated in order to sustain the required change.

Arguably, the most comprehensive and clearly articulated interpretation of a transformational change process was that delineated by Peter Senge (1990) as the 'Learning Organisation'. As defined by Senge (1994: 3), a learning organization is one 'where people continually expand their capacity to create the results they truly desire, where new and expansive patterns of thinking are nurtured, and where collective aspirations are set free'. It is argued that a learning organization is one that promotes continual organizational renewal by weaving a set of core processes that nurture a positive propensity to learn, adapt and change (Jamali, Khoury and Sahyoun 2006). Within his conception of a learning organization, Senge (1990) proposes new organizational understandings with his emphasis on attaining a 'shared vision' rather than an imposed outcome. He contends that this represents a means of motivating and aligning organizational activity, of learning how to personally create 'mental models' or internal pictures of what constitutes quality organizational activity instead of relying on formally documented roles and responsibilities to shape and guide a commitment to best practice, and of striving for 'personal mastery' as opposed to only adhering to imposed work standards. In addition he emphasizes essential shifts in the deepest operational structures by asserting that 'team learning' (as distinct from hierarchical control, and 'systems thinking') needs to be at the fore of successful organizational development.

Despite its initial widespread appeal, many scholars now perceive the learning organization as an ideal instead of a fully achievable outcome (Argyris 1992; Jamali, Khoury and Sahyoun 2006; Johnson 2002). To date, few organizations have been able to fully achieve the necessary characteristics that support it being a learning organization. Again, Snowden's view would be in accord with this claim by these authors because his decision-making framework extends beyond just the 'simple', 'chaotic' and 'complicated' forms of organizational change. In other words, there is far more to leading successful organizational change than merely the transactional and transformational approaches. Thus, it is important to note the views of Hamel and Zanini (2014: 1) that transformational change has a 'dismal track record' and the research by the eminent Harvard Business School professor, John Kotter, suggesting that nearly 70 per cent of large-scale transformational change programmes in organizations have not produced the expected outcomes. In response to this data, Hamel and Zanini (2014: 1) posit that 'today's organizations were simply never designed to change proactively and deeply – they were built for discipline and efficiency, enforced through hierarchy and routinization'. Furthermore, within this particular organizational design, managerialism thrives on control so that what gets changed and how the culture is understood and modified remains the prerogative of the formal leaders. At the same time, because predictability is paramount, change is minimized to more of an episodic activity amid the status quo – something that is designed, initiated and managed from the top of the hierarchy in order to minimize any interruption. This means that the desired change is often reactionary – a delayed fix to a slowly recognized and acknowledged problem – rather than a proactive initiative to a foreseeable challenge. For those employees charged with the task of actually making the change happen, the unexpected and poorly understood change can induce fear and anxiety rather than enthusiasm and commitment, and hence resistance. Instead of seeing the good in the change, many see the uncertainty of successful change as well as the possible loss of personal job security when new workplace knowledge and skills are required.

What a commitment to transformational organizational change overlooks is the need to address the internal dimension of the individual attached to the organization. That is to say, such organizational change overlooks the need to adjust the natural personal thinking processes of each person within the organization. To this end, the concept of complexity theory (Black and Edwards 2000; Maguire and McKelvey 1999; Styhre 2002; Tsoukas 1998), or complex adaptive systems theory (Englehardt and Simmons 2002), has been drawn upon to further advance understandings of how to successfully lead organizational change. Essentially, complexity theory argues that the only substantial form of organizational change occurs naturally through the interaction of the people within the organization (Beinhocker 1997). By necessity, any form of organizational change needs to enable and encourage positive and constructive interpersonal interaction throughout the organization. Hence, promoting effective organizational change is extremely complex because it requires paying attention to how the individual thinks, which is influenced by their personalized feelings, beliefs, values, perceptions and sensitivities.

The book *Presence: Exploring Profound Change in People, Organizations and Society*, by Senge et al. (2007), stresses the primacy of attending to the internal individual dimensions of organizational change as featured in complexity theory. In this way, this book arguably redresses deficiencies inherent within the learning organization literature. For these authors, it became clear that a learning organization cannot form unless the people within the organization are able to develop the most appropriate feelings, beliefs, values, perceptions and sensitivities, by being readily and willingly engaged in the most creative, rewarding and productive interpersonal relationships with their co-employees. The employees need to be able to change the way they think about themselves, their work, their co-employees, and their organization. Senge et al. (2007) posited a new organizational change initiative with the potential to overcome the inherent deficiencies in the establishment of a learning organization. In *Presence: Exploring Profound Change in People, Organizations and Society*, the authors provide a clear and compelling argument for people changing the way they think, expanding their consciousness, as they go about fulfilling their role in an organization. Essentially, this book argues that, in order to promote profound organizational change, each individual's thinking must adopt the 'sensing', 'presencing' and 'realizing' processes (Senge et al. 2007: 88).

Simply stated, sensing is about 'inner knowing' (Senge et al. 2007: 89) whereby the person's more informed, cognisant, attentive and vigilant awareness enables the production of a unique and comprehensive, but intrinsic, perspective of the whole situation. Sensing means getting in touch with your subjective response to what is happening because it entails the 'need to feel out what to do. You don't act out of deduction; you act out of your inner feel, making sense as you go' (Senge et al. 2007: 85). Briefly, presencing is 'being fully conscious and aware in the present moment [through] deep listening, [and] of being open beyond one's preconceptions and historical ways of making sense' (Senge et al. 2007: 13). Presencing is about paying close attention to whatever is unfolding here and now rather than repeating past habitual ways of thinking. It is about thinking differently whereby both objective and subjective data from the immediate experience is brought into awareness and, together, these inform the person's deliberations. The final phase, 'realizing', is described as 'bringing something new into reality ... but comes from a source that's deeper than the rational mind' (Senge et al. 2007: 91). Realizing is an ongoing, dynamic act of 'co-creation between the individual or collective and the larger world' (Senge et al. 2007: 92). These three processes are explicit approaches to self-reflection and, thus, expanding consciousness. By, first, helping the person to develop their sensing, presencing and realizing capabilities, organizational change is more likely to occur because the individual's personalized thinking processes are more readily able to nurture productive interpersonal relationships with their co-employees. This in turn cultivates more creative, conscientious, skilful and beneficial work practices and a far more harmonious, collegial, enjoyable and productive organizational culture.

From within Snowden's decision-making framework, such an approach to leading organizational change is categorized also as 'complex' change. For Snowden, complex change is characterized as presenting with a sense of there being no apparent viable solutions; the problem is engulfed by flux and unpredictability. While the problem is clearly visible, its possible causes seem variable, at least, if not non-distinguishable. Similarly, there are as many predictions about the likely cause of the problem as there are suggestions as to how it might be solved. In such a complex organizational circumstance, Snowden stresses the importance of the leader being able to facilitate change processes that allow solutions to emerge from the employees rather than they having a solution thrust upon them by the leader or an outside 'expert'. Such processes provide the employees the freedom not only to openly discuss and discern what might be the key features of the problem but also to share, analyse and create viable ways for overcoming the problem. By means of such an inclusive, cooperative and purposeful process, all who work in the organization can unify their understanding of why the problem exists, what can be done to try and rectify the problem, and how to implement ways to address the problem. In this way, the actual organizational change process automatically overcomes employee resistance, builds employee confidence in and engagement with the strategies, and enables creativity and initiative to be applied and shared.

As with the process for overseeing transformational change, the leader should not facilitate the complex change process but, rather, needs to be an integral part of the communal discernment process. Hence, it is wise for an appropriately knowledgeable and skilled external facilitator to be employed to manage the required process. Such a facilitator would utilize one or more ways for engaging the leader and as many of the employees as practicable in a process that first builds a common understanding of what are the observable features of the problem and then, in groups (usually of 8–10), creates a way for individuals and groups to devise potential solutions and means for enacting the solutions. These multiple solutions are then presented collectively to the whole community, and are analysed and critiqued so that a multifaceted change strategy is formed and can be implemented. Through maximizing involvement in the decision-making process, employee involvement in the change implementation process is also maximized. It is only through the implementation of the multifaceted change strategy that a better understanding can be found of the actual cause–effect relationship. This would then enable a far more directed change strategy, such as a transformational change, to be implemented.

This discussion of the different types of organizational change strives to highlight the importance of the organizational leader knowing that there are these types of change and that each requires its own way of being led or facilitated. If such knowledge is ignored then failure and employee resistance are both likely. Often, employee resistance is only considered from its detrimental effect upon the change process, but it can also have a detrimental impact upon the acceptance of the leader. It is easy for the employee to automatically align a specific failed change process with a more general view of poor leadership. If a change process fails, then trust in the leader is significantly diminished. Hence, it is not surprising that many in formal leadership positions try to avoid overseeing organizational change because they fear looking bad in the eyes of those they are leading. But avoiding organizational change is a recipe for disaster. Knowing the different types of organizational change and how to successfully facilitate them is one way to successfully lead change. Also, a better understanding of the nature of employee resistance provides additional insight into how it can be minimized. The following section provides some of these insights.

Overcoming employee resistance to organizational change

As has been previously argued, one of the main reasons that approximately 70 per cent of intended change process fail is that most of the attention is directed on creating the most ideal plan while insufficient attention is directed to the culture and those who have to create the change. Moreover, if the change fails to eventuate then, more often than not, those charged with the responsibility of making the change happen are blamed and not the plan, because a change plan always looks perfect on paper. Also, in such circumstances it is easier for the person who devised the plan to label those involved as change resistors than to acknowledge any weaknesses in the plan. These narrow-minded views of unsuccessful change do not redress the fundamental problem – that the leader needs to see how change actually happens. People create the change, not the plan – any leader wishing to lead organizational change more successfully needs to understand how such change is likely to affect those who have to bring about the change and incorporate this understanding into how the change is to be implemented.

To begin to form this better understanding of organizational change it is helpful to appreciate its inherent explicit and implicit duality (see Bridges 2009). Clearly, the explicit dimension is the desired 'change' itself, which often involves some sought of observable outcome such as a situational move, or a structural reorganization, or a performance revision, or a role refinement, or some other tangible alteration to the status quo. However, within each and every case of organizational change is the implicit dimension of 'transition', which is the process that people go through as they internalize and come to terms with their new situation that the change has brought about. Fundamental to this process of transition is each person's subjective interpretation and critique of the proposed reasons for the change, their personal analysis of how the change will impact upon their self, and their internalized determination of how they will behaviourally respond to the change plan. Causal Reasoning Theory (see, for example, Martinko, Gundlach and Douglas 2002) provides further insight into an employee's thinking when faced with a proposed organizational change. First, the employee internally evaluates the quality of what is being asked of them within the change – is it fair, just, logical, achievable, relevant, beneficial, reasonable. Secondly, based upon these personal change 'quality' judgements, the employee then internally evaluates the personal impact of the proposed organizational change – will they remain successful in the work they do, will they be sufficiently supported during the change, will their future career pathway be maintained, will their role be adversely affected, will they be doing work that interests them, will they be working with co-employees of personal benefit and interest (for more detailed descriptions see Branson 2010). It is upon these internal reflections that the employee decides how they will behaviourally respond to the proposed change plan – support, reluctantly comply, passively resist or actively resist.

Based upon this insight, a leader who is seeking to become more successful when leading organizational change would be wise to adopt two essential practices into their change strategy. First, become far more inclusive and open in the very beginning phase of considering a possible change. Enact a growth mindset approach by allowing those who will be involved in bringing about the change to actually contribute in the discernment process of reviewing the need for a change, of determining what the change, if any, will be, and how the change will unfold if it is thought necessary. In this way, the initial 'quality' phase of the employee's causal reasoning process is constructively subdued if not dismantled because they are fully aware of why the change is being considered and what the outcome might be. Their inclusion makes the process fair and just, and any co-constructed change that might be initiated will automatically appear far more reasonable, logical, relevant, beneficial and achievable. Secondly, by maintaining a close, actively involved, relational approach, the leader can enact a far more flexible and employee-centred change process in which the plan is seen as a guide and not a prescription. Such a leader ensures that adequate resources are supplied so that the individual employees and the change plan both are well supported with the required resources. Furthermore, by being intimately involved, the leader can acknowledge and affirm the progress being made so as to encourage and motivate continued commitment to the change process. The process can also be adjusted to ensure that everyone is able to maintain involvement and that the devised strategies are producing the intended outcomes.

What is being described here is the call for *transrelational* leadership to be guiding organizational change. A leader committed to enacting a transrelational approach to their leadership practice will automatically be well placed to be able to successfully lead organizational change. Any other approach to the demands of leading organizational change will most likely result in failure. However, the premise in this discussion is that organizational change is always an episodic event – an intrusion into the status quo in order to create something new, different and better about the organization. But, as described above, people are reluctant to change. We like to feel safe and secure, these are basic human needs, and so control, predictability, stability and continuity are much preferred workplace qualities. Thus, any form of episodic organizational change, no matter how transrelationally led it is, may still have the potential to generate resistance in some individuals and varying degrees of uncertainty in others. For this reason, and given that organizational change is a necessary constant, there is now a pervasive call within the literature for a move away from a dependency on episodic organizational change to the establishment of a change culture, or a platform whereby the organizational culture automatically and continually produces in each employee the knowledge, skills and disposition to embrace evolving change as an ongoing personal opportunity to learn, grow and achieve. This new way of leading successful organizational change and its alignment with transrelational leadership is described more fully in the next section.

Where to for organizational change?

Hamel and Zanini (2014) call for the 'reimagining' of the way organizational change is conceptualized and practised. More specifically, they describe this new image as moving from a top–down to an activist-out process. 'To make deep change proactive and pervasive, the responsibility for initiating change needs to be syndicated across the organization' (Hamil and Zanini 2014: 2). This is about the leader creating an organizational culture in which constructive and purposeful change is able to emerge from anywhere and at any time in the organization because all who work in the organization are readily and actively wanting to be continually improving themselves and thereby the organization. Thus, this involves leadership that 'invites' others to solve acknowledged organizational problems rather than 'selling' a prescribed change process to them. Furthermore, this form of change leadership moves away from the traditional episodic format to that which nurtures a culture that is very evolving. Rather than being 'managed,' the culture is said to become 'organic'. This is less about 'building a powerful project-management office and more about building self-organizing communities that identify, experiment, and eventually scale new initiatives' (Hamil and Zanini 2014: 2).

The bedrock of such an organizational culture is what some have termed 'antifragility' – it is argued that rather than working on becoming resilient and robust, we must become anti-fragile (Hollingworth 2016). A robust person resists change and stays the same; the resilient person survives the change and is left changed; the anti-fragile person embraces the change and uses it to get better. The pragmatic implication for leaders wishing to nurture anti-fragility as an outcome of the organizational culture is around information and meaning. As Wheatley highlights (2006: 107), 'An individual without information cannot take responsibility, but an individual who is given information cannot help but take responsibility. Information provides true nourishment; it enables people to do their jobs responsibly and well.' Moreover, where the leader is a 'part of their group' they not only readily and continually provide information to those they are leading but also they are far more attuned towards knowing what information to be providing. Information that is about current achievements as well as information about what is happening elsewhere that is of importance and relevance.

A leader accomplishes anti-fragility by being able to regularly 'align the group's identity to its wider reality' in an agreeable, non-controversial and unremarkable way. This is about organizational sense making – helping each employee to make sense of what is happening in their organization so that they have the personal freedom and responsibility to create ongoing workplace security for their self and, thereby, the organization. In taking this approach the leader is encouraging each individual to be far more personally creative in how they design and perform their work. The employee is being invited to listen carefully to what is happening in and around their workplace, to contribute towards the development of a common understanding of what this means for the organization, to determine what this means now and in the future for their own contribution to the sustainability of the organization, and accordingly to work with their line manager and workplace colleagues to consolidate and grow their workplace knowledge and skills. This automatically invokes a need for creativity, which is about turning new and imaginative ideas into reality.

Creativity is the ability to perceive the world in new ways, to find hidden patterns, to make connections between seemingly unrelated phenomena, and to generate solutions. Moreover, where there is creativity there is meaning. Life becomes far more meaningful when we feel creative in what we are doing and we all seek to be doing something that is meaningful. As described by Wheatley (2006: 133), 'With meaning as our centering place, we can journey through the realms of chaos and make sense of the world. With meaning as an attractor, we can re-create ourselves to carry forward what we value most.' This is about the leader encouraging each of those they are leading to be continually helping to reshape the organization's identity by being personally responsible for continually reshaping their own workplace identity. As they continually change for the better, so too do their workplace colleagues as well as the organization as a whole. Change is endemic and welcomed but it takes a transrelational leader to achieve such a desirable and beneficial organizational outcome.

Conclusion

Successful organizational change is consistently illusive across all contemporary contexts, including that of higher education. Despite a plethora of how-to-fix-it type of literature, the learning of how to lead successful organizational change remains unacceptably lacking. In this era of managerialism, and its emphasis of fiscal responsibility and accountability, it is a scurrilous contradiction for any organizational leader to ignore the overwhelming data of change failure and avoid looking to learn how to ensure greater success. For those who lead higher educational institutions where 'learning' is the core business, it is imperative that this failure is confronted. It is totally irresponsible and unscrupulous to continue to spend extraordinarily large amounts of money on faulty change management processes when there are clearly articulated alternative change leadership processes that will prove successful. Ignorance of how to lead successful organizational change can no longer be an excuse, if it ever was. If organizational change is a constant, as we all accept that it is and needs to be, then it behoves each and every higher education leader to learn the knowledge, skills and dispositions that will ensure success. Leading successful organizational change is about learning how to be a transrelational leader. Whether it is leading an episodic change process, or leading an organization to develop an ever-evolving change culture, it is the acquisition of transrelational skills, knowledge and dispositions that are the required leadership qualities.

We acknowledge that for many organizational leaders, and higher education leaders in particular, change is a very important but of secondary concern to that of performance. It seems that most leaders feel that dealing with change is more periodic whereas concern about the quality of performance is constant. Change is about the future whereas performance is about the here and now. Also, the assumption is that the organization might well be able to survive a failed change process but it won't survive poor employee performance. Although these thoughts and assumptions are fraught with misconceptions and misunderstanding, the reality is that many leaders prioritize dealing with employee performance over knowing how best to lead successful organizational change. Hence, the next chapter specifically addresses the issue of performance management, as it is so commonly referred to in the literature.

Seeking High Performance

Abstract

In today's highly competitive world, those organizations that are not striving to achieve high employee performance are most likely the ones that are in decline or disappearing. Hence, a leader's capacity to ensure that their organization's culture is enabling high performance among its employees has become essential. Importantly, however, it is now acknowledged that enhanced organizational sustainability is aligned with high employee performance in the areas of creativity, ingenuity, inventiveness and risk-taking. Thus, the importance of this chapter is its use of research literature from a variety of fields to illustrate how transrelational leaders are far more able to nurture creativity, ingenuity and inventiveness. This is about encouraging risk-taking by accepting unsuccessful outcomes as opportunities to learn rather than actions to be avoided. Moreover, this is about favouring a growth mindset in which the open sharing of alternative opinions and perspectives is actively encouraged and embraced by all. Hence, trust between the leader and employee is absolutely fundamental, but trust is also an integral component of transrelational leadership. If there is no trust, there is no transrelational leadership.

Introduction

In today's highly competitive world, those organizations that are not striving to achieve high employee performance are most likely the ones that are in decline or disappearing. Hence, leaders' capacity to ensure their organization's culture is enabling high performance among its employees has become essential. However, although seeking high performance is an extremely important contemporary requirement, it is not an entirely new focus. Indeed, actions by an organizational leader to improve employee efficiency and effectiveness, and thereby quality of performance, has arguably been an integral part of organizations since 1911, with the scientific management work of Frederick Winslow Taylor used to change employee practices. Essentially, this involved (1) adopting scientific measurements to break jobs into series of small, related tasks and develop a standard time for each task, (2) using systematic methods for selecting workers and training them for specific jobs, (3) establishing clear division of responsibility between management and workers, where management sets goals, plans and supervises, and the workers execute the required tasks, and (4) establishing a discipline where management sets the objectives and the workers cooperate in achieving them. Moreover, it is essential to acknowledge the significance of these historical roots of performance management as the process for achieving high performance. In many respects it is understandable that early-twentieth-century organizational leaders sought to apply management strategy that would help workers to learn how to better perform in an entirely new and evolving business and industrial world. The application of these early performance management systems played a large part in helping the adjustment of the employee to become familiar, confident and capable in much larger, more complex and more technologically sophisticated working environments. Yet, although today's employees do not have to adjust to the same dramatic structural and production changes as were experienced in the first half of the last century, they are still largely being controlled by performance management systems by organizational leaders wanting to maintain high performance. In 2006, around 90 per cent of 278 multinational corporations in fifteen countries reported that they have performance management systems (Cascio 2006). In Australia it was 96 per cent of companies (Nankervis and Compton 2006). Performance management continues to be the accepted way for organizational leaders to influence the achievement of high performance. But should it?

As early as 1994, J. B Arthur warned that where performance management is moderated from managerial 'control' to that of supporting and developing employees, it results in higher productivity, efficiencies and lower employee turnover. Arthur argued for a change in how employees were viewed by their leaders – from one that saw the employee as a passive resource to be manipulated and directed into performing in a prescribed way to one that saw the employee as a dynamic and active contributor because they are naturally committed to doing their best for the organization and so, if given the freedom and resources, can be trusted to carry out their work to the best of their ability.

More recently, Webb (2017: 1) urged leaders to 'stop telling people what to do' and highlighted that 'telling people what to do feels like we're in control and being helpful – but it doesn't often work'. Supporting this view, Gruman and Saks (2011) found that less than a third of employees believe that their organization's performance management process assists them in improving their performance, and performance management regularly ranks among the lowest topics in employee satisfaction surveys. Instead they argue the need to focus on fostering employee engagement to lift employee performance. This is not a lone voice. A survey of almost 1,000 HRM professionals' performance management systems found that they are not always successful and do not always lead to the intended results (Nankervis and Compton 2006). Furthermore, a Deloitte 2015 survey of executives revealed that 58 per cent believe that their current performance management approach drives neither employee engagement nor high performance (Buckingham and Goodall 2015). This Deloitte survey also drew attention to the view of these executives that their 'current process for evaluating the work of our people – and then training them, promoting them, and paying them accordingly – is increasingly out of step with our objectives' (Buckingham and Goodall 2015: 42).

The growing abundance of similar research data is causing the business world to re-evaluate the role and requirement of performance management systems. It is becoming clear to many organizations that performance management systems may actually be diminishing rather than increasing the achievement of employee high performance. For these organizations, the increasing realization is that it is attention to employee engagement rather than performance management which will have the desired effect. This chapter first explores and critiques the concept and application of performance management as a means for achieving high performance. Then, in concert with the aforementioned change in focus towards employee engagement, this concept is also explored and critiqued.

Limitations of performance management

The problem with performance management is that it focuses on the task and the performance of the task and does not typically take account of the social/behavioural aspects of a person and a group of people (team) including the social exchange, networking, trust, mentoring and influence (Aguinis 2008). Nor does it take account of the culture of the team/group. For most people, work is a very social activity even if the task at hand is very individualistic. The performance of a person's work is not entirely isolated from the influence of those around them or even from others who are not even employed in the same organization. An individual's workplace performance has social and emotional dimensions and not just a physical and cognitive dimension (Clayton et al. 2016). In other words, at any given time the quality of a person's workplace performance is more than the sum of what they think and do with respect to their specific task at hand. It is also affected by what they are thinking and feeling about many other things, including, what others are doing around them, what they believe about the alignment of their strengths and talents with what is required of them by their current task, what is happening in their life inside and outside of the organization, what they are desiring for their future career, what they believe about their line manager, what they think of the resources they have been provided with, and so on. Any specific performance measurement only captures the product of all such influential forces. Hence, any response to this form of performance measurement that only attends to changing the behaviour is grossly deficient.

Invariably, a key component of performance management systems are performance-based goal-setting and reviewing processes. According to Ordóñez et al. (2009), goal setting is one of the most replicated and influential paradigms in performance management based upon the widely held belief that goals are powerful drivers of behaviour. However, research now shows that 'the beneficial effects of goal setting have been overstated and that systematic harm caused by goal setting has been largely ignored. We identify specific side effects associated with goal setting, including a narrow focus that neglects non-goal areas, a rise in unethical behavior, distorted risk preferences, corrosion of organizational culture, and reduced intrinsic motivation' (Ordóñez et al. 2009: 1). Furthermore, Barsky (2007) claims that there is a relationship between the harmful effects of goal setting and organizational culture, in that the managerial objectives create a focus on the ends rather than the means. This in turn impacts on the ability of employees to recognize unethical leadership behaviour, so that the actual goal-setting process provides an unacknowledged rationale for unethical behaviour. Fleming and Zyglidopoulos (2008) agree that goal setting and culture are connected and that goal setting may create a climate ripe for unethical behaviour and covertly alter culture. Aiuinus and Pierce (2008: 143) elaborate upon how some unethical actions associated with performance management systems can occur by asking, 'Within the context of such performance management systems, how do group dynamics affect who measures performance and how performance is measured? How are team-level goals established? What mechanisms and processes could be implemented so that team-level performance is assessed accurately and fairly?' Other limitations of goal-setting processes include the competition between goals because there is rarely consensus across an organization on a set of goals to pursue (Aithal and Suresh Kumar 2016), and a fixation on a goal marketed as an idealized future can be destructive but used to justify face-saving behaviour (Kayes 2006).

The insidious outcome of performance-based goals also provides the ideal conditions that foster two unhelpful workplace conditions – inter-employee competition (Colligan and Higgans 2008) and fixed mindsets (Dweck 2006). Inter-employee competition caused by performance management processes is a major contributor to employee stress. Colligan and Higgans (2008) identify some causes of employee stress that include a toxic work environment and climate, isolation, role ambiguity, lack of autonomy, difficult relationships, barriers to career development, and the assumption of managerial bullying. The result is likely to be increased absenteeism and decreased work productivity.

Fixed mindsets arise because employees are encouraged to select goals that they know they can achieve within the time limit, that they can measure and can report on in their next performance review, and thereby they can avoid being judged as under performing. As described by Dweck (2006), a fixed mindset is one that is about proving you are smart or competent by ensuring you remain in control and avoid doing unusual or unexpected activities where you might fail. Employees with fixed mindsets believe they prove themselves to be highly competent and successful by not failing to achieve a goal, especially at an annual review. Employees with fixed mindsets are unwilling to try something new, especially if there is uncertainty about the outcome. Thus, the annual goal-setting process at the heart of a performance management system tends to encourage employees to only create achievable goals year after year. They adhere to the principles of SMART goals that are specific, measurable, achievable, realistic and time-bound. While this approach creates a predictable and measurable organizational result, it does little or nothing to create learning and growth in the individual and the organization. Thus, performance management and goal setting effectively work to maintain the status quo.

There is growing evidence that goal setting and performance reviews only improve employee performance by as little as 2 per cent. Consequently, many organizations are now doing away with these traditional performance processes altogether (Patel 2015). For example, in contrast to a goal-setting performance management regime, the Deloitte 2015 survey of high-performing employees revealed that working to strengths every day was the most powerful motivator. Deloitte has now responded to this finding by adopting an approach that separates high-performance decisions from performance measurement processes and instead creates processes that encourage closer connections between line managers and employees. These connections enable clearer insight into progress through quarterly or per-project performance-snapshots, and weekly check-ins with line managers, which together not only keep employee performances on course but actually enhance them.

Thus, in the business sector there are calls for change in approaches to attain high performance. The manner by which managerialism strives to achieve high performance has had its day. Again, the business sector is noting the more far-reaching advantages of a relational approach to performance management as the genesis for achieving high performance from employees. More specifically, attention to employee engagement is proving to be of greater importance than performance management as organizations seek to maintain high performance. Hence, this chapter concludes with a discussion of employee engagement – its nature and achievement. Before this, however, it is important to review the impact of performance management within the higher education environment.

The impact of performance management in higher education

As described in some detail in the introductory chapter, higher education institutions appear to be positioned on a rising curve of managerialism as they attempt to cope with the massive changes in the sector. We posited that higher education around the world finds itself under intense fiscal pressures driven by increasing governmental involvement and expectation, global and local competition for students, rapidly changing technologies and an ever-diminishing pool of research funding. In response, most higher education institutions have felt compelled to adopt a managerial-based approach to leadership. As a result, the days of academic freedom and autonomy have been replaced by academic marketability and pressures to attract and diversify income streams in an environment of unprecedented levels of scrutiny from politicians, policy makers and key stakeholders (Taylor and Baines 2012). Academic endeavour is now moderated by managerial approaches as senior leaders implement private sector methods into the public sector organizations, with resulting immense frustration for academic workers (and colleagues).

Higher education institutions across many countries have implemented performance measurement systems for academic work. For many higher education leaders there seems to be no alternative as the continuation of government funding becomes increasingly contingent upon evidence of academic performance in research and teaching, obtained via assessments and audits, including value for money, student satisfaction and performance audits (Ter Bogt and Scapens 2012). With the pressure associated with the growing importance of marketability and international ranking systems, higher education leaders are increasingly focusing on the performance of academic departments and of the individuals within those departments. According to Mathews (2011), this growing administrative control over the work of academics as generated by managerialism is nothing but a 'self-perpetuating bureaucracy'.

Yet, however we regard it, this move to managerialism raises an important question: Has academic productivity explicitly increased as a result of the introduction of performance measurement and management processes? There is no agreement on answers to this question. Some researchers suggest that performance management processes in the right doses and contexts do have positive results in terms of the quality of performance of academics (e.g. Chan 2001). Decramer, Smolders and Vanderstraeten (2013) found that performance management systems introduced in a Flemish university were able to achieve academic employee satisfaction provided the process involved high levels of internal consistency and communication. These performance management systems worked where the academic employee was able to influence the process to ensure that it was directly related to the work being done. However, others argue that performance management processes produce the opposite effect (e.g. Bryson 2004; Davis and Thomas 2002) and create the situation of 'managerialism contradiction' (Smeenk et al. 2006) whereby high performance is reduced rather than increased. In an English university, Melo, Sarrico and Radnor (2010: 233) found that 'in spite of a substantial increase in the measurement of performance in most areas, there seems to be a lack of action, especially regarding individual performance'. They also report upon the decline of academic-voice in institutional decision-making, decline in academic freedom as a result of the introduction of performance management processes, and parallel growth in the importance of the work of the non-academic employees who oversee the various components of the performance management processes.

Edgar and Geare's (2013) inquiry into the Performance Based Research Fund performance management practice, which aims to lift research productivity in New Zealand universities, identified that autonomy and egalitarianism within a strong cultural ethos supporting achievement and individualism was far more effective than a prescribed performance management system in developing high-performing academics, departments and faculties. This said, it cannot be assumed that all universities in New Zealand have succeeded in fostering this cultural ethos. Ter Bogt and Scapens (2012: 451) summarize the concern about the use of performance management processes in higher education by arguing that

> we see an increasing use of judgemental forms of performance evaluation and, in particular, the use of more quantitative performance measures. The use of these more judgemental quantitative systems is seen to have various effects. Although these systems emphasise objective quantitative measures, they relocate subjectivities (usually at a greater distance from the subject), rather than remove them. This creates uncertainty and anxiety about how the systems are used. There is a danger that the new systems could inhibit creativity in teaching and limit contributions to the world outside the university. Furthermore, they could damage creativity and innovation in accounting research – as researchers play safe in getting the publications they need.

The problems caused by performance management systems are certainly not limited to academic employees within higher education institutions. Pick, Teo and Yeung's (2012) research identified that these processes also create an array of stressors for administrative support staff that negatively impact on their work environment creating reduced job satisfaction. They also found that administrator work conditions might be improved by employee participation, improved communication and employee performance support. Importantly, these authors argue that the prevailing climate of managerialism, and its narrow focus on performance management processes, was not conducive to such improvements. As the business sector, the higher education arena has found not only that performance management processes are counterproductive towards achieving high performance but also that any beneficial outcome can only result from these processes if there is far more personal involvement in the focus and structure of such processes. Processes that are less about performance measurement and more about aiding employee engagement are far more effective in achieving high performance in higher education institutions. Hence, there is a need to better understand the concept of employee engagement and its capacity to achieve high performance.

The currency of employee engagement in the business world

It is no secret that employee engagement is a headline issue in the business sector today. In their Human Capital Reports since 2012 Deloitte identify that engagement is in the top five most pressing issues for organizations. In 2013 Deloitte identified the need to sustain employee engagement/morale as the second most pressing human resource concern for businesses around the world. By 2016 the Deloitte Human Capital report stated that 'an overwhelming majority of executives (85%) ranked engagement as a top priority' (Deloitte 2016b: 6). The 2016 report also identified that the percentage of executives who believe their organization are 'fully ready' to deal with engagement issues increased from 31 per cent in 2015 to 34 per cent in 2016. This executive concern is backed up by decades of data that describe a disengagement crisis. Rates of employee engagement vary around the world ranging from 29 per cent in North America to 6 per cent in East Asia (Table 6.1).

The Gallup data shown in Table 6.1, with research participants numbering in the millions and collected over decades, indicate globally that people are disengaged in their work in endemic proportions. Worldwide, just 13 per cent

Table 6.1 Employee engagement by region 2011–2012: An illustration of the distribution of the percentage of engaged, non-engaged and disengaged employees by region based on Gallup research data

Region	Engaged (%)	Not engaged (%)	Actively disengaged (%)
North America	29	54	18
Australia and New Zealand	24	60	16
Latin America	21	60	19
Western Europe	14	66	20
South East Asia	12	73	14
Central and Eastern Europe	11	63	26
Middle Eastern North Africa	10	55	35
South Asia	10	61	29
Sub-Saharan Africa	10	57	33
East Asia	6	68	26

Source: Crabtree (2013)

of employees are positively involved in, enthusiastic about and committed to their work and organization; 63 per cent are non-engaged and 24 per cent are actively disengaged (Mann and Hartner 2016). Non-engaged workers are not involved in their work, nor are they committed emotionally to their job and organization – they merely put in time on the job. Actively disengaged workers act out their discontent with counterproductive behaviours which include: theft, abuse, sabotage, damaging the brand, negatively influencing their co-workers, absenteeism and driving customers away through poor service (Yu 2014). Disengaged employees work to the minimum required. They do not innovate, they ridicule those who try to make changes; they resist change and put effort into maintaining the status quo (Yu 2014). Conversely, Williams (2012) claims that where people are engaged in their work there is a 2.2 per cent increase in profit. There are also lower rates of staff turnover and absenteeism, customer satisfaction increases as do workplace safety and the quality and efficiency of production, and employee theft decreases. Indeed, Gallup reports that there is 28 per cent less theft in business units where employees are engaged.

The impact of disengagement on productivity is illustrated in this data relating to Germany. In Germany, 16 per cent of workers are engaged in, or emotionally and behaviourally connected to, their jobs – and this has more or less been the case since 2001 when data were first collected (Nink 2016). Gallup estimates the cost to the German economy to be between 75 and 99 billion euros annually in lost productivity (Nink 2016). Gallup also reports that the 'economic damage caused by workers who are not engaged is an estimated additional cost to the [German] economy of 139.1 billion to 187.9 billion euros. The total estimated cost would range from 214.7 to 287.1 billion euros each year' (Nink 2016: 1). Although these data focus solely on the financial costs of disengagement in Germany alone, extrapolating the data illustrated in Table 6.1, in addition to considering somewhat similar results worldwide, it is clear that the current incapacity of organizational leaders to maximize employee engagement is a serious concern.

Disengagement not only impacts on the local and the global economy, it has negative effects on the health and well-being of the disengaged employee, their co-employees and on the organization. For example, in the research by Nink (2016) around 50 per cent of actively disengaged employees answered 'yes' when asked if they felt stressed at work yesterday (48 per cent), compared with just 20 per cent of the engaged employees (Nink 2016). Absenteeism is 67 per cent higher among disengaged employees than engaged employees (Gallup). Brand damage is also a problem. According to Gallup only 3 per cent of actively disengaged employees strongly agree that they would recommend their company as a place to work compared with 75 per cent of engaged employees. Similarly, only 16 per cent of disengaged employees would recommend their company's products or services.

While all the data discussed here are based on the business sector, it also points to a disengagement crisis in higher education institutions, particularly as they struggle with what Ernst and Young describe as 'being on the cusp of profound change' associated with disruptions to traditional core functions (Ernst and Young 2012) such as the loss of autonomy resulting from increasing government regulation and the need to forge new business models (PWC 2017). Although higher education institutions now operate as businesses and have been doing so for the past decade or more, employee engagement in academic institutions occurs (or not) at different scales. When the culture is healthy, academics may be highly engaged in their professions, networks, research and with their students. They connect well to colleagues in their local unit. Their engagement however diminishes at the broader scale of school and faculty to the point where they are disconnected and disengaged at the organization level. When the culture is toxic their engagement in their work drops to minimum as they cope with the loss of academic freedom and their autonomy.

Defining employee engagement

Given the observations made and statistics presented above, it is not surprising that organizations have sought to find out as much as they can about employee engagement. Employee engagement is a phenomenon, not a concept. It might be better understood as human endeavour, which has served humans well throughout time as people have innovated to solve problems and to discover the world around them. This kind of endeavour or engagement is an essential characteristic of being human. In the past we have treated engagement as if it is a concept and therefore missed the intrinsic human essence of engagement that makes it a naturally occurring phenomenon. Thus, we have attempted multiple ways to understand it from a motivational perspective. We thought we could judge it from the observation of behaviours or practice and the amount or quality of work done and then measure it against predetermined outcomes. While we are still missing the full understanding of engagement as a human phenomenon there continues to be a major problem of disengagement around the globe. It is all very well to talk about lifting performance and managing performance, but organizations have yet to come to terms with the underlying problem of poor performance; people are not being engaged in their work.

William Kahn (1990) first developed the 'concept' of engagement to explain that employees provide different degrees and dimensions of their selves to their work according to some internal considerations that they consciously and unconsciously make. This view was born out of the traditional studies of workplace motivation, which assumed that workers were either on or off track, that is, they were seen as being either motivated or not motivated. More recently, Kahn (2010: 22) posits that engagement in the workplace manifests as

> people focused on their tasks. They stay with them. They show that they care about them. They work hard to accomplish them as best as they can, they bring all sorts of data – their thoughts, feelings, hunches, experiences – into play as they go about their work. They fully inhabit their roles, not just do their jobs. They do not need to do this in a showy way, designed to make others stop and applaud them. They are just very present in doing their work.

From a psychological perspective, employee engagement has been seen through the lens of what a good employee might look like. For example, employee engagement was aligned with Organisation Citizenship Behaviour (OCB) and the Good Soldier Syndrome as proposed by Organ (1988) and describes the positive and constructive behaviours that employees engage in, of their own volition, which support co-workers and benefit the organization. Specifically, such behaviour was said to be identified by personal characteristics including altruism (being helpful), courtesy (being polite and preventing conflict), conscientiousness (doing more than just the minimum and minimizing error), civic virtue (showing interest and involvement in the organization, keeping up to date and defending organizational policies and practices), and sportsmanship (accepting change and working without complaint). Since first proposed by Organ (1988), multiple authors have attempted to quantify the specific drivers of these behaviours as a means for being able to create the conditions by which employees choose to either extend their discretionary behaviours beyond their expected normal duties (Podaskoff et al. 2000; Pradhan, Jena and Kumari 2016), or to more willingly develop their predisposition towards naturally enacting organization citizenship behaviour (Yu 2014; Finkelstein 2006).

Over the years, multiple definitions and models have sought to capture the essence of employee engagement and to manipulate it for productivity outcomes. Macey and Schneider (2008) describe engagement as a fulfilling psychological state characterized by vigour, dedication and absorption in one's work. Meanwhile Keating and Heslin (2015: 329) propose that 'mindsets are a personal resource that may influence employees' engagement via their enthusiasm for development, construal of effort, focus of attention, perception of setbacks, and interpersonal interactions'. It is important to note that these perspectives were from the position of the leader and the organizational advantages that could be gained if employee engagement could be constructively influenced externally. This is summed up nicely by the Linley, Harrington and Garcea (2010: 158) definition of employee engagement, which is typical of a multitude of commercial definitions, as 'a heightened emotional connection that an employee feels for their organisation, that influences them to exert greater discretionary effort in their work'. In the light of such a definition it is not surprising that organizations and their leaders have been keen to know more about what creates or drives employee engagement.

Exploring the likely drivers of employee engagement

Thirty years of research has produced an abundance of literature with various theories and proposals about what drives, contributes to or explains employee engagement. Most of the research has focused on engagement in the workplace but how and why people engage is relevant to all aspects of social connection including family, sports teams and community groups. Many explanations of employee engagement are based on the fundamental theories that explain the human character and what makes us tick. For example, we are described as social creatures and hence we like to be connected and belong and so we prefer to work in groups rather than alone (Castells 2000) and so our group membership is important for how we feel about being at work. We also like control over our own life, to be self-determined. Self-determination theory (SDT) (Ryan and Deci 2000; Deci and Ryan 1995) proposes that we have a natural inclination to do a job properly and so we seek to be autonomous so that we can make informed, un-coerced decisions about how to best do our work and we willingly seek connections with others to help us in this endeavour. Luthans et al. (2007) refer to this as the psychological capacity of a person, which is a combination of hope (the sense of control to work towards our own goals), self-efficacy (the sense of self-confidence in our own ability to achieve the goal), resilience (our positive ability to cope with adversity or stress), and optimism (the sense that one can succeed now and in the future). Meanwhile, the field of neuroscience contributes to our understanding of employee engagement by illustrating how the human brain responds to external conditions, which are interpreted as being either a 'reward' or a 'threat'. These responses appear across the five domains of human experience of perceived status relative to that of others, of certainty or predictability, of level of autonomy and control over events, of a sense of safety with others, and of the perception of fair exchanges between people. Clearly, each of these domains of human experience exist in every workplace such that an employee is constantly judging whether the current experience is a 'reward' or a 'threat' and reacts accordingly. For example, as explained by Rock (2008), while people are threatened by uncertainty or unfairness, they interpret this as a threat and so will be unwilling or resistant to being engaged.

McClelland and Atkinson's research in the early 1950s recognized that human motivation was a personal drive for success and the avoidance of failure. Importantly, they advanced the view that employees desperately seek autonomy because they prefer working in an environment in which they are able to assume responsibility for solving problems, to take moderate risks in order to learn how to do things better, and have continuous recognition of how well they are doing. More recently Ryff and Singer (2002) propose that autonomy is a dimension of well-being, which is essential for being able to fully apply one's self to a task. In addition to autonomy, Xanthopoulou et al. (2009) research in the fast food industry showed that coaching and team climate are directly related to employees' levels of (self-efficacy, self-esteem, and optimism) work engagement.

'Purpose' also crops up time and again as a driver of employee engagement. Gallup-Healthways (2016) identify purpose, which they define as liking what you do each day, as one of the five essential elements of the employee engagement. In order to be fully engaged, employees need to know that their effort is important in achieving organizational goals and that they believe in what they are doing. Purpose is also about clarity of one's role and the confidence to complete it. Surprisingly, according to research from Gallup, only half of the employees involved in its research strongly agree that they understood what was expected of them at work and their line managers were equally at a loss to explain their own jobs. In order to feel purposeful, employees need to understand how their work aligns with the organization's mission and goals – and from that they find purpose in their effort and achievements. In a more comprehensive way, the work of Pink (2009) distils employee engagement into the three essential components of autonomy (the urge to control the who/what/where/when of work), mastery (working to strengths and the drive to get better and to find innovative solutions to challenges) and purpose (the sense of connecting to something bigger that we believe in).

Despite this breadth of research insights, Saks and Gruman (2014: 155) recently concluded that 'there continues to be a lack of consensus on the meaning of employee engagement as well as concerns about the validity of the most popular measure of employee engagement. Furthermore, it is difficult to make causal conclusions about the antecedents of employee engagement.' Thus, we argue that employee engagement is not a universal human construct but an artefact of the organizational culture. Its derivatives are contextual rather than general. While there may well be some common factors such as autonomy, mastery, purpose and support these are interwoven with contextually specific social and political phenomena. This implies that the knowing of possible drivers of employee engagement will not be solely sufficient to ensure employee engagement. The establishment of a conducive organizational culture is just as important if not more so. Rather than trying to manipulate the beliefs and attitudes of the employee in order to create the impression of autonomy, mastery, purpose and support, an organizational leader would be far more successful in achieving employee engagement by ensuring that the organizational culture naturally supports these and any other requirements that will generate employee engagement.

Towards a more holistic understanding of employee engagement

Rather than viewing employee engagement in a similar way to performance management – that it is the responsibility of the individual employee to get it right – the most recent research highlights the importance of a collaborative and relational responsibility. Specifically, the Gallup (2015) research identifies the primary determinant of an engaging and high-performing workplace as the line manager. Importantly, every formal leader in an organization is essentially a line manager in the sense that they have explicit responsibility to lead a particular group. Even the higher education institution leader is the line manager of each of their leadership group members. Gallup reports that as much as 70 per cent of the variance in the employee engagement can be traced back to the influence and practices of the line manager. Alfes et al. (2013) also found line manager behaviour and perceived HRM practices to be linked with employee engagement. Employees become disengaged from management practices that include micromanagement and the loss of autonomy, ignoring staff, providing unclear purposes, poorly managed change, favouritism and unfairness, inequity in opportunities and workload.

In response to its employee engagement data, Gallup proposes that line managers need to create environments where employees take responsibility for their own and team's engagement to build workplaces that are sites of productivity and profitability. Figure 6.1 below provides a more specific illustration of the respective responsibilities that work in tandem of all those who are able to contribute towards enhancing employee engagement.

According to Buckingham and Goodall (2015) one simple way that a line manager can begin to enhance employee engagement is to ensure they check-in regularly with each employee. These authors suggest that check-in conversations keep priorities in focus and give the employee the opportunity to talk about how best to do their work. Too frequent check-ins might become

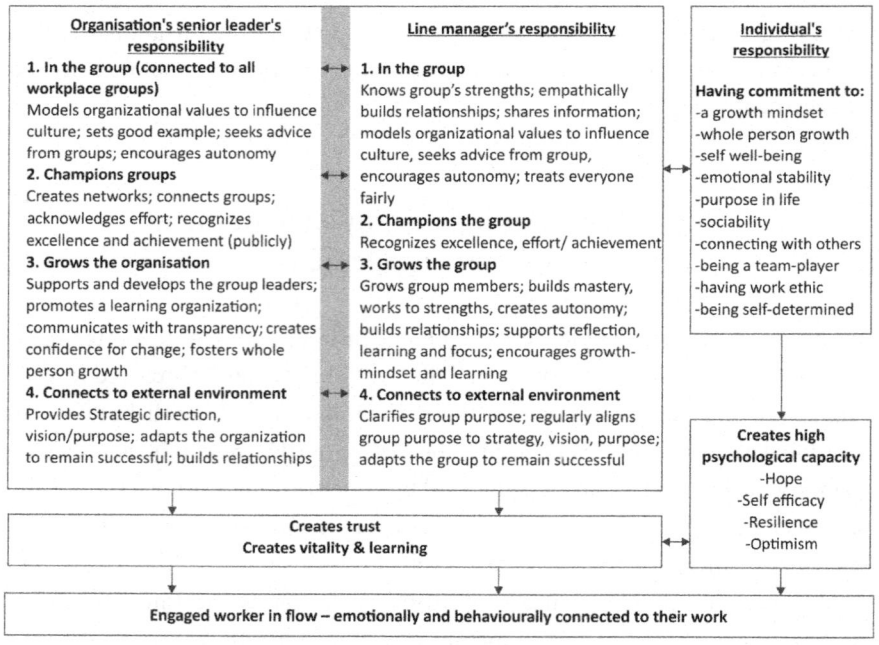

Figure 6.1 An illustration of the respective responsibilities of all those involved in the enhancement of employee engagement

micromanagement, which Buckingham and Goodall (2015) call the 'team leaders killer app' because the net result of micromanagement is disengagement. The micromanagement problem stems from the line manager not being able to accept that employees are specialist in their own particular work and therefore are more knowledgeable if they are free to be working to their strengths. This understanding is supported by decades of Deloitte research where it has been regularly found that the most significant variable explaining the differences between high-and low-performing employees was how they responded to the question: 'At work I have the opportunity to do what I do best every day.' Where employee engagement was strengths based, the organization was 44 per cent more likely to earn high customer satisfaction scores, 50 per cent more likely to have low employee turnover, and 38 per cent more likely to be productive (Buckingham and Goodall 2015).

Arguably, the opposite of micromanagement is trust. Rather than strictly controlling what an employee does, the line manager needs to show that they trust that the employee will do their best if provided with the necessary support. Levene (2015) refers to knowing that you are completely trusted by your line manager as being in a state of vitality and learning where the freer the employee feels from repression and conflict the more energy they have for creativity and vitality. Vitality refers to being in a state of aliveness that brings a sense that one's actions have meaning and purpose. From this sense of vitality employees also feel energized and in a higher psychological state which Levene (2015) describes as *'thriving'*. When vitality and energy are present, then the employee is wide open to learning how to improve upon what they are doing, even if this involves the risk of getting it wrong, and this provides the basis for creative initiatives. Where there is opportunity for such self-guided workplace learning, employee engagement is heightened. Goleman (2013) refers to this state of engagement as 'flow'. His model (Figure 6.2) predicts that being in a state of 'flow' occurs when brain activity is at a peak and it results in high performance. Brain activity declines, as does productivity, if the employee has too much work and they become 'frazzled'. The non-engaged employee has low brain activity and low performance. According to Goleman, the employee's capacity to clearly focus upon the task is the hidden driver of excellence (flow); it requires attention, and attention is a skill that can be strengthened.

Similarly, recent neuroscience advancements provide a compelling insight into the importance of trust being the foundation of the relationship between a line manager and each employee they are explicitly leading. According to

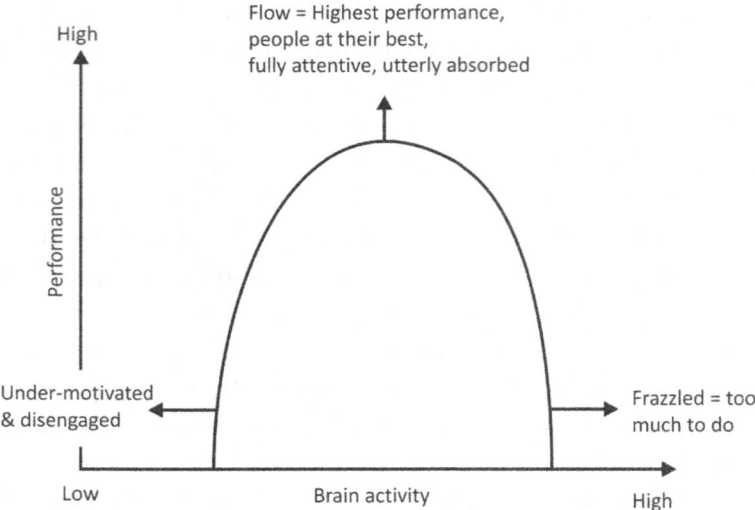

Figure 6.2 Relationship between brain activity and productivity

Zac (2017), when an individual feels trusted they produce oxytocin, and when trust occurs with purpose these mutually reinforce each other to produce an extended release of oxytocin, which produces happiness. From this research, Zac (2017) also identified eight leader behaviours that foster trust:

1. recognizing excellence which has the largest effect on creating trust especially if it is a public recognition and it occurs immediately after the achievement;
2. promoting networking within a team to find solutions as this intensifies focus and strengthens social cohesion and trust;
3. encouraging autonomy which promotes innovation and gives a sense of satisfaction of being trusted;
4. enabling job crafting so that employees can focus on their passions/ strengths;
5. sharing information because poor communication leads to mistrust;
6. intentionally building relationships because when employees build social ties at work they become more trusting;
7. facilitating whole person growth and encouraging growth mindsets in place of performance reviews;
8. showing vulnerability and asking help from others instead of always deciding on what things need to be done.

We argue that, together, these eight behaviours provide the essential ethical culture, which is the prerequisite bedrock for the maximization of employee engagement. An ethical culture is based upon the shared values of trust, openness, transparency, honesty, integrity, collegiality and fairness (Branson 2014c). This is a culture in which all have a sense of safety and security because they each feel that they can rely on each other, but especially their leader, in order to achieve their best. Working together becomes more meaningful and purposeful because each employee's strengths are recognized and utilized for the benefit of all. Moreover, individual weaknesses are accepted as either opportunities for future personal growth or opportunities for networking with the strengths of another employee in order to overcome it. Thus, being an ethical leader is about being fair, which is the most fundamental element of transrelational leadership. The onus is explicitly on the line manager's responsibility to create this ethical culture within their business unit/organization. Riivari and Lämsä (2014) argue that there is a pay-off for the organization if it is ethical because aspects of an ethical culture encourage innovation. This implies that the highest effect on organizational innovativeness, and thereby success and sustainability, is the behaviours of the leaders and line managers and the example they set.

Conclusion

The argument developed in this chapter is that the search for high performance, which is an essential aspiration for each and every organization striving for success and sustainability including those in higher education, needs to refocus attention away from performance management to that of employee engagement. Research has shown that performance management processes invariably achieve the opposite of what they are intended to achieve. Most performance management processes lower performance rather than raise it. Only highly relational, and far less prescriptive, performance management processes actually achieve some success. In contrast, organizations focusing on enhancing employee engagement are far more successful in building a commitment to high performance and thereby increasing productivity and profitability.

In support of this move, there is ample evidence of the factors that promote the level of employee engagement. Yet despite this substantial research effort engagement remains a major organizational and personal issue. Why is this so? We propose that employee engagement needs to be understood by leaders as a relational phenomenon that is influenced by the actions of the leader. If leaders focus on trying to measure and improve some of the key integral elements of employee engagement, such as autonomy or mastery or purpose, then disappointment is most likely. Employee engagement cannot be differentiated into its constituent parts with each to be separately attended to. This would be like a car driver saying that they will only pay attention to the use of the footbrake and nothing else. Good, safe driving requires the simultaneous attention to a myriad of sensory experiences. Similarly, employee engagement requires a unified attention to all of its integral building blocks. Simply, it requires the right organizational culture – an ethical culture – to be properly addressed. This ethical culture provides the fertile ground for whole-self-engagement and growth. It is a workplace culture where employees are emotionally and behaviourally connected to their work and they care about their work, colleagues and the organization. This means that the employee is not just concerned with earning money but more with being fully engaged in meaningful tasks so that they feel they truly belong and they can connect with others.

Importantly the only way in which this can be achieved is through people-centred, and not product and/or profit-centred, leadership. This is transrelational rather than managerial leadership. Keeping people fully engaged in their work is not complicated. All it requires is the discarding of last-century managerial thinking, structures, policies and practices that constrain and suppress engagement. It requires transrelational leaders who naturally create ethical cultures throughout their workplace because they put the interests of people first. However, the leader and line managers alone cannot achieve the establishment of such an ethical culture. This insight acknowledges the critical role of the organization's HRM structure and processes in supporting, modelling, creating and spreading this culture across the whole of the organization. Through the actions of the HRM personnel the higher education leader can more readily spread all of the desired effects of their transrelational approach to leadership, including that of increased employee engagement and thereby high performance, across their institution. Hence, the following chapter describes how this ideal outcome can be achieved through a reinvention of HRM.

Reinventing Human Resource Management

Abstract

This chapter focuses on the challenge that organizations, including higher education institutions, face to bring about the foundational change that is necessary if transrelational leadership is to be embraced. In most large organizations, the Human Resource Management (HRM) department functions to maintain the status quo by implementing standardized policies, practices and systems that aim to unify and control employees' behaviour, attitudes and performance. Hence, this chapter argues that a change to transformational leadership in higher education requires a simultaneous refinement in the focus of HRM. To this end, the growing awareness within HRM of the concept of 'corporate socially responsible' (CSR) organizations is described and aligned with the nature and practices of transformational leadership.

Introduction

The focus of this chapter is on highlighting the challenge that organizations (including higher education institutions) face when attempting to bring about the foundational change required if transrelational leadership is to be embraced. Pragmatically, most large organizations seek to achieve a leader's vision, and the organization's strategic purpose, via its HRM department. Simply defined, HRM refers to the policies, practices and systems that influence employees' behaviour, attitudes and performance. Hence, it is through the actions of the HRM department that the desired leadership wishes and intentions are translated into policies, practices and systems, and are thereby 'filtered down and across' the organization. Invariably, achievement of the intended outcomes is also overseen by an HRM department that is charged with the responsibility of ensuring not only that the desired policies, practices and systems are implemented but also that the required employee commitment to these is maintained.

We do acknowledge that there is a growing trend in higher education to use an alternative name for this department. For example, quite a number of institutions are now preferring to use the department title of 'People and Culture' while others have applied the name of 'Human Capital Systems'. However, what is far less obvious is a commitment within these institutions of there being a significantly different approach or departmental culture accompanying the name change. Although this raises serious concern, it is beyond the scope of this book to explore this matter. But what is explored are the widely used traditional strategies and processes that are common to most higher education institutions, including many of those who have had a name change. Thus, for ease of discussion these will be categorized together under the term of HRM.

The past three Deloitte annual reports on global human capital trends are very pertinent to this discussion of HRM. The reports present findings from comprehensive longitudinal studies of various organizational topics and include the tracking of the performance of HRM structures and practices. Notably, each of the three reports highlights very deep concerns with HRM departments worldwide and across all sectors. For example, the 2014 Deloitte publication reports that 42 per cent of business leaders believe their HRM teams are underperforming and 'less than 8% of HRM leaders have confidence that their teams have the skills needed to meet the challenge of today's global environment and consistently deliver innovative programmes that drive business impact' (2014: 107). More specifically, the Deloitte report identifies that HRM needs to 'develop an understanding of the needs of the 21st-century workforce' (2014: 107). Moreover, after business leaders rated HRM with failure or barely passing grades, the 2015 Deloitte's Global Human Capital Trends report lifted the urgency for improved HRM performance to fourth highest of the ten most urgent organizational needs. This report posits that most HRM departments seem to be 'stuck in neutral and unable to use analytics capabilities to address complex business and talent needs ... and calls for a dramatic change in strategies for leadership, talent, and human resources' (Deloitte 2015: 2). According to this particular report, HRM needs to be 'reinvented' because it needs an 'extreme makeover'. The 2016 Deloitte report again ranked the need for HRM to change in its top ten trends, reflecting that HRM needs to become far better at assisting organizations to adjust to the fact that 'sweeping global forces are reshaping the workplace, the workforce, and work itself' (2016b: 1).

Collectively the reports reflect that HRM's past ways of managing employees as a resource, and not a person, have well and truly gone. The traditional HRM approach to employees is strictly transactional and has no place in, or congruence with, a modern organization or leadership approach, least of all with transrelational leadership. Yet despite this, HRM departments seem to be desperately clinging on to the command-and-control approach that is now no longer helpful. Ironically, while HRM is the traditional 'gatekeeper of performance management', HRM's own performance has been declining markedly to the point of hindering organizational engagement and productivity. Hence, this chapter argues that a change to transformational leadership in higher education requires a simultaneous refinement in the focus of HRM. This is to argue that HRM needs to be reinvented. To this end, the growing awareness within HRM of the concept of CSR organizations is described and aligned with the nature and practices of transformational leadership.

The foundations of HRM

The *Encyclopedia of Human Resource Management* defines HRM as 'the term used to describe formal systems devised for the management of people within an organization. The responsibilities of a human resource manager fall into three major areas: staffing, employee compensation and benefits, and defining/ designing work. Essentially, the purpose of HRM is to maximize the productivity of an organization by optimizing the effectiveness of its employees' (Inc 2017: 1). To achieve this purpose, HRM activities can be distilled down to three core areas of focus:

1. carrying out activities such as recruitment, retention of talent, managing employee performance through goal-based performance management, managing redundancies and change;
2. measuring explicit outcomes such as employee satisfaction, stakeholder appeal, service satisfaction and other such metrics; and
3. creating the policies and processes to reinforce and implement core activities and monitoring/measuring.

In theory, it is presumed that these core activities all work to improve the overall performance of the organization as determined by increased sales, improvements in market share, increased productivity and profit growth. Boselie, Dietz and Boon (2005: 73) argues that HRM 'can be viewed as a collection of multiple, discrete practices with no explicit or discernible link between them. The more strategically minded system approach views HRM as an integrated and coherent "bundle" of mutually reinforcing practices created for the purpose of achieving organisational goals.'

Figure 7.1 below provides a further illustration of the more typical diverse roles, responsibilities and actions of a traditional HRM department. The figure shows how current traditional HRM processes strive to support the leader's implementation of any new strategic direction for the organization and the goals to achieve it. It is the responsibility of HRM to implement the new goals, which essentially means 'getting people to do things differently' where required. Typically, HRM first consider the implications of the new direction in terms of the competencies and capabilities of the organization to achieve the desired result. Then largely through the HRM-devised mechanism for the annual process of personal goal setting, each employee is explicitly directed towards contributing to the implementation and accomplishment of the leader's strategic direction. In

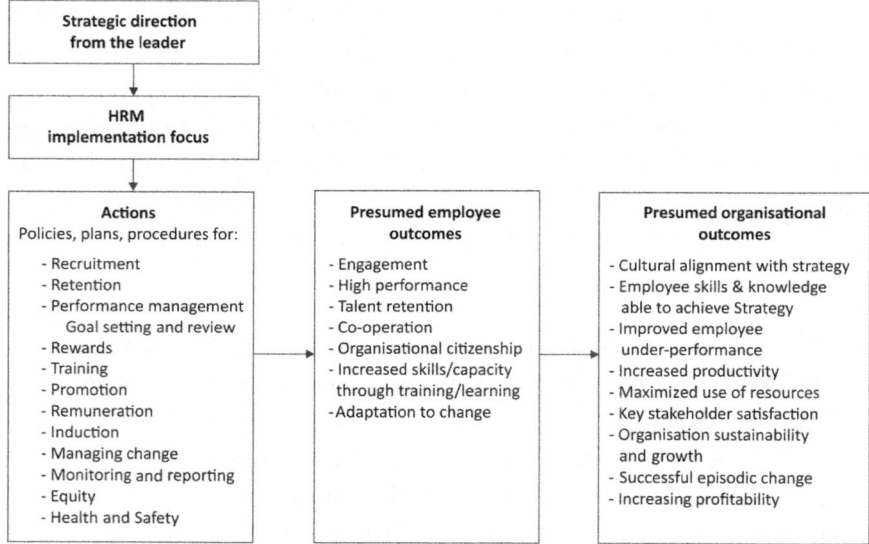

Figure 7.1 An illustration of the traditional model of HRM

theory, the goals of each employee should align with what is required in the new direction. Where there are perceived shortfalls in organizational capacity and capability, attention may be directed to recruitment and/or the retention of key employees. The overall assumption is that through a combination of rewards, training, incentives and change management actions, every employee will eventually adapt to all required changes and furthermore, will become engaged, high-performing and willing contributors to the improved organization. As a consequence, it is presumed that the organization will grow and profit from upskilled, highly productive employees who have adjusted to the change.

While the assumptions built into the model may at one level appear reasonable and logical, the lived reality is very different. Critically, the model ignores the human component. Also, it ignores the reality that the successful implementation of the strategy all comes down to the 'boots on the ground' because it is the people and not the strategy that brings about the change. This model produces a very managerialistic approach to the attainment of the leader's strategic direction. Employees are treated like cogs in a machine that are all manipulated and controlled so that they turn in the right direction. Hence, a common employee response is to resist any changes, or to comply with what is required of them only when it might achieve a personal benefit. As a result, the strategic direction struggles to gain a strong foothold across the organization (70 per cent of change initiatives fail – see Chapter 6) and presents as something of a failure. The employees are more often than not targeted as the 'problem' and needing to be performance managed, instead of the deficiencies in the leader, leadership approach and in HRM being acknowledged.

Within this managerialistic approach, performance management, and all that it entails, are the key HRM tool for trying to gain positive employee engagement with any new requirements. Literature from both management and strategic human resource management view the purpose of performance management as being to improve employee performance, with the aim of positively affecting organizational success (e.g. Mondy, Noe and Premeaux 2002) by creating high- performance work systems (e.g. Appelbaum et al. 2000). Cardy (2004) argues that performance management is critical for organizational effectiveness yet, as described in the previous chapter, decades of research and a substantial body of empirical evidence have failed to provide conclusive evidence of HRM processes resulting in markedly improved employee performance Boselie, Dietz and Boon (2005: 73).

The relationship between HRM and performance summarized in Figure 7.1 shows that these processes tend to follow a logical cause-and-effect sequence with the goal of increasing the performance and behaviour of individuals to grow the performance of the organization. Here performance management is understood as 'a continuous process of identifying, measuring, and developing the performance of individuals and teams and aligning performance with the strategic goals of the organisation' (Aguinis and Pierce 2008: 29). It is a process with several identifiable elements or stages, including performance planning and goal setting, performance assessment, appraisal of performance against the achievement of the goals, performance review and performance renewal (Aguinis and Pierce 2008). Theoretically it is an integrated process in which managers work with employees to set expectations, measure and review results and then reward performance (den Hartog et al. 2004) and it is assumed that, by having high-performing employees, organizational goals are achieved.

Yet, what we have described represents a very technical understanding of performance management. Furthermore, it is an orientation that struggles with the challenges that organizations have in defining what constitutes high performance and, therefore, in being able to stimulate employees to perform and then accurately measuring the quality of the performance (den Hartog, Boselie and Paauwe 2004). If the essence of the desired effect (high performance) cannot be clearly articulated then it is nigh impossible to determine what causes (employee performances) need adjusting in order to achieve it. To further understand the growing dissonance between what traditional HRM strategies and processes are trying to do and what they are actually doing, as a foundation argument for the reinvention of HRM, the following section provides a more in-depth review of contemporary HRM.

A review of contemporary HRM

Despite the abundant business literature (Buckingham and Goodall 2015; William 2012; Yu 2014) clearly identifying the problems and causes of disengagement and the subsequent underperformance, HR departments and chief executives around the globe still seek to follow outdated thinking, particularly regarding organizational development. For example, an international advertising organization advertised recently for a human resources manager with the capability to run strong performance management processes and to manage performance issues, disciplinary actions, grievances and to implement an array of new policies and processes. This was despite the organization's goal to have innovative, productive and happily involved workers. This is one example, typical of advertised organizational development positions across sectors, which appears to recognize that there are serious organizational problems but fails to understand the actual nature of these problems. Hence, they erroneously believe that past ways will still work. As a result, the knowledge and skills of those being appointed to these new positions are completely misunderstood by HRM and so the wrong person will gain appointment and the problems are most likely to persist.

Examples such as that above indicate that the current model of HRM does not have either the capacity or the philosophical foundations to move beyond its traditional focus on processes and transactions. This problem largely stems from the organizational behavioural home of HRM and the human motivational theories of Douglas McGreggor (1960). These very early motivational theories proposed that the basic human person is lazy, self-centred, lacking ambition, resistant to change and wants to be told what to do (Aithal and Suresh Kumar 2016). But far more modern insights into human nature as provided by psychology, sociology, behavioural studies and philosophy now throw considerable doubt on the credibility of McGreggor's early theories. Simply, some of the fundamental principles, upon which traditional HRM strategies and practices are founded, are outdated and unhelpful.

It is important to also acknowledge that these HRM processes originated in support of very different forms of leadership. Indeed, many were introduced at a time when transactional leadership practices were almost universally accepted and employed. Thus, it is quite understandable that the aligned HRM strategies and processes were similarly transactional in design and intent. However, as described in previous chapters, the transactional, managerial approaches to organizational leadership are no longer working. The unacceptable levels of employee non-engagement and disengagement described in the previous chapters show this understanding to be abundantly true. Thus contemporary HRM faces massive change to meet the needs of our twenty-first-century organizations that have been described by Deloitte (2016b: 1) as having 'very different design' because these need to be built 'around highly empowered teams, driven by a new model of management, and led by a breed of younger, more globally diverse leaders'. This approach follows the holacracy model founded by Brian Robertson and Tom Thomison in 2007 (see Robertson 2015). Holacracy provides a team-based peer-to-peer model as an alternative to the industrial-age hierarchical model with its centralized control and top–down planning. According to Robertson (2015), it is absolutely essential for today's organization to have the capacity to establish a new HRM social framework for governing and operating as a united and productive organization.

As organizations are forced to change, HRM needs to be able to not only 'drive' the required changes but also, just as importantly, be able to do this in a commensurate way so that the people flourish and innovate. Because this is, by and large, yet to be the case, there is an ever-increasing employee voice via employee surveys and social tools saying that HRM needs to listen to and take note of the needs of employees (Deloitte 2016b). This voice claims that HRM has not yet 'reinvented' itself to keep pace with the changing organizational environment but rather has become a conglomerate of traditional managerialism tempered by listening apps, digital know-how, HRM analytics and scorecards. Thus, from the view of many employees, while 'Rome' is burning, most leaders are jumping from 'fires' into 'frying pans' and HRM is 'fiddling about' at the edges persisting with outdated and unhelpful performance policies and processes in the same way it has done for decades. As Margaret Wheatley (2005: 65) points out, 'With so much evidence supporting the benefits of participation, why are organizations not using self-managed teams to cope with turbulence. Instead organizations are cluttered with control mechanisms that paralyze employees and leaders. Where have all the policies, procedures, protocols, and regulations come from? And why do we keep creating more and more?'

Unfortunately, organizational development in the hands of HRM in its traditional form is not able to adequately help bring about the changes required. From this traditional perspective, organizational development is an effort that is:

1. Planned
2. Organization-wide
3. Managed from the top
4. Leading to increased organization effectiveness and health
5. Uses behavioural science knowledge to guide organizational interventions and processes (Organizational Development Network 2017).

Within this process the stated focus is about developing organizational capability through alignment of strategy, structure, management processes, people and rewards and metrics (OD network 2017). As such, it is strictly managerial – there is no mention of leadership or culture or relationships, and certainly no acknowledgement that organizations have and are evolving. Instead, the organization is being treated the same way as it always has been. According to Harvard Business School's management expert, Gary Hamel (2007), 'Instinctively, we know that management is out of date. We know its rituals and routines look slightly ridiculous in the dawning light of the 21st century.' Edgar

Schein, a world authority on organizational culture identifies that it is of critical importance for successful organizations to align the various sub-cultures within an organization. He states,

> Building an effective organization is ultimately a matter of meshing the different subcultures by encouraging the evolution of common goals, common language, and common procedures for solving problems. It is essential that leaders recognize that such cultural alignment requires not only cultural humility on the leader's part, but skills in bringing different subcultures together into the kind of dialogue that will maintain mutual respect and create coordinated action. (Schein 2010: 271)

It is this work where organizational developers in HRM need to focus and assist the leader.

Similarly, the seminal work of Peter Senge (2006) examining how and why organizations learn, grow and develop is missing from the traditional HRM organizational development strategies. Senge argues that organizational learning can only occur where people continually grow their capacity to create the results they desire – where new and expansive patterns of thinking are nurtured, where collective aspiration is set free and where people are continually learning how to learn together. Clearly, these essential principles for the successful achievement of organizational development are not embedded in the traditional HRM strategy. Thus, it is not surprising when Margaret Wheatley (2005) proposes that organizations not only have a severe disability in solving organizational problems, but all attempts to resolve a problem results in unintended consequences that worsen the original problem because decisions are based on power rather than intelligence. This includes damaging relationships and increasing unwillingness by people to consider alternatives. Decisions become based on power rather than intelligence. Laloux (2014: 4) believes that

> the way we try to deal with organizations' current problems often seems to make things worse, not better. Most organizations have gone through many rounds of change programs, mergers, centralizations and decentralizations, new IT systems, new mission statements, new scorecards, or new incentive systems. It feels like we have stretched the current way we run organizations to its limits, and these traditional recipes often seem part of the problem, not the solution.

Observations such as these highlight that currently there seems little understanding within HRM departments of the fundamentals of how people function in their workplaces and how best to help employees to adjust to the demands of new organizational cultures and new approaches to leadership. The next section seeks to respond to this state of affairs.

Where to next for HRM?

As indicated in our introductory chapter, in this era of unprecedented global change and volatility, organizations face a future marked by grave uncertainty and strong competition as they strive to remain viable, productive and sustainable. Surely the critical element for success in this challenging environment is adaptability: the ability of the organization through the guidance of its leader to create a workplace culture, which fosters employees who are willing and able to adjust to and embrace change so that innovation can thrive. As top international executive Pablo Isla puts it, 'Motivating people and generating a sense of spirit inside a company are essential parts of the CEO's role. We need to appeal to our employees' emotions to help create an environment where they can innovate' (Ignatius 2016: 54). As change and uncertainty in organizational culture now appear 'the norm' and, arguably, need to be accepted as such, the questions for HRM as it reinvents itself are:

1. How can HRM support the transrelational leader to facilitate the organization's 'new design'?
2. What does HRM need to do, and how does HRM need to be, to ensure people are psychologically well and fully engaged in their work?
3. How can HRM provide processes that encourage rather than suppress employee creativity and innovation which are essential for organizations during times of such uncertainty and change?
4. How can HRM move from the rhetoric of diversity to appreciating and including the fullness of diversity in organizations of today and tomorrow?
5. In what ways do HRM processes need to adjust to ensure these are relevant for the different generations of employees in the workplace?
6. What implications for HRM arise from the development of an ethical culture across the organization?

These questions result from the arguments and discussion throughout this book and not just from within this particular chapter. This recognizes the critical and unique role that HRM contributes towards ensuring that what has been previously described about leadership, organizations and culture are able to take effect. While the focus of this book is essentially the nature and practice of leadership, it is acknowledged that while the actions and dispositions of the leader are paramount in determining much of what happens in an organization, ultimately leaders are not solely responsible. HRM is a key means through which the leader's influence is spread across and throughout the organization. Thus the very different approach to leadership and organizational culture that is foregrounded in this book requires HRM to help promote and disseminate the necessary changes, but doing this requires a distinctly different HRM philosophical and practical foundation. This calls upon HRM to embrace the new social contract that is developing between organizations and employees, which is driving major changes in the employer/employee relationships (e.g. Karnes 2009). This mandates a relational approach to HRM rather than the policy-driven controlled approach, and this means that each and every HRM process must be seen to be valuing people as creative contributors to a common goal rather than humans to be managed as a resource. Indeed, if the fundamental role of HRM in today's organizations is to align all of the sub-cultures with the desired culture across the whole organization then it, too, must model that very same culture in all that it does. If the new approach to leadership is transrelational, then HRM's work with all in the organization must also be transrelational.

In supporting the search for attaining high performance, HRM must also address employee engagement, which can only be achieved through the nurturing of an ethical organizational culture. As argued in Chapter 6, organizations now need to consider nurturing employee engagement rather than managing employee performance if high performance is the ideal. It is not possible to mandate employee engagement, although such engagement polices do exist in some organizations. Although managing for engagement and performance might appear to make sense from a rational, logical-sequential, managerial perspective, the actual creation of systems to manage and manipulate engagement are counterproductive because these invariably overlook cultural norms and practices that are additional important influences upon engagement.

Is HRM up to the task we have outlined? This task is not only to support new organizational models but also to help drive organizations in a way that breaks down the very managerial structures, processes and culture that create division, disharmony and disengagement. HRM's traditional approaches of creating highly hierarchical and clinical systems and policies for processes such as recruitment, performance management and professional development need to go. So too does any form of the coercive power previously wielded by HRM; power that not only creates subliminal fear that one's job is on the line if one does not toe the line, but also is reinforced by policies that seem to police rather than support performance. As noted in the previous chapter, this is the very climate that results in toxic culture, disengagement and counterproductive behaviours and unhealthy levels of stress (Colligan and Higgins 2008). As noted above, a complete makeover is called for that includes very different approaches to dealing with employees, including those in senior positions. To this end, we present a reinvented HRM model, as illustrated in Figure 7.2.

The essential differences between this reinvented model and the traditional model (Figure 7.1) is that it acknowledges that employees work best in teams. Hence, HRM must focus on supporting the success of the team and helping the team, and the individual team members, to be able to assess progress and success. Rather than managing, controlling and measuring the individual, HRM must work in partnership with the team and its members, which is a major shift in the role of HRM. Guided by relational line managers, teams work to achieve specific strategically aligned purposes, and they are largely autonomous in how they go about achieving the team purpose; all of which ensures engagement and high productivity. Growth mindsets are the norm for all, including the HRM personnel, and employees are encouraged to use their natural workplace strengths in order to be creative and to innovate.

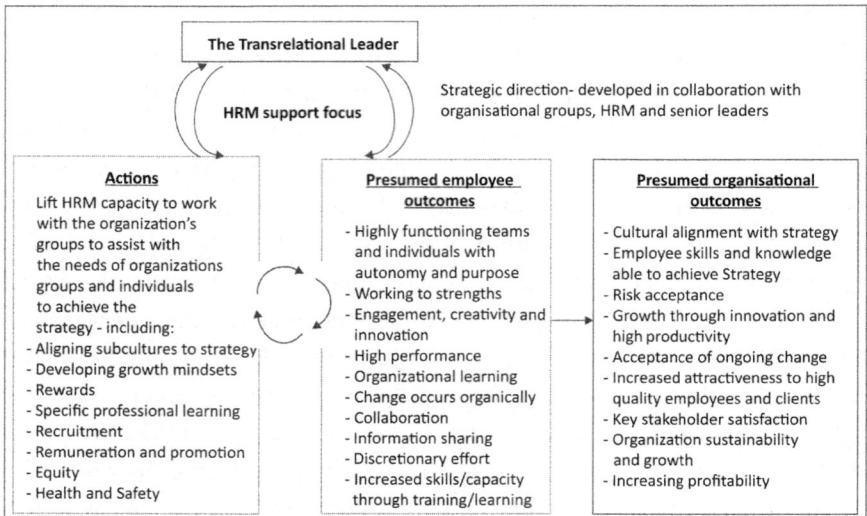

Figure 7.2 A reinvented HRM model illustrating what and how HRM must now be supporting new organizational cultures and different approaches to leadership

This model proposes that when the new strategic direction is announced by the leader it has already been discussed with, and strengthened by, all of those teams who will be required to implement the changes. In this model the role of HRM is as support for teams rather than being the implementation systems controller of the new direction via processes such as goal setting, performance management and managing the change. Instead, within this reinvented model HRM works to ensure that the culture of the various teams is aligned to the new strategy. As the new direction has already been openly and widely discussed by the leader, employees in their teams understand what is expected of them. Importantly, they have already been able to influence how the change will impact on the work of their team and explore how the team can best implement the change. They are thus far less likely to feel challenged by the change. Supporting the implementation of the change is no longer a thorn in the side of the involved employees or HRM or the leaders. In this way, the beneficial outcomes for the organization are higher levels of engagement, increased growth mindsets and the experience of being part of the change process. All of this helps to create a change culture within the organization whereby change becomes far less episodic as it is ingrained in the everyday workplace life. Hence, the disruptive and divisive influence of employee resistance is significantly minimized.

Such support by HRM of building 'team culture' across the organization is proving to be successful. For example, speaking from experience, Hollie Delaney, head of HRM at Zappos, an organization that adopted holacracy, suggests that senior management in the company needs to throw down their authority and give it to the employees who are doing the day-to-day jobs. This is necessary because the goal is to create a workplace where employees pick up that authority and make decisions without looking to a manager or supervisor for approval. From this, people become innovative and engaged with their jobs (see Gray 2015). For Delany, the work of HRM has changed in that instead of simply implementing independently rationalized processes, the work now includes active involvement in employee circles, teams and projects; organizing staff events; developing talent acquisition schemes that create a pool of people looking to work at the company rather than people just looking for a job; encouraging employees to adapt to the new systems; establishing values-based recruitment and training opportunities; and encouraging senior leaders to let go of authority in order to become far more relational (Gray 2015). The new HRM ethos is about not just doing the work, but getting to know all of the employees better so that mutually supportive collaborations can unfold, from which creative innovations are born and engagement and productivity are increased. According to Delany, the new look of HRM isn't just about holding people to rules, it's a lot more than that. It's about making sure employees are represented in the company's decisions and are supported in living up to their potential. It's about HRM being part of something much bigger than before because it takes on the responsibility of creating an organizational culture, which becomes a great place to work.

Where to next for higher education organizations?

Today's higher education institutions need to respect the diverse needs of all stakeholders and not just those that encourage and support managerialist outcomes. This includes the diversity of needs of academic and non-academic staff, the student populations, local and national social and economic interests, and the higher education profession. Importantly, creating the workplace environment in which all employees are able to give their very best is at the very heart of accomplishing this essential outcome. As comprehensively described in the introductory chapter, this is clearly not being achieved at present. Arguably, the residual structures and processes that have resisted the influence of managerial leadership are producing the best of today's higher education outcomes. But the strong message from the introductory chapter is that managerialism is slowly but surely diminishing the capacity of higher education institutions to successfully complete the core businesses of teaching, research and professional publications.

Rather than going backwards, a new transrelational approach to higher education leadership is required. This will enable the right balance to be gained among the demands of income generation, fiscal responsibility and high performance. Transrelational leadership can build on the natural strengths specific to higher education instead of suppressing these through managerialist practices. Two of these natural strengths are the existence of 'teams' and 'unique individual skills and knowledge'. The concept of a 'network of teams', as an ideal organizational model (see Deloitte 2016b; Robertson 2015), is gaining universal traction in business and government sectors. More importantly, this is an ideal model for higher education institutions because these are essentially team based (be they 'teams' formed by committees, faculties, disciplines, schools, departments, institutes, boards and so on). But, as previously explained, for success, 'teams' need transrelational leaders, not managers. They require leaders who provide them with autonomy, with the opportunity to set their own goals and make their own decisions, with the required resources, and with regular acknowledgement and encouragement.

Alongside the appropriate leadership, teams also need the right team members. The best teams comprise a diversity of skill, knowledge, experiences and dispositions because this creates the deepest pool of wisdom, creativity and innovation. Where there is diversity of abilities and knowledge, a team has the potential to come up with new ideas, innovations and opportunities to learn (Molleman and Timmerman 2003). Here, again higher education institutions have a natural advantage because of the incredible array of unique academic and non-academic individual skills and knowledge at their disposal. People are employed in higher education largely because of their unique and desirable skills and knowledge. Used to its maximum, this diverse array of skills and knowledge provides higher education with an enviable resource pool for creativity and innovation that few if any other organizational sectors have access to in searching for a productive and sustainable future. The challenge for higher education lies in being able to create the culture that enables the full use of this resource. Until that happens, higher education is wasting its potential.

Thus the future challenge for HRM in higher education centres on reinvention. The reasons for this are not only those generic organizational reasons described earlier in this chapter, but also to meet the specific needs of higher education. The reinvented HRM in higher education needs to be capable of helping to connect the right employees into successful teams and to support these teams towards enhanced success. This responsibility will have its genesis in HRM processes that maximize the innate diversities of higher education institutions. These diversities are inclusive of ethnicities, genders, generations, attitudes, knowledge, experience, beliefs and skills. Importantly for HRM this endeavour encompasses an essential role in helping to create teams, but also in being able to clearly and authentically model teamwork both within its own department and in how it supports the teams. This implies that the future critical challenge for HRM in higher education is to relinquish its hierarchical, technical, procedural reputation in order to embrace and enact far more relational, employee-centred, supportive attributes.

Finally, higher education needs to acknowledge its own specific role in establishing the reinvention of HRM. The irony for higher education institutions is that they continue to proliferate HRM practitioners in the same form that is not in its own best interests. Institutions around the world continue to graduate thousands of new HRM professionals based on outdated and unhelpful principles and practices. These courses must start producing graduates attuned to and confidently able to practise the knowledge and skills as illustrated in Figure 7.2 and described above.

Conclusion

There is no doubt that some HRM functions are now and will remain strictly transactional. These include the legalities around employment law, health and safety, ethics and duty of care. However, activities relating to the managing of people will shift from transactional to transrelational, from control to support. This new reinvented HRM design requires a depth of understanding of, and commitment to, leadership and culture (see Chapters 1 and 2). Equally significant, it requires new thinking and different capabilities for HRM to enable it to support and create workplaces that are places where people want to be, where they are valued, where they feel they belong and where they can be their best – fully engaged and innovative.

One of the very important responsibilities of HRM in this new organizational environment is preparing future leaders who can be authentically transrelational. Our past ways of developing leaders will not work – these will only train ineffective leaders at best or managerial leaders at worst. So how is it possible to develop transrelational leaders? This vitally important information is provided in the next chapter.

Learning for Future Leadership

Abstract

This chapter presents details and findings of a research project that sought to develop a transrelational way of understanding the nature and practice of leadership among a group of aspiring leaders in a New Zealand university. Higher education institutions are concerned about leadership and are inclined towards improving its practice. However, promotion within higher education is still more aligned to professional outputs and outcomes within one's field of study than with leadership skills and knowledge. Hence, academics are often appointed to a formal leadership role without any specific knowledge and understanding of leadership theory and practice. The research reported in this chapter sought to respond to this reality. The chapter describes some of the experiences of a group of prospective future higher education leaders following their participation in a comprehensive transrelational leadership-learning programme. The chapter provides a critique of the challenges that might arise in higher education when trying to change the approach to leadership but argues that these can be readily addressed if the appropriate means, as described, is applied.

Introduction

Higher education, once seemingly sheltered from the influences of neo-liberal policies and practices, has more recently seen a dramatic shift. As described previously in this book, there has been an ever-increasing focus on outcomes and accountability, instantiated by means of managerialism. This process, as well as its deleterious effects on academics, has been extensively documented across a range of countries by writers including Deem (1998; 2004), Bolden, Gosling and O'Brien (2014) in the UK, Sievers (2008) in Sweden, and Yielder and Codling (2004) in Australia and New Zealand.

Importantly, the development of leadership has changed in this environment. Traditionally, aspiring or potential future leaders were likely to have risen from the ranks of academics, were chosen or endorsed by them, and were likely to have held limited-term leadership roles, while at the same time continuing as teachers and researchers (Black 2015; Smith 2007). Some argue that this is a necessary and positive way for the development of leaders so that the once 'insular' (Davies, Hides and Casey 2007), 'inward looking and collegial' leaders (Black 2015) were made to lead in a way that prioritizes accountability and effective management. However, a number of scholars are not so positive about the suitability of this means for developing higher education leaders, suggesting that there is now little recognition of leadership in contemporary higher education institutions. Stefani (2015: 2166), for example, claims that 'little or no attention is paid to developing the leadership capabilities of individuals with responsibilities to lead, be a leader and show leadership' in higher education. Ekman, Lindgren and Packendorff (2017) speak of a 'discursive void' – 'a void that is "filled" with notions of instrumental management rather than the enthusing and motivating aspects usually associated with "leadership"' (Ekman, Lindgren and Packendorff 2017: 3). There is also some uncertainty and debate about what leadership in higher education now entails (Black 2015; O'Connell 2014).

Alongside the above diminished presence and practice of leaders and leadership in higher education, there is an increasing bureaucracy where academics themselves come to feel somewhat sidelined from the business of leading other academics. There appears to be a favouring of 'management over academic leadership within a hierarchical structure, with "management teams" primarily consisting of staff holding managerial positions who are not necessarily academic leaders' (Yielder and Codling 2004: 322). This process of reconfiguring or restructuring units within higher education institutions, and appointing people to a position of managing those units, is common and widespread, and has been in train for some time (see, for example, Bolden, Gosling and O'Brien 2014; Harman 2002; OECD 2003; Yielder and Codling 2004). Bolden, Gosling and O'Brien (2014: 764) explain its impact:

> As universities have consolidated schools and departments into larger business units (believed to be better able to respond to fluctuations in market demand and government policy) they have recognized a need to 'professionalize' their financial, marketing and support processes. In order to do this they have recruited increasing numbers of professional staff with qualifications and experience considered appropriate to this new definition of the task and streamlined allegedly cumbersome and inefficient processes such as the committee structure.

Here Bolden et al. are pointing to the current reality of significant changes to, or the removal of, leadership committees which traditionally have operated in a representative or democratic way, giving a voice to academics and academic leaders. This reflected that 'the traditional model of governing universities is collegial and consultative in nature, with large and broadly representative bodies and forums open to all academic members of the university' (OECD 2003: 71). The affected committees range from those at unit and or faculty level to those at university level. For example, a relatively recent and government-mandated change in New Zealand to university councils has seen student representation removed and staff representation diminished, so that the national government could make more appointments supposedly to increase the business interests on the councils.

Within this era of managerialism in higher education many academics have been sidelined from governance and leadership experiences, and have increasingly come to feel disengaged and disconnected from their institutions (Bolden, Gosling and O'Brien 2014; Siever 2008). This has severe consequences precisely because, in times of change, organizations need not only committed, engaged and resilient staff but also highly knowledgeable, competent and experienced leaders across the institution who know and are committed to its mission. The OECD cautions that, "it would be hard for a university to retain a true sense of mission if significant numbers of academics become alienated from the institution' (OECD 2003: 73). This state of affairs, in concert with all that has been previously described and discussed in this book, calls for an urgent re-examination of leadership, and leadership-learning possibilities in higher education. Hence, we first argue that rather than eschewing the importance of academic leadership we should be promoting it and exploring how to support *all* academics to show leadership in various ways in their everyday practice. Secondly, and of primary importance in the context of this book, we argue that the particular approach to leadership to be learnt must be transrelational. This chapter presents the principles upon which such leadership learning must be based.

Why learning and not development?

As well as the many ways of thinking about work-related learning, there are also a large number of widely used terms that are associated with this complex concept. While many of the meanings overlap and intersect, each has emerged from a specific set of circumstances and perspectives. The nomenclature used to describe the learning workers do during their careers may be used interchangeably but each term connotes a slightly different idea about how adults develop their work-related skills and understandings over the passage of a career. Training and development, in-service education, professional development, continuing education, lifelong learning and professional learning are all terms that have been used to describe the means by which adults have gained new work-related knowledge and skills (McRae et al. 2001). Perversely, while 'the language used to name and describe [work-related] learning is undoubtedly significant, the same words spoken by different people can mean different things' (Doecke, Parr and North 2008: 9). Hence, it is important to clarify why we have chosen to use the term 'leadership learning' rather than something like 'leadership development'.

Much research has established that the development of links between work-related learning and change (rather than continuity) is critical to corporate success (Sefton, Waterhouse and Cooney 1995). Traditionally, however, work-related learning was underpinned by 'a common concern with continuity of practice' (Billett 2007: 56). Unfortunately the result of linking work-related learning to change, particularly in times of rapid change, has seen an emphasis on 'the obsolescence of present knowledge ... [reinforcing] the view of learning as "filling up" a reservoir of knowledge in a professional's mind that will run dry if left too long' (Webster-Wright 2009: 712). Simply, this approach to work-related learning essentially maintained the status quo because it reproduced current knowledge, skills and dispositions. The focus was on developing the workplace learner to do what others were already doing. There was little consideration of how the impact of the workplace environment might undermine the new learning. Hence, the actual developmental experience was time-bound – it only had to provide sufficient knowledge and skills to enable the person to begin applying these and to then continue their learning through experience and with ad hoc support from those already practising it in the same workplace. This enabled external 'expert practitioners' to be used as either off-site or on-site trainers/facilitators of the learning experience. Consequently, this form of experience was essentially 'development' and not 'learning'.

By contrast, and with the advent of more in-depth understandings of the nature of adult learning, far more sophisticated forms of work-related learning have evolved. Instead of the mind of the worker being regarded as a passive 'semi-empty' vessel waiting to be 'topped up' with new knowledge that will help them to perform better or differently, new theories of adult learning have been underpinned by assumptions that the learner was mature and brought rich life experiences to formal learning. Adult learners were thus understood to possess 'a repository of information, consisting of direct experimentation and realities' (Ahedo 2009: 67) that they bring to any work-related learning. Furthermore, they are recognized as being more motivated to learn when there is a clear practical application of the learning to the work they are doing. Such learning was encouraged if it was problem centred and linked to changes in the learners social roles (Malone 1990) since these factors act as significant motivators for the adult learner. Learning experiences were felt to be far more worthwhile if the worker was challenged to apply the new knowledge and if the new knowledge had the potential to enhance their workplace status in some way.

Also in contrast to traditional thinking, it was recognized that not all learning had to occur at a given specific time, but rather could occur subsequent to any formal learning and be self-directed in the workplace. Self-directed learning embodied the idea of everyday learning that, while organized, did not rely on an instructor or facilitator. It was argued that the self-directed aspect motivated the learner and fostered transformational learning (Brookfield 1986) through critical reflection (Mezirow and Associates 2000) and promoted emancipatory learning and social action (Cranton 1994). Self-directed learning forms the basis for much of the work in the field of adult learning and 'remains a viable arena for theory building related to adult learning' (Merriam 2001: 11)'.

More recently, theories of adult learning have focused on the interactions between the learner and the contexts within which learning takes place. This view of the adult learner takes 'a holistic view of learning as involving the whole person within his or her sociocultural community' (Webster-Wright 2009: 706). While learning is fundamentally an individual activity, the learning by many individuals is recognized as prospectively benefitting the whole group and/or organization. Although individuals within any organization complete specific tasks, this is most often done in collaboration or association with other workers. Simply, the work that one person does must fit with, align with or complement that done by others. Thus, any new work-related learning gained by one individual must also fit with, align with or complement that done by others if any benefits are to be gained. This form of team or network learning is more than the sum of the parts; it is a synthesis of the work that each and every person can contribute (Kekäle and Viitala 2003).

Such team or networked learning is said to create organizational learning (Senge 1995). Individual learning is a necessary first step, but it is not sufficient to achieve organizational learning (Argyris and Schon 1978). A linchpin for turning individual work-related learning into organizational learning is the dissemination of knowledge among individual workers. This entails the sharing of knowledge, skills and insights in a collaborative exchange of differing perspectives and understandings (Shaw and Perkins 1992). When employees view knowledge as a public good belonging to the whole organization, knowledge flows easily (Ardichvili, Page and Wentling 2003). By establishing conditions for individual workers to learn and to share their learning within the organization, the value of the organization's human capital is substantially increased.

With these new understandings, the most ideal form of work-related learning is a far cry from the traditional model; it 'is situated in the system of ongoing practices of action in ways that are relational, mediated by artifacts, and always rooted in a context of interaction. Such knowledge is thus acquired through some form of participation, and it is continually reproduced and negotiated; that is, it is always dynamic and provisional' (Nicolini, Gherardi and Yanow 2003: 3). This definition provides the foundational principles for how to best prepare higher education personnel to become transrelational leaders. Thus, we talk about *leadership learning* rather than leadership development.

Leadership preparation programmes in higher education

Planning, organizing and facilitating leadership preparation often falls within the purview of HRM divisions in higher education, that tend to adopt traditional approaches (Smith 2007). Most often, these leadership preparation programmes are provided by 'experts', sometimes from within the higher education institution but also as often from outside the organization, 'based on the notion that knowledge and expertise are best updated outside the day-to-day work context' (Gerken, Beausaert and Segers 2016: 136). These can be characterized as training approaches (Deem and Brehony 2005; Inman 2009; Smith 2007). Schein (2010), a world authority on organizational culture, identifies the aligning of the various sub-cultures within an organization as being a critically important leadership responsibility. He states,

> Building an effective organization is ultimately a matter of meshing the different subcultures by encouraging the evolution of common goals, common language, and common procedures for solving problems. It is essential that leaders recognize that such cultural alignment requires not only cultural humility on the leader's part, but skills in bringing different subcultures together into the kind of dialogue that will maintain mutual respect and create coordinated action' (Schein 2010: 271)

It is this work where organizational developers in HRM need to focus and assist the leader.

These approaches are underpinned by a certain view of knowledge – that resides in the expert and is to be passed on to less experienced and knowledgeable individuals. They focus on a non-differentiated generic view of a learner and the uptake of a circumscribed body of knowledge. In knowledge transmission, knowledge itself is seen as bounded, factual and somewhat static. Workshops and seminars can be seen as 'knowledge transmission practices and events' (Franken et al. 2015: 194). Yet, 'knowledge detached from its context becomes meaningless' (Bosua and Scheepers 2007: 95), and transfer to workplace practice is limited. In addition, knowledge transmitted in formal learning arrangements does not always 'keep up with the high-speed developments in practice' (Gerken, Beausaert and Segers 2016: 147). In Smith's (2007) study, head-of-department participants reported topics such as 'health and safety, equal opportunities or the university's administrative systems as examples of such generic and not immediately useful knowledge' (Smith 2007: 6).

Furthermore, this type of knowledge, and the manner of its presentation, represent an autonomous view of learning – to borrow a term from literacy studies (Street 2000), where learning considerations are removed from the context. However, learning is fundamentally a situated and social process. It is also a process that can occur in a spontaneous way in daily work practice (Eraut 2004; Gerken, Beausaert and Segers 2016). Learning that is 'not organized, unstructured and without systemic support' (Gerken, Beausaert and Segers 2016: 136) is potentially of immense value to learning leaders because of its 'here and now' quality. Noe, Tews and Marand (2013) estimate that informal learning accounts for up to 75 per cent of learning that occurs within organizations. Informal learning has received much research attention but it is not always easy to instantiate given that it is often taken for granted and not noticed as learning, learners find it difficult to describe, and the knowledge that arises from it is often subsumed as part of a person's general capability (Eraut 2004). The learning arrangements we advocate later in the chapter draw heavily on the affordances of informal learning.

More specific to the content of these higher education leadership preparation programmes, for much of last century our leadership theories concentrated on informing leaders about what to do in order to gain a desired outcome be it for the benefit of the organization, the leader, or the employee. Towards the end of the century there was an acknowledgement of the affective side of leadership, including the role of values, motives, beliefs and ethics. However, the preparation of leaders remained essentially tied to the practical, tangible and measurable characteristics. Indeed, many organizations and systems developed leadership frameworks – models or illustrations of those constituent elements that together constituted ideal leadership. Although well intentioned, these frameworks narrowed the focus of leadership preparation to explicit behaviours already seen in those deemed to be 'successful leaders'. Development of leaders thus tended to reproduce current leadership practices and maintained the status quo in organizational leadership.

Influential examples of leadership frameworks in higher education include Black (2015) and Bryman (2007). Bryman's framework incorporates a list of thirteen behaviours and practices associated with effective leadership of university departments. Black's more recent framework is more comprehensive (with forty-one capabilities nested in four areas) and detailed (with clear actions) adapted from a non-higher education context (Black, Groombridge and Jones 2011), and tailored for higher education. Black (2015) links aspects of the framework explicitly to analyses of contemporary challenges faced in higher education leadership including, for example, globalization and internationalization, bureaucracy which stifles innovation and creates inefficiency and ineffectiveness, and conflicts between management and research aspects of academic leader roles. This was a significant enhancement as 'any leader development framework for the twenty-first century must encompass the capacities projected for future leader effectiveness' (O'Connell 2014: 186). Black's framework includes behaviours related to 'vision and goals' (e.g. set clear, short-term achievable goals), 'hands on leadership' (e.g. check results with staff and empower them to get the job done), 'improvement and learning' (e.g. expect, and support, staff to strive for-high standards), and 'work details and the big picture' (e.g. integrate management flexibility alongside professional and academic rigour).

In discussing the value of leadership frameworks, Black (2015), himself, expresses some caution. Such frameworks can specify what skills or practices are needed but do not specify how they can be developed. They also often incorporate competing items within lists of skills and practices and are not greatly nuanced to account for specific context. Thus, the practices specified in them may be observed without critical consideration of the needs and goals of the organization being led. Black's framework certainly reads like an inventory and appears to need to be supplemented and unified by the inclusion of values and beliefs (as in O'Connell 2014), more relationally oriented competences (as in Hill 2007: 29), as well as a more careful consideration of context. However, as a reference point for reflecting on one's actions after the fact, it would appear useful to leaders who are learning. But, leadership frameworks based on capabilities are a limited form of theory, and as Raelin comments, 'Theory has time to create a level of order and clarity that is seldom experienced when living forward, which tends to be unpredictable and dynamic' (Raelin 2011: 198). We revisit the usefulness of theory in a later section when we consider the role of theoretical knowledge in influencing conceptual change in those learning to lead.

Leadership frameworks focus on the desired behaviours and practices of an individual leader, and this reflects the traditional tendency to focus on the individual and the development of prescribed leadership traits without reference to the specificity of the context and the people to be led. As mentioned above, this approach aligns with *leader development* and, not surprisingly, it is an approach that has been critiqued by a number of authors over the last decades. (See, for example, Alvesson 1996a,b; Alvesson and Sveningsson 2003; Evers and Lakomski 2001, 2012; Haslam, Reicher and Platow 2011.) Gronn (2003) described this approach as creating 'designer' leaders, highlighting the incongruous homogeneity of this way of preparing future leaders, given that no two leaders will ever be in the very same context. Nigel Wright (2011) was far less polite with his criticism, labelling the approach as creating 'bastard leadership' (2011: 347). This was because of its technical/skill emphasis, at the expense of a moral/values underpinning, and the consequent tendency to produce leaders who readily comply with managerialist practices, to the serious detriment of those they are meant to be leading. Turnbull James explains that 'development that is focused on leader attributes alone will be insufficient to bring about desired organisational change' and reiterates that 'leadership development needs to be deeply embedded and driven out of the context and the challenges that leaders in the organisation face collectively' (Turnbull James 2011: 4).

In the light of such criticisms, there have been numerous attempts to describe more holistic leadership preparation programmes. For example, Bolden et al. (2014: 766) argue that 'when organisations (universities and others) claim that they need better or more leadership they are generally referring to leadership of the institution, with most attention directed at how to improve productivity and reputation'. Good leadership is often assessed on the basis of a leader's performance in these areas. 'A focus on organisational purpose is the primary test of good leadership' (Black 2015: 58). Braun et al. (2009) likewise comment that leadership development programmes should specifically support leaders to 'articulate and align personal practice with university strategy' (Braun et al. 2009: 197). However, in describing his leadership programme, Arsenault (2007) stressed the importance of supporting leadership learners to be true to their own values and beliefs and not feel as if they exist merely to accept and carry out the bidding of the organization. Myerson refers to this as enabling the leaders to become 'tempered radicals', who are 'people who want to succeed in their organization but want to act as agents of deviation that instigate small wins, challenge and question assumptions, and experiment to do what is doable' (Arsenault 2007: 19–20).

A critical and reflective perspective may mean that a leader does not necessarily buy into all aspects of an externally preferred model of leadership, but rather sees themselves as acting for, and as part of a collective of 'engaged citizens' (Bolden, Gosling and O'Brien 2014). The concept of engaged citizenship sees a leader's behaviour being influenced by them identifying themselves as 'citizens' of the organization, which evokes within them 'ideals and feelings associated with belonging to a collective defined not by organisational goals and outputs but by community membership; drawing attention to responsibilities and duties as well as rights and obligations' (Bolden, Gosling and O'Brien 2014: 765–6). Finally, a suggested balanced approach is offered by Hill (2007: 29–30) who describes how important it is for a leader preparation programme to include 'at least three core beliefs: (1) the institution is more important than any single individual, including himself or herself; (2) the leader's job is to help others succeed; and (3) first and foremost in making decisions, the organization's future and sustainability must be considered'.

In sum, these criticisms of the commonly used higher education leadership preparation programmes point to the need to replace such leadership training or development experiences with a far more comprehensive and coherent 'leadership learning' programme. In accordance with the previously offered definition of learning (Nicolini, Gherardi, and Yanow 2003), the contention is that the most appropriate leadership preparation programmes must be deeply embedded in its particular context in order to be situated in the system of ongoing practice. Programmes must also be underpinned by morals and values in order to be relational and rooted in the context of interaction so that the leader is better prepared to consider and address the needs of those they lead. Finally, a truly effective leadership preparation programme should awaken the leader to the myriad of organizational-cultural artefacts, which need to be acknowledged and understood beyond simply their own beliefs and preferred behaviours, if they are to be accepted as, and become, the leader. What would a leadership-learning programme then look like?

As indicated previously, a carefully constructed leadership-learning progr-amme is a crucial prerequisite for transrelational leadership. As described in

Chapter 2, the observable practices of a transrelational approach to leadership are founded upon critically essential internal, non-observable phenomenon. Leadership becomes transrelational when the leader's practices are influenced by the quality of their relational interactions with those they are leading. Moreover, the entity perspectives, how well the leader is able to overcome their natural tendency to selectively relate to others, do not solely determine this quality. These entity insights only provide knowledge and understanding predominantly from the leader's understanding. Of even more importance is the relational perspective, whereby the leader's thoughts and assumptions are constructed in the context of ongoing conversations and relations. In this sense, the forming of a relationship is not a moment-in-time happening – a moment when two or more people either form or don't form a relationship – but evolves over time based not only on the entity thoughts and assumptions but also, and perhaps even more importantly, as a product of the interplay of ongoing conversations, social connections and professional networking.

These understandings point to a requirement for a far more uniquely constructed leadership preparation programme – that is, one that not only provides specific knowledge and skills but also, and more essentially, presents opportunities for self-reflection and the building up of mindful consciousness over a much longer period of time than that usually provided. Such a programme would need to help the leader to learn how to become self-reflective and mindful and, through opportunities to share and discuss their learning and applications, also enable them to openly share with other co-learners what they are learning about their self as leader, how this is influencing their relationships with those they are leading, and what impact this is having on desirable organizational outcomes. Traditional leadership frameworks are simply not able to provide the required knowledge, skills, disposition and learning that are mandatory for transrelational leadership preparation.

The fundamental principles of a leadership-learning programme

In order to explain how learning happens, and specifically how people come to learn how to be leaders, we draw on Hodkinson, Biesta and James (2007: 27), who espouse 'a theory of learning cultures and a cultural theory of learning'. These dual theoretical aspects complement each other. On the one hand, the theory of learning cultures acknowledges the contextual or situational influences that impact on learning. On the other hand, the cultural theory of learning acknowledges the individual's influence on their context. By placing the individual in the learning context, Hodkinson, Biesta and James's (2007) position represents a sociocultural one – not one in which the cognitive is acknowledged separately from the social. In addition, Hodkinson, Biesta and James's (2007) position encompasses the Deweyian view that learning resides not just in the mind\head, and does not just represent a change in what one knows – but rather it is embodied and impacts on how one is, how one behaves and how one acts in their world. In other words, 'Learning involves participation in its widest sense, and any conceptual change is but a part of this wider social and embodied picture' (Hodkinson, Biesta and James 2007: 31).

In support of Hodkinson, Biesta and James's (2007) theory of learning cultures, Salomon and Perkins (1998: 2) describe learning as 'a collective participatory process of active knowledge construction emphasizing context, interaction, and situatedness'. Learning about leadership (like any learning) needs to be situated, social and relational. This view aligns with the strong emphasis on leadership-as-practice (L-A-P). Raelin (2017) explains an L-A-P perspective on leadership development: 'At the outset, it would require an acute immersion into the practices that are embedded within social relations and between people, objects, and their institutions. It needs to be a learning associated with lived experience that occurs within specific historical, cultural, and local contexts' (Raelin 2017: 217). In simple terms, experiencing and interacting lead to learning, and this learning changes what we experience and how we interact with others. 'A person learns through becoming and becomes through learning' (Zukas and Kilminster 2012: 203). A person learns in a learning culture, and a learning culture 'should not be understood as the context or environment within which learning takes place. Rather, learning cultures stand for the social practices through which people learn' (Hodkinson, Biesta and James 2007: 34).

Seeing learning as occurring in 'learning cultures' is consistent with a view that sees leadership as relational, embodied and instantiated in practice, rather than residing within an isolated individual. We also need to see leadership learning as a long and ongoing process that has precedents before the present, and which will continue on a daily basis and into the future. 'We need to understand learning at any one time as part of a lengthy on-going process, where the past life history of the individual and the past history of the situation strongly influence that current learning' (Hodkinson, Biesta and James 2007: 28). What an individual brings to a learning culture will impact on what one does and can learn from that culture. As Zukas and Kilminster (2012: 203) explain, 'Opportunities to learn depend on the nature of the learning culture and the individual's position, disposition and capitals in interaction with each other.' It is undeniable that each individual 'has had an earlier learning life that strongly influences his or her current learning' (Bloomer and Hodkinson, as cited in Hodkinson, Biesta and James 2007: 37), and, thus, how they will understand, interpret and focus their learning about leadership.

In so doing, the individual influences their context as posited by Hodkinson et al.'s cultural theory of learning. In other words, the theoretical knowledge the individual acquires as the result of a learning experience is turned into personalized behaviour, which then impacts upon others and the culture. Theoretical knowledge gained from some form of new learning can be defined as 'the cognitive resource which a person brings to a situation that enables them to think and perform' (Eraut 2000: 114). Most often, this theoretical knowledge originates from some type of codified form and includes academic papers, guidelines, books and institutional documentation. Leadership theory has been extensively codified in a plethora of books and articles thereby providing a rich pool of theoretical knowledge and a powerful force upon an individual to adopt a conceptual change – to learn – about how to lead (Hodkinson, Biesta and James 2007). But, to better understand theoretical knowledge we need to acknowledge the different types of knowledge upon which it is formed. Quite simply, there is more to theoretical knowledge than simply the codified theory.

According to Eraut, the individual also contributes to the formation of theoretical knowledge. Eraut's view is that the totality of theoretical knowledge an individual eventually forms about a particular focus incorporates 'procedural knowledge and process knowledge, experiential knowledge and impressions in episodic memory', as well as skills and 'representations of competence, capability or expertise' (Eraut 2000: 114). In terms of a particular individual's theoretical knowledge of leadership, this is likely to be formed from:

1. knowledge of how leaders have done things in the past or how leaders do things presently (procedural and process knowledge);
2. prior experiences of being led and even of having to lead others (experiential knowledge and memory); and
3. knowledge of what is expected of them if they are to be judged as an effective leader by their particular organization (representations of competence, capability or expertise).

Although not always an assured outcome, this new theoretical knowledge can ultimately impact practice, and thus contribute to behavioural change

(Cooper, Scandura and Schriesheim 2005). However, there needs to be an explicit connection made between the theory and the practice (Middlehurst 2013; Raelin 2011). Simply, theoretical knowledge is more likely to induce a behavioural change if the theoretical knowledge is 'tuned' to the context by the personal experience of its 'owner' (Eraut 2003). It is this process of tuning to the context or selectively and critically applying understandings to their own specific context that connects theory and practice. Eraut names this process 'resituation' – the theory has to be resituated into the specific context if it is to become meaningful and purposeful, and so of sustainable benefit.

Key features of effective learning arrangements for leadership

Thus, we hold the view that 'any form of leadership learning must mediate and integrate the learner's pre-existing leadership understandings with both their perceptions of their current organizational context and the principles and precepts proffered by general leadership theory; and that this process best occurs over a period of time' (Franken, Branson and Penney 2016: 10–11), and in a collaborative context. Drawing on the literature, and our own learning projects (Franken, Branson and Penney 2015, 2016), we conclude that an effective learning programme for transrelational leadership must include the following elements:

1. A comprehensive introduction to all relevant theoretical knowledge.
2. An ongoing iterative process that continually supports a theory to practise connection so that any learning is contextualized and personalized, and the theory is used to guide current and future practice.
3. Regular opportunities for theoretical mediation and brokering, and collaborative knowledge and experience sharing with others, so that self-reflection/mindfulness is cultivated, feedback is provided, and other possibilities shared and critiqued.
4. A relational learning culture so that learners are affectively supported and become mutually engaged, and transrelational leadership practice is modelled.
5. A programme flexible enough to be bespoke and tailored to each individual's specific context.

Each of these key elements is now described in more detail and with reference to the application of these to a learning programme for aspiring leaders provided in a New Zealand higher education institution.

Theoretical knowledge learning

As defined earlier in this particular chapter, theoretical knowledge is described as 'the cognitive resource which a person brings to a situation that enables them to think and perform' (Eraut 2000: 114). Theoretical knowledge is the touchstone upon which a person can begin to become a leader. It provides the specific knowledge upon which personal beliefs, attitudes, motives, preferences, perceptions, judgements and decisions can be compared and contrasted in order to be validated, confirmed, varied or ignored. Without access to such theoretical knowledge, proper leadership behaviour is more likely to be accidental, erratic, discriminatory and self-centred. This is due to the many misconceptions about the nature of leadership. Because we experience some form of leadership every day, it is easily assumed that we know what constitutes leadership and, thereby, how to practise it. Like many complex tasks, it looks far easier to practise leadership than it actually is.

There are five misconceptions of leadership that we wish to highlight. First, leadership is a phenomenon and not a concept. It is not possible to define and package leadership into some simple concept or formula, which can be universally enacted by almost anyone. Leadership is a phenomenon because it evolves from the interplay of theoretical, personal and contextual knowledge. It is the idiosyncratic outcome of both objective and subjective knowledge drawn together by a person within a particular context. We add that leadership needs to be seen as a phenomenon because it is fundamentally relational and not technical/rational. Thus, being able to truly understand and appreciate what constitutes leadership requires specific discipline knowledge, which is not widely present in common sense. It is a misconception to think that a person can 'step up to leadership' without knowing what actually constitutes leadership.

But knowing what constitutes leadership for today and tomorrow's world can only be deeply understood by knowing the evolution of leadership theory. Leadership is an evolving and not a static phenomenon. Few would wish to be led as was generally accepted in society early last century. As society and cultures change, so has our understanding of leadership. A serious leadership misconception is that it is a static concept whereby leadership practices of thirty or forty years ago are still effective. This highlights that leadership is a complex rather than a simple phenomenon. It is complex because it requires the leader to be fully attuned to the needs of others and the changing nature of their environment. Leadership is not the sole prerogative of the leader. It is a negotiated phenomenon and this adds to its complexity.

Finally, and very importantly, it is a serious misconception to view leadership as an independent rather than an interconnected phenomenon. Too often leadership has been developed in isolation from the key functions of a leader. This perspective assumes that once the particular leadership concept has been developed it can be applied to any task and it can address any particular problem. In this sense, the development of leadership is seen as being independent from the tasks and problems to be faced. In contrast, leadership seen as an interconnected phenomenon aligns theoretical knowledge with contextually important knowledge – leadership knowledge is aligned with organizational culture knowledge and organizational change knowledge and employee engagement knowledge and so on. Overcoming these leadership misconceptions is a prerequisite for the proper preparation of all contemporary organizational leaders, including those in higher education. Importantly, these perspectives guided both the creation of the New Zealand leadership-learning programme and the structure of this book.

Reflection on theory and practice

While theoretical knowledge is the touchstone for leadership learning, it is grossly deficient without the additional processes that enable it to influence practice. The first of these is that the process must continually support a theory to practise connection. *Reflection* has long been an indispensable feature of most learning arrangements, particularly for those working to learn from and in practice (Boud 1994; Boud, Keogh and Walker 1985; Eraut 2004; Inman 2014). Reflection, often synonymous with experiential learning, generally focuses on learners retrieving, attending to and interpreting experiences with a view to utilizing insights to guide future action (Boud 1994; Kolb 1984; Schön 1987). Similarly, Eraut (2004: 49) advocates sharing of 'emotionally rich situations ... to focus attention on extracting key issues and addressing them in a manner that leaves participants better prepared for any similar incidents in the future'. We believe that for learning leaders there is much to be gained on reflecting not just on personal experiences but on theories that can guide the interpretation of experiences, and provide options for future action. As discussed above we can use leadership theories as a *touchstone* for our practice, if they are structured into our reflective cycles. As Raelin (2011: 198) explains, theory can 'enlighten practice', especially when we choose 'to reflect on our actions to improve them in which case we may rely on theory as a way to predict the consequences of our next actions'.

Reflection can be both a solitary or interactive process. Eraut (2004) is of the view, as are we, that reflection in interaction with others is best. He offers three criterial features: having sufficient time, having a quality relationship within the group and having a facilitator with expertise. In the leadership-learning arrangement upon which this book was founded, we believe those three criteria were met. One of the authors acted as the facilitator of the reflective cycles that took place over a period of time with the participating aspiring leaders. Reflection over time, in a group with 'relational bonds' (Raelin (2011)), and with a facilitator, allowed the leadership learners to be aware of leadership-as-practice – to recognize the leadership required in even everyday and seemingly simple acts and practices. The shared discussion of decision-making and action in the discussion sessions brought this to the fore in particular, and allowed the facilitator to comment on their connection to leadership theory, and why decisions and actions made counted as leadership-as-practice. We consider that the recognition of leadership-as-practice is a crucial role of reflection, and one that moves leaders beyond reacting by using long-established, albeit usually tacit, coping skills and resorting to managerialist practices. We would see that this supports 'leaderful practice' (Raelin 2011) and forms the bedrock for the embodiment of transrelational leadership.

Mediation, brokering and knowledge sharing

The leadership-learning arrangement described above enabled mediated leadership learning rather than the instilling of leadership theory. We draw on pedagogical understandings of mediation 'where it refers to the process of a teacher bringing a text within the realm of understanding of his/her students by analyzing, deconstructing, and personalizing it' (Franken, Branson and Penney 2016: 8). Eraut in his 2004 statement of critical features of effective reflection does not define the role of the facilitator (a mediator of sorts) nor does he specify the nature of their expertise. In the description of our leadership-learning arrangement (Franken, Branson and Penney 2016), we extended and further defined the role of the facilitator in reflection as one of a 'theory broker'. Our view is that a leadership-learning reflection in a group is enhanced by the presence of an expert with knowledge of leadership theory and theories.

In the pedagogical literature again, mediation is a key process undertaken by 'literacy brokers', who assist others to engage in text and to understand it (Mihut 2014). 'Literacy brokers are, by definition, those who have knowledge or expertize of the text, and who share that expertize with the reader' (Franken, Branson and Penney 2016: 8). We see a theory broker's role to be one of assisting others to understand leadership theory, to recognize the leadership required in even everyday and seemingly simple acts and practices, and most importantly to interpret it from a theoretical perspective, that is, to personalize it. In other words, they facilitate resituation, the process of tuning a learner's theoretical knowledge to context (Franken, Branson and Penney 2016). The brokering we described in Franken, Branson and Penney (2016) challenges the view that brokering represents an asymmetrical relationship in which one person is the more knowing, and is helping the other(s) (Lillis and Curry 2006). As we explained, 'in effect the learning relationship involved a type of mutual brokerage', in that those learning to become leaders mediated the world of practice for the theory expert. 'All … participants were investing in a process that was seeking to challenge and extend existing understandings – and to collectively support each other in that process' (Franken, Branson and Penney 2016: 8).

The learning arrangements described above range from informal, semi-structured and somewhat unplanned to more structured and planned. The next section discusses how learning arrangements need to occur in a relational learning culture.

Relational learning culture

Bosua and Scheepers (2007), in their work on knowledge management in complex organizations, distinguish between knowledge transfer and relational learning. Knowledge transfer occurs when knowledge moves from one to another supported by a joint understanding of the context. It thus represents a more effective learning arrangement than the transmission of knowledge from an outside expert to less-knowing others; however it still incorporates a dimension of transmission in that it is one-way. Relational learning, on the other hand, is 'a dual process of enquiring and contributing to knowledge through activities such as learning by observation, listening and asking, sharing ideas, giving advice, recognizing cues, and adopting patterns of behaviour … . [It] is both an individual and collective activity, involving explicit and tacit exchanges between people' (Bosua and Scheepers 2007: 95).

Relational learning can occur in both formal learning arrangements and informal contexts, but its key feature is that knowledge is shared in a two-way relationship. Relational learning is an important collaborative activity, as through it individuals are able to 'engage with their colleagues to acquire new insights and to find innovative solutions to their complex problems' (Ahmad 2017: 139). Some specific practices that support relational learning are social networks, collaboration and dialogue 'for the purpose of collectively constructing new meaning and improving the skills and knowledge that result in action' (Gerken, Beausaert and Segers 2016: 136). Relational learning actions identified by Gerken, Beausaert and Segers (2016: 139) include 'acting upon feedback, information seeking and help seeking'. Eraut (2004) provides more specific detail again by suggesting three actions (relating respectively to the past, the current situation and future actions) which he deems to be effective and which lie at the more formal end of the spectrum as they are carried out with conscious deliberation or reflection. They include: 'Discussion and review of past actions, communications, events, experience; engagement in decision making, problem solving, planned informal learning; and planning learning opportunities and rehearsing for future events' (Eraut 2004: 250).

Our experience has also shown us the value of informal, less structured and more dynamic interactions that do not constitute an organized learning arrangement per se (Franken, Branson and Penney 2015). We represented a specific instance of a learning arrangement that we participated in 'as information grounds' (Fisher, Landry and Naumer 2007; Franken, Branson and Penney 2015), where people may initially find social engagement or mutual support but eventually it becomes a place where they come to experience significant knowledge sharing, from which they can benefit along physical, social, affective and cognitive dimensions. An information ground provides what others (e.g. Laksov and Tomson 2016) maintain that a 'community of practice does, or what a personal knowledge network does' (Ahmad 2017: 140). We believe that it better captures a social arrangement that is dynamic and flexible, and that has dimensions beyond the social and cognitive, and it is somewhat aligned with Bourdieu's notion of 'field' (1985), albeit on a small scale.

In Franken, Branson and Penney (2016), we describe a semi-structured, and thus not an informal, leadership-learning arrangement, with a number of specific features that we believe support the process of drawing on or making use of theoretical knowledge to inform practice. Two of the features discussed above (based on Franken, Branson and Penney 2016) are reflections on theory and practice and mediation and brokering. While they focus on the importance of theoretical or conceptual knowledge, they also represent knowledge sharing.

Bespoke leadership-learning opportunities

From the description already provided it is clear that we are ever mindful of the fact that leadership theory and practice are contingent on context. Middlehurst (2008: 325–6) exemplifies this when she describes the following scenarios:

> An Anglo-Saxon dean of a UK higher education institution would recognize instantly, no doubt, the need for different approaches to leadership from those of a dean of a Chinese university; a corporate-sector leader moving to take up the role of university vice-chancellor would notice the impact of context on what

can or cannot be done; or how quickly it can be done, and individuals who have undertaken 360-degree reviews of their leadership performance in more than one setting will often have direct feedback that successful behaviours and actions in one setting do not necessarily achieve the same results in a different place.

Leadership learning is also contingent on context. By definition, informal learning opportunities are bespoke and tailored to context and audience, but as we continue to see formal arrangements used ubiquitously, it is important to consider how to make them more effective. One way of tailoring learning arrangements to audience is to consider where leaders are in their careers. Much leader development in higher education is geared towards more senior staff who are in, or are closer to being considered for, leadership positions. Less attention is paid to those in early career stages. Hill (2007) recognizes this and suggests, 'Junior faculty would benefit from mentoring and periodic coaching early in their career' (Hill 2007: 30). Given the relative scarcity of mentoring and coaching in higher education, Hill questions, 'Who in our institutions is currently prepared to coach them on the leadership aspects of their work?' (Hill 2007: 30)

We argued previously (Franken, Branson and Penney 2015: 2016) that leadership-learning opportunities should be 'bespoke'. We retain the view that this is the approach needed to facilitate and support the growth of transformational leaders and leadership. The Leadership Foundation for Higher Education (LFHE) (n.d., p.2) offers what they call a bespoke programme and describes it in the following way. It is:

1. Strategic: the programme can be directly linked to your leadership development strategy.
2. Responsive: bespoke programmes can be based upon your own 360° feedback data and organizational climate surveys.
3. Targeted: we can design programmes for specific groups of participants in your organization (such as registrars, academics, research staff, professional services, etc.).
4. Diverse: we can design and run programmes for mixed groups of academic and professional staff.

Conclusion

The contemporary higher education context in which people come to be leaders is, as we have comprehensively described, undergoing significant change and in that change process there is uncertainty about what leadership is and what it is that leaders do. Regrettably, within this uncertain milieu the application of managerialism has found an advantageous foothold. Furthermore, this foothold has become a stronghold due to the deficiencies of leadership frameworks in adequately preparing leaders. We maintain that these frameworks potentially perpetuate the status quo of leadership practice and, thereby, organizational problems. Thus, rather than just being concerned about the effectiveness of leadership there are also concerns with the ineffectiveness of organizational change, the quality of employee performance, the rate of employee engagement, the unhelpfulness of organizational culture to adequately support core business, and the ineffectual influences of HRM strategies.

In response to this unsustainable situation we provide a holistic solution encompassed within the introduction and application of a transrelational approach to higher education leadership. But this would require a very different leadership preparation programme, which emphasizes learning how to become and be a leader within a particular context. As comprehensively explained in this chapter, a leadership-learning programme is significantly different from one that focuses on leadership development and leadership training. A leadership-learning programme supports the essential relational foundation of leadership by embracing knowledge sharing, reflection on leadership theory and practice, and the mediation and brokering of theoretical knowledge. These are prerequisite ingredients for the provision of a relational, situated and more contextually aligned arrangement for leadership learning. It is in this way that current and future higher education leaders will be able to embody and enact a transrelational approach to their leadership.

Conclusion: What Might Tomorrow Bring?

Introduction

This final chapter provides a summative review of the nature and practice of transrelational leadership within the context of higher education and takes a closer look at its possible adoption. The chapter therefore highlights the perceived benefits, as well as the likely challenges, for higher education institutions that might seek to introduce this new form of leadership. In conclusion, the chapter raises concerns about whether or not higher education actually has a choice in this regard. It emphasizes not only the need for the essential place of leadership-learning programmes for aspiring leaders in higher education but also that such programmes must be founded upon the conceptualization of leadership as fundamentally transrelational.

Why leadership in higher education needs to change

Few would argue that the organizational world of higher education is extremely complex and challenging not just because of numerous national and international pressures but also because of the traditional structural, procedural and attitudinal variability across its multidisciplinary units and hierarchical employment arrangements. Undoubtedly, leadership within higher education is a demanding responsibility. Thus, it requires the most effective and efficient form of leadership or else the task of leadership will be decidedly more difficult. It is absolutely essential that today's higher education leaders need to learn how to lead in the most suitable, efficient and effective way.

Sadly, as described in the early chapters of this book, many higher education leaders come to their positions with little understanding of what constitutes true leadership. They make misinformed assumptions based upon past experiences, observations and interpretations. Thus, their attention tends to focus on personal beliefs and perceptions about what a leader needs to do, which draws them into management and not leadership. This less-than-ideal situation has been compounded following the advent of neo-liberal pressures upon higher education institutions. As governments worldwide have forced higher education to become far more financially independent and entrepreneurial, they have adopted a largely free-market, business-like administrative model. Consequently, as described in the introductory chapter, many researchers and writers are now describing higher educational leadership as having become managerialism whereby the dominant concerns relate to productivity, accountability and performativity.

Although the adoption of managerialism might seem appropriate during this era of globalization in which economic outcomes dominate national and international political agendas, its impact upon the core business of higher education is devastating. Moreover, the view that managerialism works well in the business/corporate world and therefore must be used in higher education has been clearly shown to be a falsehood. As described herein, the world's largest business research companies like Deloitte, Forbes, McKinsey and Ernst and Young are calling for new forms of business leadership because managerialism is failing to bring about successful organizational change, or maximize employee engagement, of achieve high performance, or create organizational cultures that encourage creativity and ingenuity, or establish organizations that attract the best employees. Indeed, we argue that managerialism, especially in the context of higher education, fails on its very own fundamental criteria – fiscal responsibility – because the detrimental outcomes from its enactment are adding enormous organizational costs (as described in Chapter 6, for example). It is not fiscally responsible to use managerialism as the preferred model for leadership in higher education.

This book has sought to move beyond describing what's wrong with managerialism in higher education, to provide, justify and explore in detail an alternative, transrelational, approach to leadership in higher education. This approach builds on what is currently known to be working in higher education but provides a far more comprehensive and coherent description of it as well as providing a deep insight into how it can be introduced and the breadth of its influence across the institution.

Building on what is known to work

Although there is a wealth of research literature from around the world highlighting the detrimental impact of managerialism upon the culture and core business of higher education, a number of authors have taken a slightly different path, illustrating the aspects of leadership that are and can work successfully in higher education. In early chapters we described how Professor Jean Lipman-blumen argued that, contrary to the popular assumption promoting managerialism, the business world needs to learn how to use the form of leadership that works well in higher education, which she referred to as connective leadership. A connective leader is described as being willing to share decision-making with their faculties and reaching out to those they are leading, to treat them like a co-leader, and entrust them to share burdens and enhance the leader's vision. This involves the leader being inclusive and flexible, acknowledging their own limitations, seeing strength and wisdom in others, and being willing to be guided by those who know more or can do things better. Similarly, Burnes, Wend and By (2014) believe that collegiality is a far better foundation for higher education leadership than the business-inspired managerialism. In particular, these authors argue that the type of leadership that does work in higher education is the form that seeks to marry the need for central decision-making with local involvement in and control over all of the important organizational processes. Both Shattock (2010) and Gray (2008) share this same belief that it is by enhancing collegiality and collaboration within the culture of higher education institutions that the ills of managerialism can be overcome.

Finally, such leadership characteristics of connectivity, collegiality, coope-ration, inclusiveness and so on have been drawn together by many authors (as presented in Chapter 2) into promoting the essence of leadership as being a relational phenomenon. This book argues that where successful leadership in higher education exists it does not arise out of any particular action that the leader decides to take based upon their personal beliefs, feelings and judgements. Essentially, such leadership is constructed in the common daily social interactions among the leader and those they are tasked with leading. This implies that the individualism and detachment of managerialism needs to be challenged. Rather, higher education leadership needs to be co-constructed such that the effectiveness of the leader is not measured by their achievement of certain practical competencies but more on how well they are able to establish mutually beneficial relational processes with those they are leading.

Without a more comprehensive, coherent and defensible description of the nature and function of such a relational approach to leadership, it becomes far too easy to dismiss its principles and premises as ideological and impracticable. Thus the nature and practice of transrelational leadership is presented as a detailed explanation, elaboration and application of these perspectives.

The essence of transrelational leadership

As emphasized earlier, we stand by the view that leadership is leadership is leadership (see Chapter 3). We are not adding a new leadership theory but rather describing in detail how it is possible for a leader in today's higher education context to achieve what is expected of someone in that role. But in order to practise leadership, the person must first become the accepted leader. For a transrelational leader, the four fundamental qualities (see Chapter 2) that need to be to be accepted as the leader are: become an 'in-group' member, champion the group, shape the group's identity and align the group's identity to its wider reality.

As explained in this book, becoming the leader does not necessarily result in remaining as the leader. To be the leader, the person must be accepted as the leader and such acceptance is an ongoing construction. Those being led are continually determining whether or not to accept the person as their leader. Specifically, those being led are determining whether or not they can continue to trust the person to lead them. If trust is lost, then the leader's acceptance is simultaneously lost. This means that each and every key action of the leader must reinforce and not undermine such trust. To this end, Chapter 4 described four fundamental issues associated with the leader being able to continually model being authentically transrelational. First, the transrelational leader willingly acknowledges that their power to influence others emanates from the relational trust others have in them. Of pivotal importance in the maintenance of this trust is the transrelational leader having a growth mindset whereby they are willing to have an open and transparent discussion among those they are leading about how well the organization is achieving its goals and strategy.

Second, the issue of an employee's perceived duty to the organization needs to be re-envisaged. From a managerial perspective, issues associated with employee duty, obligation and loyalty to the organization have been explored as the expected response from the employee as a result of being given employment. A form of implied contractual obligation – the leader provides an important benefit to the person with employment and a source of regular income, and the employee in response provides high-quality work output, which is an important benefit to the organization. Moreover, within a managerial perspective, it is the leader who determines the degree to which this implied duty to the organization is being met. However, from a transrelational position, this understanding of duty is understood as self-forming motivation, and calls upon the need to create the conditions in which each employee has the freedom to reflect and question their workplace circumstances, to nurture a kind of curiosity about how to better their workplace skills and knowledge within these circumstances, and to seek ways to become more productive in these and future circumstances.

Third, the transrelational leader is required to adjust how they interpret and attend to the employees' level of commitment to the organization. From a managerial standpoint, a key responsibility of the leader is to implement policies, principles and processes that foster employee discipline, punctuality, efficiency, rationality and order. This is about striving to control, manipulate, measure and produce employee commitment. Instead, the transrelational leader, as described in more detail in Chapter 4, recognizes the potential in every employee to be committed, provided the conditions are conducive. Such conditions are those that enable them to work productively with other co-employees. Thus a transrelational leader does not try to control employee commitment but rather, they encourage connections, interrelationships, among all of those they are leading in unpredictable, dynamic, strategic, fluid, creative and emergent ways. They seek to create as many co-employee connections as possible and all based upon equality, respect, collegiality, support, encouragement and empathy.

The fourth, and final, fundamental issue associated with the leader being able to continually model being authentically transrelational is that of employee responsibility. Managerialism assumes that employees cannot be fully trusted to take responsibility to work to the best of their ability and so it is necessary to implement accountability procedures in the form of performance management processes. Under managerialism, it is presumed that it is the leader's role to determine how well people are doing their jobs and to implement a way of holding the employee accountable for the quality of their workplace performance. Whereas, a transrelational leader trusts that the employee will take responsibility for working to the best of their ability if the organizational culture encourages employee engagement, commitment, creativity, ingenuity, determination and personal responsibility. Then responsibility becomes personal and spontaneous.

The challenges and benefits of transrelational leadership

Each of the issues just described are countercultural for most organizations and, as such, raise considerable challenges especially for current leaders. Regardless of how a person chooses to lead, trust is the cornerstone of its effect on others –

the greater the trust, the more influential and successful the leadership. Also, the building up of trust can take a great deal of time. Thus, to gain the reputation of being an authentically transrelational leader, which is founded on deep trust, is a journey and not a destination – it will require much time and considerable patience, resources that are not always readily available to a leader facing many and diverse responsibilities. But the pay-off is worth the time and effort. To continue with a non-effective form of leader is to invite even more serious organizational problems in the long term.

More specific benefits are those described in this book around the important leadership responsibilities of organizational change, employee engagement and high performance (see Chapters 5 and 6). In these respects we have illustrated just how unsuccessful managerialism is, in both the business and higher education sectors, in achieving desired change. In an organizational environment known to be experiencing constant change, this is a dreadful acknowledgement. We confidently argue that the combination of transrelational leadership and a broader understanding of the different types of change will rectify this unsustainable situation. But, again, this requires a commitment by the leader to not only learn how to be, and to become, a transrelational leader but also to learn more about the intricacies and variability of organizational change. Furthermore, the more complex the required change, the more time it will take to implement and complete the change successfully. Often, leaders want changes to occur quickly because the unwanted situation can be divisive and disruptive – but quick fixes invariably deal with the symptoms and not the cause, and do not tend to change what needs to be changed.

In Chapter 5 we illustrated the failing of managerialism in this regard. The introduction or strengthening of performance management regimes often founded upon an annual goal-setting and review strategies deals with a symptom – less than expected performance output and/or quality – and not the cause. Chapter 6 provides ample evidence that the issue is employee engagement and not performance management. Managerialism looks to performance management while transrelational leadership seeks to improve employee engagement. Importantly, it was highlighted that 70 per cent of engagement is influenced by how the employee experiences their leader/line manager. A leader willingly enacting a transrelational approach to their leadership practices will automatically and dramatically increase employee engagement and, simultaneous, develop high performance outcomes. Yet again, this implies that the leader/line manager is willingly making time to interact and talk with those they are directly leading in order to support, affirm, encourage, advise and show interest in what the employee is contributing to the organization.

Finally, and arguably one of the most difficult challenges to the inculcation of transrelational leadership into higher education institutions is in being able to positively and constructively change the organizational culture in a way that is commensurate with being transrelational. The culture must not only support but also promote and distribute a transrelational approach to all levels of leadership across the institution. To this end, the well-established role of the HRM department comes into focus, but not through its traditional strategies and processes. This department must undergo its own cultural change, too. Given its close alignment to the implementation of the institution's leadership vision and strategy, HRM tends to reflect these in its structure, policies and practices. If institutional leadership appears to be managerialist, so too does HRM in the opinion of most employees. It is therefore significant that numerous higher education institutions are now changing the name of their department from Human Resource Management to that of People and Culture or Human Capital Management. This suggests to us that the leaders of these institutions are realizing the discrepancy between what this department should be doing and how it actually goes about doing it.

But changing the name doesn't mean that the culture of the department will automatically change. As Covey quite rightly argues, 'You can't talk your way out of something you have behaved yourself into.' If higher education leaders 'soften' the name but don't change the culture, the deceit will be obvious to all and trust in the department and the leader will be dramatically reduced. Although we see much benefit in changing the name of this department, it is far more important to change its culture. Then, and only then, will the right name become obvious. To this end, Chapter 7 provides a very comprehensive insight into what needs to change in HRM departments. Essentially, this chapter details the required reinvented form of the HRM department that is needed in higher education. HRM needs to adopt new thinking and different capabilities so that it becomes able to support and create workplaces that are places where people want to be, where people are valued, where they feel they belong and where they can be their best – fully engaged and innovative. All who work in this important department need to learn how to model transrelational practices in all that they do. This includes the essential responsibility of preparing future leaders who can be authentically transrelational. This is a monumental shift for HRM departments. There is no pretence that it will be quick or easy to achieve.

It will take up a great deal of time, a great deal of professional re-learning for the personnel, and a great deal of rethinking about best practice.

Preparing higher education leaders to be transrelational

Wishing for different leadership won't actually create it – proactive action is required. If we want a different approach to leadership in higher education institutions, then it is time to start preparing people to become such leaders. If one of the current problems with higher education leadership is that many have no formal learning in leadership, then it is hypocritical to want a new form of leadership but not establish learning programmes to bring it about. Thus the previous chapter provided a comprehensive description of how it is possible to prepare and support current and future leaders to be transrelational.

The key features of this preparation and support programme were that it is founded upon learning and not training or development, it was personal rather than generic, and it was closely interdependent with the learner's context. This transrelational leadership-learning programme supports the essential relational foundation of leadership by embracing knowledge sharing, reflection on leadership theory and practice and the mediation and brokering of theoretical knowledge. As described in this chapter, these are the essential prerequisite ingredients for the provision of a relational, situated and more contextually aligned arrangement for leadership learning. It is in this way that current and future higher education leaders will be able to embody and enact a transrelational approach to their leadership.

Concluding comments

We recognize that this book is asking much of higher education institutions. Leadership is like a foundation stone and it could seem that we are asking for it to be removed to be replaced by a completely different 'stone'. The fear, of course, is that everything will fall down in the interim. If there is no foundation stone, will not the building collapse? But, if the foundation stone is faulty, or worse decaying, the building is still likely to collapse. What we are suggesting is that leadership in higher education is far too important an influence across the whole institution for its faults and ineffectiveness to be ignored. Fear of what managerialism will ultimately bring to higher education institutions must be much greater than the fear of working towards changing it to transrelational leadership.

Those who have worked in higher education institutions for some time would acknowledge that managerialism has crept into becoming the dominant leadership paradigm. Arguably, it has taken some twenty or more years to gain its now substantive and pervasive place. Thus, there is no reason to think that its suppression and removal would take much less time. To change higher education leadership to that of a transrelational approach must be by evolution and not revolution or else its means of adoption will undermine its basic principles. Compulsion can never encourage cooperation. Regulation can never encourage relationships. Tumult can never encourage trust. In the case of establishing a transrelational approach to the enactment of leadership and to the nature of the organizational culture, the means must justify the ends.

However, we firmly believe that while this end point might be some considerable time away, there are other more immediate and readily achievable outcomes arising out of this book, which will pave the way by beginning and extending the change to the establishment of transrelational leadership and culture in higher education.

First, this book, with its comprehensive application of research data from both the higher education and business/corporate sectors, will immediately challenge and debunk many unsubstantiated and misguided claims held by current higher education leaders wishing to maintain a commitment to managerialism. These can be couched in opinions that include but are not limited to the following:

1. *Only doing what successful businesses are doing;*
2. *I didn't know there are different ways to lead;*
3. *I didn't know how to do things differently;*
4. *Managerialism hasn't had a detrimental effect on higher education;*
5. *We can only be fiscally responsible if we apply managerialism;*
6. *But universities are different and need managerialism;*

Such opinions can no longer be stated unchallenged. In this way, we believe that this book provides the impetus for a groundswell of energy, commitment and knowledge that can initiate and commence the processes leading to how higher education institutions are led.

Second, a highly desirable and achievable outcome promoted by this book is the critical need for explicit leadership-learning programmes for all who hold leadership positions in higher education and for those who aspire to such leadership positions. However, we do acknowledge that many higher education institutions have, in good faith, implemented professional learning opportunities for these personnel but we question the focus of many of these programmes. Too many, in our opinion, are aligned to management and, thereby managerialism, rather than to the nature and practice of leadership. Moreover, through the arguments presented in this book, we add that the approach to leadership learning in these programmes must be about that which is aligned to the specific characteristics of the higher education context and which will provide the most desirable form of leadership for higher education institutions into the future. To this end, we have promoted transrelational leadership as just such an approach.

Third, it seems to us to be a complete contradiction for any higher education institution not to be universally promoting and supporting a growth mindset. Surely an institution with 'learning' as its core business has to model this in its culture and practices, which implies the need for all, especially the leaders, to embrace and apply a growth mindset. Arguably, the implementation to establish a growth mindset culture could be the first 'small step' by an institution towards ultimately adopting a transrelational approach to its leadership and culture.

Fourth, upon the establishment of a growth mindset culture comes the opportunity for the higher education institution to utilize its natural pool of creativity and ingenuity to greatest advantage. In today's highly competitive and challenging organizational environment, the application of creativity, ingenuity and skilful problem-solving capacities is universally essential. Undoubtedly, higher education institutions have these in abundance because these are the very capacities associated with its core business of creating new knowledge. Furthermore, higher education institutions have enhanced capacities due to the unique breadth and diversity of skills and knowledge across such a wide number and variety of disciplines, generations and career pathways. We argue through this book that the stability and sustainability of a higher education institution can be far better achieved via transrelational leadership's capacity to appropriately access the existing natural pool of creativity and ingenuity among its employees than any commitment to managerialism could ever hope to achieve.

Fifth, our discussion in Chapter 7 of the misguided and misdirected processes and practices currently maintained by HRM departments, or similar but rebranded departments, is an issue that requires serious attention. We wonder whether such departments, through which employee performance management processes are controlled, ever comprehensively review their own performance for its impact on employee engagement. The negative employee engagement statistics provided in Chapter 6 should be the impetus, at least, for a review of HRM practices. But rather than simply highlighting a serious problem, we have presented a solution with our reinvented model of HRM. Eventually, such departments may be renamed when it becomes far more obvious as to what the work and outcomes should be for the good of employees, leaders and organizations, but until that occurs we urge for a progressive change in their culture, strategies and processes, which are aligned with a transrelational approach to higher education leadership. In this way, these departments would make an invaluable contribution towards ensuring that higher education institutions are workplaces in which people want to work and which attract the best people.

Finally, if these achievable outcomes are embraced and successfully implemented, then a transrelational culture will surely follow. Transrelational leadership will become the norm and a far more conducive learning environment will be established, not just for the students but for employees and leaders too. We argue through this book that transrelational leadership is what higher education institutions need now and into the foreseeable future.

References

Abbasi, E. and N. Zamani-Miandashti (2013), 'The Role of Transformational Leadership, Organizational Culture and Organizational Learning in Improving the Performance of Iranian Agricultural Faculties', *Higher Education*, 66 (4): 505–19.

Abel, C. F. (2005), 'Beyond the Mainstream: Foucault, Power and Organization Theory', *International Journal of Organization Theory and Behavior*, 8 (4): 495–519.

Aguinis, H. and C. A. Pierce (2008), 'Enhancing the Relevance of Organizational Behaviour by Embracing Performance Management', *Journal of Organizational Behavior*, 29: 139–45.

Ahedo, M. (2009), 'Comparing the Principles of Adult Learning with Traditional Pedagogical Teaching in Relation to the Use of Technology: The Tacit Dimension in ICT-Based University Teaching', *International Journal of Web-Based Learning and Teaching Technologies*, 4 (4): 66–81.

Ahmad, F. (2017), 'Knowledge-Sharing Networks: Language Diversity, its Causes, and Consequences', *Knowledge and Process Management*, 24 (2): 139–51.

Aithal, P. S. and P. M. Suresh Kumar (2016), 'Organizational Behaviour in 21st Century – "Theory A" for Managing People and Performance', *Journal of Business and Management*, 18 (7): 126–34.

Alfes, K., C. Truss, E. C. Soane, C. Rees and M. Gatenby (2013), 'The Relationship Between Line Manager Behavior, Perceived HRM Practices, and Individual Performance: Examining the Mediating Role of Engagement', *Human Resource Management*, 52 (6): 839–59.

Allan, K. (2011), *The Social Lens: An Invitation to Social and Sociological Theory*, 2nd edn, Thousand Oaks, CA: Sage.

Altizer, T. E. (2010), 'Motivating Gen Y Amidst Global Economic Uncertainty', *Journal of Learning in Higher Education*, 6 (1): 44–54.

Alvesson, M. (1996a), *Communications, Power and Organisation*, Berlin: Walter de Gruyter.

Alvesson, M. (1996b), 'Leadership Studies: From Procedure and Abstraction to Reflexivity and Situation', *Leadership Quarterly*, 7 (4): 455–85.

Alvesson, M. and Sveningsson, S. (2003), 'The Great Disappearing Act: Difficulties in Doing "Leadership"', *The Leadership Quarterly*, 1 (3): 359–81.

Anderson, G. (2006), 'Carving Out Time and Space in the Managerial University', *Journal of Organisational Change*, 19 (5): 578–92.

Appelbaum, E., T. Bailey, P. Berg and A. Kalleberg (2000), *Manufacturing Advantage: Why High-Performance Work Systems Pay Off*, Ithaca, NY: Cornell University Press.

Ardichvili, A., V. Page and T. Wentling (2003), 'Motivation and Barriers to Participation in Virtual Knowledge-sharing Communities of Practice', *Journal of Knowledge Management*, 7 (1): 64–77.

Argyris, C. (1992), *On Organizational Learning*, Cambridge, MA: Blackwell Publishers.

Argyris, C. and D. Schon (1978), *Organisational Learning: A Theory of Action Perspective*, San Francisco, CA: Jossey-Bass.

Aronson, E. ed. (1995), *The Social Animal*, 7th edn, New York: W. H. Freeman.

Arsenault, P. M. (2007), 'A Case Study of a University Leadership Seminar', *Journal of Leadership Education*, 6 (1): 14–27.

Arthur, J. B. (1994), 'Effects of Human Resource Systems on Manufacturing Performance and Turnover', *The Academy of Management Journal*, 37 (3): 670–87.

Avery, G. C. (2006), *Understanding Leadership*, London: Sage Publications.

Avolio, B. J. (2007), 'Promoting More Integrative Strategies for Leadership Theory-Building', *American Psychologist*, 62 (1): 25–33.

Avolio, B. J., F. O. Walumbra and T. J. Weber (2009), 'Leadership: Current Theories, Research, and Future Directions', *Annual Review of Psychology*, 60: 421–49.

Ayers, D. F. (2014), 'When Managerialism Meets Professional Autonomy: The University "Budget Update" as Genre of Governance', *Culture and Organization*, 20 (2): 98–120.

Baert, P. and A. Shipman (2005), 'University Under Siege? Trust and Accountability in the Contemporary Academy', *European Societies*, 7 (1): 157–85.

Balda, J. B. and F. Mora (2011), 'Adapting Leadership Theory and Practice for the Networked, Millennial Generation', *Journal of Leadership Studies*, 5 (3): 13–24.

Balkundi, P. and M. Kilduff (2005), 'The Ties that Lead: A Social Network Approach to Leadership', *The Leadership Quarterly*, 16 (6): 941–61.

Barsky, A. (2007), 'Understanding the Ethical Cost of Organizational Goal-Setting: A Review and Theory Development', *Journal of Business Ethics*, 81 (1): 63–81.

Barth-Farkas, F. and A. Vera (2014), 'Power and Transformational Leadership in Public Organizations', *The International Journal of Leadership in Public Services*, 10 (4): 217–32.

Bauman, Z. (1992), *Intimations of Postmodernity*, London: Routledge.

Bauman, Z. (1999), *In Search of Politics*, Cambridge: Polity Press.

Beinhocker, E. D. (1997), 'Strategies at the Edge of Chaos', *The McKinsey Quarterly*, 1, Winter, 24–39. Available online: https://www.researchgate.net/profile/ Eric_Beinhocker/publication/235361202_Strategy_at_the_Edge_of_Chaos/ links/02bfe51387b9a0668f000000/Strategy-at-the-Edge-of-Chaos.pdf (accessed 28 June 2017).

Bellamy, S., C. Morley and K. Watty (2003), 'Why do Business Academics Remain in Australian Universities Despite Deteriorating Work Conditions and Reduced Job Satisfaction: An Intellectual Puzzle', *Journal of Higher Education Policy and Management*, 25 (1): 13–28.

Berk, R. A. (2013), 'Multigenerational Diversity in the Academic Workplace: Implications for Practice', *Journal of Higher Education Management*, 28 (1): 10–23.

Billett, S. (2007), 'Exercising Self Through Working Life: Learning, Work and Identity', *Technical and Vocational Education and Training: Issues, Concerns and Prospects*, 5 (2): 183–201.

Bingham, S. (2017), 'If Employees Don't Trust You, It's Up to You to Fix It', *Harvard Business Review*, 2 January. Available online: https://hbr.org/2017/01/if-employees-dont-trust-you-its-up-to-you-to-fix-it (accessed 28 June).

Black, J. A. and S. Edwards (2000), 'Emergence of Virtual or Network Organizations: Fad or Feature', *Journal of Organization Change Management*, 13 (6): 567–76.

Black, S. A. (2015), 'Qualities of Effective Leadership in Higher Education', *Open Journal of Leadership*, 4: 54–66.

Black, S. A., J. J. Groombridge and C. G. Jones (2011), 'Leadership and Conservation Effectiveness: Finding a Better Way to Lead', *Conservation Letters*, 4 (5): 329–39.

Blenkin, G., G. Edwards and A. Kelly (1997), 'Perspectives on Educational Change', in A. Harris, N. Bennett and M. Preedy (eds), *Organizational Effectiveness and Improvement in Education*, 216–30, Buckingham: Open University Press.

Bodenhausen, C. and C. Curtis (2016), 'Transformational Leadership and Employee Involvement: Perspectives From Millennial Workforce Entrants', *Journal of Quality Assurance in Hospitality and Tourism*, 17 (3): 371–87.

Bolden, R., J. Gosling and A. O'Brien (2014), 'Citizens of the Academic Community? A Societal Perspective on Leadership in UK Higher Education', *Studies in Higher Education*, 39 (5): 754–70.

Bolman, L. G. and T. E. Deal (2008), *Reframing Leadership: Artistry, Choice, and Leadership*, 4th edn, San Francisco, CA: Jossey-Bass.

Bordia, P., S. L. D. Restubog and R. L. Tang (2008), 'When Employees Strike Back: Investigating Mediating Mechanisms Between Psychological Contract Breach and Workplace Deviance', *Journal of Applied Psychology*, 93 (5): 1104–17.

Boselie, P., G. Dietz and C. Boon (2005), 'Commonalities and Contradictions in HRM and Performance Research', *Human Resource Management Journal*, 15 (3): 67–94.

Bosua, R. and R. Scheepers (2007), 'Towards a Model to Explain Knowledge Sharing in Complex Organizational Environments', *Knowledge Management Research and Practice*, 5 (2): 93–109.

Boud, D. (1994), 'Conceptualising Learning from Experience: Developing a Model for Facilitation', in *Proceedings of the 35th Adult Education Research Conference*, 49–54, Knoxville, TN: University of Tennessee.

Boud, D., R. Keogh and D. Walker (1985), 'Promoting Reflection in Learning: A Model', in D. Boud, R. Keogh and D. Walker (eds), *Reflection: Turning Experience into Learning*, 18–40, New York, NY: Nichols.

Bourdieu, P. (1985), 'The Genesis of the Concepts of "Habitus" and "Field"', *Sociocriticism*, 2 (2): 11–24.

Branson, C. M. (2009), *Leadership for an Age of Wisdom*, Dordrecht, the Netherlands: Springer Educational Publishing.

Branson, C. M. (2010), *Leading Educational Change Wisely*, Rotterdam: Sense Publishers.

Branson, C. M. (2014a), 'Maintaining Moral Integrity', in C. M. Branson and S. J. Gross (eds), *Handbook of Ethical Educational Leadership*, 263–81, New York, NY: Routledge.

Branson, C. M. (2014b), 'Deconstructing Moral Motivation', in C. M. Branson and S. J. Gross (eds), *Handbook of Ethical Educational Leadership*, 294–312, New York, NY: Routledge.

Branson, C. M. (2014c), 'If it isn't Ethical, it isn't Leadership', in C. M. Branson and S. J. Gross (eds), *Handbook of Ethical Educational Leadership*, 439–454, New York, NY: Routledge.

Branson, C. M., M. Franken and D. Penney (2016), 'Reconceptualising Middle Leadership in Higher Education: A Transrelational Approach', in J. McNiff (ed.), *Values and Virtues in Higher Education Research: Critical Perspectives*, 155–70, Abington, Oxon: Routledge.

Braun, S., T. Nazlic, S. Weisweiler, B. Peus and D. Frey (2009), 'Effective Leadership Development in Higher Education: Individual and Group Level Approaches', *Journal of Leadership Education*, 8 (1): 195–206.

Braynion, P. (2004), 'Power and Leadership', *Journal of Health Organization and Management*, 18 (6): 447–63.

Bridges, W. (2009), *Managing Transitions: Making the Most of Change*, 3rd edn, Philadelphia, PA: De Capo Press.

Brookfield, S. (1986), *Understanding and Facilitating Adult Learning*, San Francisco: Jossey-Bass.

Brown, A. D. and M. Humphreys (2006), 'Organizational Identity and Place: A Discursive Exploration of Hegemony and Resistance', *Journal of Management Studies*, 43 (2): 231–57.

Bryman, A. (2007), 'Effective Leadership in Higher Education: A Literature Review', *Studies in Higher Education*, 32 (6): 693–710.

Bryson, C. (2004), 'The Consequences of Women in the Academic Profession of the Widespread Use of Short Term Contracts', *Gender, Work and Organisations*, 11 (2): 186–207.

Buckingham, M. and A. Goodall (2015), 'Reinventing Performance Management', *Harvard Business Review*, April, 40–50. Available online: https://hbr.org/2015/04/reinventing-performance-management (accessed 28 June 2017).

Burgan, M. (2006), *Whatever Happened to the Faculty?*, Baltimore, MD: Johns Hopkins University Press.

Burnes, B., P. Wend and R. T. By (2014), 'The Changing Face of English Universities: Reinventing Collegiality for the Twenty-First Century', *Studies in Higher Education*, 39 (6): 905–26.

Burns, J. M. (2010), *Leadership*, New York, NY: HarperCollins.

By, R. T., T. Diefenbach and P. Klarner (2008), 'Getting Organizational Change Right in Public Services: The Case of European Higher Education', *Journal of Change Management*, 8 (1): 21–35.

Cangemi, J. (1992), 'Some Observations of Successful Leaders, and Their Use of Power and Authority', *Education*, 112 (4): 499–505.

Cardy, R. L. (2004), *Performance Management: Concepts, Skills, and Exercises*, Armonk, NY: M. E. Sharpe.

Cascio, W. F. (2006), 'Global Performance Management Systems', in I. Bjorkman and G. Stahl (eds), *Handbook of Research in International Human Resources Management*, 176–96, London, UK: Edward Elgar Ltd.

Castells, M. (2000), *The Rise of the Network Society*, 2nd edn, Oxford, England: Blackwell Publishers.

Chaharbaghi, K. (2007), 'Provision of Public Services in an Age of Managerialism: Looking Better but Feeling Worse', *Equal Opportunities International*, 26 (4): 319–30.

Chan, K. (2001), 'The Difficulties and Conflict of Constructing a Model for Teacher Evaluation in Higher Education', *Higher Education Management*, 13 (1): 93–111.

Chandler, J., J. Barry and H. Clark (2002), 'Stressing Academe: The Wear and Tear of the New Public Management', *Human Relations*, 55 (9): 1051–69.

Chapman, J. A. (2002), 'A Framework for Transformational Change in Organizations', *Leadership and Organization Development Journal*, 23 (1): 16–25.

Chen, P. J. and Y. Choi (2008), 'Generational Differences in Work Values: A Study of Hospitality Management', *International Journal of Contemporary Hospitality Management*, 20 (6): 595–615.

Chou, S. Y. (2012), 'Millennials in the Workplace: A Conceptual Analysis of Millennials' Leadership and Followership Styles', *International Journal of Human Resource Studies*, 2 (2): 71–83.

Christensen, C. M., T. Hall, K. Dillon and D. S. Duncan (2016), 'Know Your Customers' "Jobs to be Done"', *Harvard Business Review*, September. Available online: https://hbr.org/2016/09/know-your-customers-jobs-to-be-done (accessed 28 June 2017).

Churchman, D. (2006), 'Institutional Commitments, Individual Compromises: Identity-Related Responses to Compromise in an Australian University', *Journal of Higher Education Policy and Management*, 28 (1): 3–15.

Clarke, M. and B. Hennig (2012), 'Motivation as Ethical Self-Formation', *Educational Philosophy and Theory*, 45 (1): 77–90.

Clayton, M. C., T. Hall, K. Dillon and D. S. Duncan (2016), 'Know Your Customers "jobs to be done"', *Harvard Business Review*. Retrieved from https://hbr.org/2016/09/know-your-customers-jobs-to-be-done

Colligan, T. W. and E. M. Higgins (2008), 'Workplace Stress: Etiology and Consequences', *Journal of Workplace Behavioral Health*, 21: 89–97.

Cooper, C. D., T. A. Scandura and C. A. Schriesheim (2005), 'Looking Forward but Learning from our Past: Potential Challenges to Developing Authentic Leadership Theory and Authentic Leaders', *The Leadership Quarterly*, 16 (3): 475–93.

Covey, S. R. (1989). *The Seven Habits of Highly Effective People: Restoring the Character Ethic*, Melbourne, VIC: Business Library.

Crabtree, S. (2013), 'Worldwide 13% are Engaged at Work', *Gallup*, 8 October. Available online: http://www.gallup.com/poll/165269/worldwide-employees-engaged-work. aspx (accessed 28 June 2017).

Cranton, P. (1994), *Understanding and Promoting Transformative Learning: A Guide for Educators of Adults*, San Francisco: Jossey-Bass.

Crevani, L., M. Lindgren and J. Packendorff (2010), 'Leadership, Not Leaders: On the Study of Leadership as Practices and Interactions', *Scandinavian Journal of Management*, 26 (1): 77–86.

Daft, R. (2010). *Organizational Theory and Design*, 10th edn, Mason, OH: South-Western Cengage Learning.

Davies, B. and R. Harré (1999), 'Positioning and Personhood', in R. Harré and L. Van Langenhove (eds), *Positioning Theory*, 32–52, Oxford, England: Blackwell Publishers.

Davies, J., M. T. Hides and S. Casey (2001), 'Leadership in Higher Education', *Total Quality Management*, 12 (7–8): 1025–30.

Davis, A. and R. Thomas (2002), 'Managerialism and Accountability in Higher Education: The Gendered Nature of Restructuring the Costs to Academic Service', *Critical Perspectives on Accounting*, 13 (2): 179–93.

Day, D. V., J. W. Fleenor, L. E. Atwater, R. E. Sturm and R. A. McKee (2014), 'Advances in Leader and Leadership Development: A Review of 25 Years of Research and Theory', *The Leadership Quarterly*, 25 (1): 63–82.

de Certeau, M. (1984), *The Practice of Everyday Life*, Berkeley, CA: University of California Press.

de Quincey, C. (2002), *Radical Nature: Rediscovering the Soul of Matter*. Montpelier, VT: Invisible Cities Press.

De Smet, A., J. Lavoie and E. S. Hioe (2012), 'Developing Better Change Leaders', *McKinsey Quarterly*, April. Available online: http://www.mckinsey.com/business-functions/organization/our-insights/developing-better-change-leaders (accessed 28 June 2017).

De Smet, A., B. Schaninger and M. Smith (2014), 'The Hidden Value of Organizational Health – and how to Capture it', *McKinsey Quarterly*, April. Available online: http://www.mckinsey.com/business-functions/organization/our-insights/the-hidden-value-of-organizational-health-and-how-to-capture-it (accessed 28 June 2017).

Deci, E. L. and R. M. Ryan (1995), 'Human Autonomy: The Basis for True Self-Esteem', in M. Kernis (ed.), *Efficacy, Agency, and Self-Esteem*, 31–49, New York: Plenum.

Decramer, A., C. Smolders and A. Vanderstraeten (2013), 'Employee Performance Management Culture and System Features in Higher Education: Relationship With Employee Performance Management', *The International Journal of Human Resource Management*, 24 (2): 352–71.

Deem, R. (1998), 'New Managerialism in Higher Education: The Management of Performance and Cultures in Universities', *International Studies in the Sociology of Education*, 8 (1): 47–70.

Deem, R. (2004), 'The Knowledge Worker, the Manager-Academic and he Contemporary UK University: New and Old Forms of Public Management?', *Financial Accountability and Management*, 20 (2): 107–28.

Deem, R. and K. J. Brehony (2005), 'Management as Ideology: The Case of "New Managerialism" in Higher Education', *Oxford Review of Education*, 31 (2): 217–35.

Deem, R., S. Hillyard and M. Reed (2007), *Knowledge, Higher Education, and the New Managerialism: The Changing Management of UK Universities*, Oxford, MA: Oxford University Press.

Deloitte (2013), *Resetting Horizons, Human Capital Trends 2013*. Deloitte University Press. Available online: https://www2.deloitte.com/content/dam/Deloitte/global/Documents/HumanCapital/dttl-hc-hctrendsglobal-8092013.pdf (accessed 28 June 2017).

Deloitte (2014), Global Human Capital Trends. Engaging the 21st-century workforce. Deloitte University Press. Available online: https://www2.deloitte.com/global/en/pages/human-capital/articles/human-capital-trends-2014.html (accessed 28 June 2017).

Deloitte (2015), Global Human Capital Trends. Leading in the New World of Work. Deloitte University Press. Available online: https://www2.deloitte.com/content/dam/Deloitte/at/Documents/human-capital/hc-trends-2015.pdf (accessed 28 June 2017).

Deloitte (2016a), The 2016 Deloitte Millennial Survey: Winning Over the Next Generation of Leaders. Available online: https://www2.deloitte.com/content/dam/Deloitte/global/Documents/About-Deloitte/gx-millenial-survey-2016-exec-summary.pdf (accessed 28 June 2017).

Deloitte (2016b), Global Human Capital Trends 2016. The New Organisation: Different by Design. Deloitte University Press. Available online: https://www2.deloitte.com/content/dam/Deloitte/nz/Documents/human-capital/gx-dup-global-human-capital-trends-2016.pdf (accessed 28 June 2017).

Den Hartog, D. N., P. Boselie and J. Paauwe (2004), 'Performance Management: A Model and Research Agenda', *Applied Psychology*, 53 (4): 556–69.

Dinh, J. E., R. G. Lord, W. L. Gardner, J. D. Meuser, R. C. Liden and J. Hu (2014), 'Leadership Theory and Research in the New Millennium: Current Theoretical Trends and Changing Perspectives', *The Leadership Quarterly*, 25 (1): 36–62.

Dobbins, M., C. Knill and E. M. Vögtle (2011), 'An Analytical Framework for the Cross-Country Comparison of Higher Education Governance', *Higher Education*, 62 (5): 665–83.

Doecke, B., G. Parr and S. North (2008), National Mapping of Teacher Professional Learning Project Final Report. Canberra, A.C.T.: Department of Education, Employment and Workplace Relations.

Dutton, J., and E. Heaphy (2003), 'The Power of High Quality Connections', in K. Cameron, J. Dutton, and R. Quinn (eds), *Positive Organizational Scholarship*. San Francisco, CA: Berrett-Koehler.

Dweck, C. S. (2006). *Mindset: The New Psychology of Success*, New York, NY: Random House.

Eacott, S. (2015), 'Problematising the Intellectual Gaze of the Educational Administration Scholar', *Educational Philosophy and Theory*, 47 (4): 312–29.

Edgar, F. and A. Geare (2013), 'Factors Influencing Research Performance', *Studies in Higher Education*, 38 (5): 774–92.

Ekman, M., M. Lindgren and J. Packendorff (2017), 'Universities Need Leadership, Academics Need Management: Discursive Tensions and Voids in the Deregulation of Swedish Higher Education Legislation', *Higher Education*. Available online: https://link.springer.com/article/10.1007/s10734-017-0140-2 (accessed 28 June 2017).

Englehardt, C. S. and P. R. Simmons (2002), 'Organizational Flexibility for a Changing World', *Leadership and Organization Development Journal*, 23 (3): 113–21.

Eraut, M. (2000), 'Non-Formal Learning and Tacit Knowledge in Professional Work', *British Journal of Educational Psychology*, 70 (1): 113–36.

Eraut, M. (2003), 'Editorial: The Many Meanings of Theory and Practice', *Learning in Health and Social Care*, 2 (2): 61–5.

Eraut, M. (2004), 'Informal Learning in the Workplace', *Studies in Continuing Education*, 26 (2): 247–73.

Ernst and Young. (2012), *University of the Future*. Available online: http://www.ey.com/Publication/vwLUAssets/University_of_the_future/$FILE/University_of_the_future_2012.pdf (accessed 28 June 2017).

Etzioni, A. (1975), *Comparative Analysis of Complex Organisations*, New York, NY: Simon and Schuster.

Evers, C. W. and G. Lakomski (2001), 'Theory in Educational Administration: Naturalistic Directions', *Journal of Educational Administration*, 39 (6): 499–520.

Evers, C. W. and G. Lakomski (2012), 'Science, Systems, and Theoretical Alternatives in Educational Administration: The Road Less Travelled', *Journal of Educational Administration*, 50 (1): 57–75.

Ewenstein, B., W. Smith and A. Sologar (2015), 'Changing Change Management', *McKinsey Quarterly*, 1–5 July. Available online: http://www.mckinsey.com/global-themes/leadership/changing-change-management (accessed 28 June 2017).

Fairholm, M. R. (2004), 'A New Sciences Outline for Leadership Development', *Leadership and Organization Development Journal*, 25 (4): 360–83.

Ferri-Reed, J. (2014), 'Leading a Multi-Generational Workforce: Learning to Leverage the Uniqueness of Every Age Group', *Journal for Quality and Participation*, 37 (2): 15–18.

Finkelstein, M. A. (2006), 'Dispositional Predictors of Organisational Citizen Behavior: Motives, Motive Fulfillment and Role Identity', *Social Behavior and Personality*, 34 (6): 603–16.

Fisher, K. E., C. F. Landry and C. Naumer (2007), 'Social Spaces, Casual Interactions, Meaningful Exchanges: "Information Ground" Characteristics Based on the College Student Experience', *Information Research*, 12 (2). Available online: http://informationr.net/ir/12-2/paper291.html (accessed 28 June 2017).

Fleming, P. and S. C. Zyglidopoulos (2008), 'The Escalation of Deception in Organizations', *Journal of Business Ethics*, 81 (4): 837–50.

Flores, L. G., W. Zheng, D. Rau and C. H. Thomas (2012), 'Organizational Learning: Subprocess Identification, Construct Validation and Empirical Test of Cultural Antecedents', *Journal of Management*, 38 (2): 640–67.

Folger, J., M. Poole and R. Stutman (1993), *Working through Conflict*, New York, NY: HarperCollins.

Ford, L. (2008), Corporate Culture: How Does it Really Work? [Video], 8 March. Available online: https://www.youtube.com/watch?v=92lg7EvwKBE (accessed 20 June 2017).

Foreman, P. and D. A. Whetten (2002), 'Members' Identification with Multiple-Identity Organizations', *Organization Science*, 13 (6): 618–35.

Foucault, M. (1997), 'Technologies of the Self', trans R. Hurley et al., in P. Rabinow (ed.), *Ethics, Subjectivity and Truth*, 223–51, New York, NY: New Press.

Franken, M., C. Branson and D. Penney (2015), 'Middle Leaders' Learning in a University Context', *Journal of Higher Education Policy and Management*, 37 (2): 190–203.

Franken, M., C. Branson and D. Penney (2016), 'A Theory-To-Practice Leadership Learning Arrangement in a University Context', *International Journal of Leadership in Education*. Available online: http://dx.doi.org/10.1080/13603124.2016.1247196 (accessed 28 June 2017).

Fredman, N. and J. Doughney (2012), 'Academic Dissatisfaction, Managerial Change and Neo-Liberalism', *Higher Education*, 64 (1): 41–58.

French, J. and B. H. Raven (1959), 'The Bases of Social Power', in D. Cartwright (ed.), *Studies in Social Power*, 150–67, Ann Arbor, MI: Institute for Social Research.

Frost, P. (2003). *Toxic Emotions at Work*, Boston, MA: Harvard Business School Press.

Gallup (2013), 'State of the American Workplace: Employee Engagement Insights for U.S. Business Leaders'. Available online: http://www.gallup.com/strategicconsulting/163007/state-american-workplace.aspx (accessed 28 June 2017).

Gallup-Healthways. (2016), 'Well-Being Index'. Available online: http://www.gallup.com/topic/well_being_index.aspx (accessed 28 June 2017).

Gardner, H. (2012), *Good Work* [Video], 6 November. Available online: https://www.youtube.com/watch?v=Bqo48PpNVbw (accessed 28 June 2017).

Gardner, S. K. (2016), 'Mentoring the Millennial Faculty Member', *The Department Chair*, 27 (1): 6–8.

Gerken, M., S. Beausaert and M. Segers (2016), 'Working on Professional Development of Faculty Staff in Higher Education: Investigating the Relationship Between Social Informal Learning Activities and Employability', *Human Resource Development International*, 19 (2): 135–51.

Ginsburg, B. (2011), *The Fall of the Faculty: The Rise of the All-Administrative University and Why It Matters*, Oxford: Oxford University Press.

Giroux, D., D. Karmis and C. Rouillard (2015), 'Between the Managerial and the Democratic University: Governance Structure and Academic Freedom as Sites of Political Struggle', *Studies in Social Justice*, 9 (2): 142–58.

Goldman, A. (2008), 'Company on the Couch: Unveiling Toxic Behaviour In Dysfunctional Organizations', *Journal of Management Inquiry*, 17 (3): 226–38.

Goleman, D. (1999). Working with Emotional Intelligence, London: Bloomsbury.

Goleman, D. (2013), *Focus, Flow and Frazzle* [Video], 20 January. Available online: https://greatergood.berkeley.edu/video/item/focus_flow_and_frazzle (accessed 28 June).

Golembiewski, R. T., K. Billingsley and S. Yeager (1976), 'Measuring Change and Persistence in Human Affairs: Types of Change Generated by OD Designs', *Journal of Applied Behavioural Science*, 12 (2): 143–55.

Graen, G. B. and M. Uhl-Bien (1995), 'Relationship-Based Approach to Leadership: Development of Leader-Member Exchange (LMX) Theory of Leadership Over 25 Years: Applying a Multi-Domain Perspective', *The Leadership Quarterly*, 6 (2): 219–47.

Gray, B. (2008), 'Enhancing Transdisciplinary Research Through Collaborative Leadership', *American Journal of Preventive Medicine*, 35 (2): S124–32.

Gray, S. (2015), 'Is "Holacracy" the Future for HR management? Exclusive Interview with Zappos 29/06/2015', 2 July. Available online: https://www.linkedin.com/pulse/holacracy-future-hr-management-exclusive-interview-zappos-stuart-gray (accessed 28 June 2017).

Greenfield, T. B. (1986), 'The Decline and Fall of Science in Educational Administration', *Interchange*, 17 (2): 57–80.

Gronn, P. (2003), *The New Work of Educational Leaders*, London: Paul Chapman.

Gruman J. A. and A. M. Saks (2011), 'Performance Management and Employee Engagement', *Human Resource Management Review*, 21: 123–36.

Gursoy, D., A. Maier and C. Chi (2008), 'Generational Differences: An Examination of Work Values and Generational Gaps in the Hospitality Workforce', *International Journal of Hospitality Management*, 27 (3): 448–58.

Hallinger, P. and K. Snidvongs (2008), 'Educating Leaders: Is There Anything to Learn from Business Management?', *Educational Management Administration and Leadership*, 36 (1): 9–31.

Hamel, G. (2007), *The Future of Management*, Boston, MA: Harvard Business School Press.

Hamel, G. and M. Zanini (2014), 'Build a Change Platform, not a Change Program', *McKinsey and Company*, October. Available online: http://www.mckinsey.com/business-functions/organization/our-insights/build-a-change-platform-not-a-change-program (accessed 28 June 2017).

Hamlin, R. G. and T. Patel (2015), 'Perceived Managerial and Leadership Effectiveness Within Higher Education in France', *Studies in Higher Education*, 42 (2): 1–23.

Handy, C. (1993), *Understanding Organizations*, 4th edn, Harmondsworth: Penguin.

Harré, R. and L. van Langenhove (1999). 'The Dynamics of Social Episodes', in R. Harré and L. van Langenhove (eds), *Positioning Theory*, 1–13, Oxford, England: Blackwell Publishers.

Harré, R. and F. Moghaddam (2003), 'Introduction: The Self and Others in Traditional Psychology and in Positioning Theory', in R. Harré and F. Moghaddam (eds), *The Self and Others: Positioning Individuals and Groups in Personal, Political, and Cultural Contexts*, 1–11, Westport, CT: Praeger Publishers.

Harré, R. and N. Slocum (2003), 'Disputes as Complex Social Events: On the Uses of Positioning Theory', in R. Harré and F. Moghaddam (eds), *The Self and Others: Positioning Individuals and Groups in Personal, Political, and Cultural Contexts*, 123–36, Westport, CT: Praeger Publishers.

Harman, G. (2002), 'Academic Leaders or Corporate Managers: Deans and Heads in Australian Higher Education 1977 To 1997', *Higher Education Management and Policy*, 14 (2): 53–70.

Haslam, S. A., S. D. Reicher and M. J. Platow (2011). *The New Psychology of Leadership: Identity, Influence and Power*, Hove, England: Psychology Press.

Hazy, J. K., J. A. Goldstein and B. B. Lichtenstein (2007), 'Complex Systems Leadership Theory: An Introduction', in J. K. Hazy, J. S. Goldstein and B. B. Lichtenstein (eds), *Complex Systems Leadership Theory: New Perspectives from Complexity Science on Social and Organizational Effectiveness*, 1–13, Mansfield, MA: ISCE Publications.

Hechanova, R. M. and R. Cementina-Olpoc (2013), 'Transformational Leadership, Change Management, and Commitment to Change: A Comparison of Academic and Business Organizations', *Asia Pacific Educational Research*, 22 (1): 11–19.

Heifetz, R. A. and M. Linsky (2002), *Leadership on the Line: Staying Alive Through the Dangers of Leading*, Boston, MA: Harvard Business School.

Henkel, M. (2005), 'Academic Identity and Autonomy in a Changing Policy Environment', *Higher Education*, 49 (1–2): 155–76.

Hersey, P. and K. Blanchard (1982), *The Management of Organizational Behaviour*, Englewood Cliffs, NJ: Prentice-Hall.

Hersey, P., K. H. Blanchard and D. E. Johnson (2001), *Management of Organisational Behaviour*, 8th edn, London: Prentice-Hall.

Hill, L. (2007), 'Leadership Development: A Strategic Imperative for Higher Education', *Educause*, January, 27–30. Available online: https://net.educause.edu/ir/library/pdf/ffp0506s.pdf (accessed 28 June 2017).

Hodkinson, P., G. Biesta and D. James (2007), 'Understanding Learning Culturally: Overcoming the Dualism Between Social and Individual Views of Learning', *Vocations and Learning*, 1: 27–47.

Hogan, S. J. and L. V. Coote (2014), 'Organizational Culture, Innovation, and Performance: A Test of Schein's Model', *Journal of Business Research*, 67 (8): 1609–21.

Holland, J. H. (1995), *Hidden Order*, Reading, MA: Addison-Wesley Publishing.

Hollingworth, P. (2016), *The Light and Fast Organisation: A New Way of Dealing with Uncertainty*, Melbourne, VIC: John Wiley and Sons.

Hopkins, D., M. Ainscow and M. West (1997), 'Making Sense of Change', in M. Preedy, R. Glatter and R. Levacic (eds), *Educational Management: Strategy, Quality and Resources*, 66–78, Buckingham, PA: Open University Press.

Hosking, D. M. (2007), 'Not Leaders, Not Followers: A Post-Modern Discourse of Leadership Processes', in B. Shamir, R. Pillai, M. Bligh and M. Uhl-Bien (eds), *Follower-Centered Perspectives on Leadership: A Tribute to the Memory of James R. Meindl*, 243–64. Greenwich, CT: Information Age Publishing.

Hosking, D. M., H. P. Dachler and K. J. Gergen (1995), *Management and Organization: Relational Alternatives to Individualism*, Brookfield, WI: Avebury.

House, E. and P. McQuillan (1998), 'Three Perspectives on School Reform', in A. Hargreaves, A. Lieberman, M. Fullan and D. Hopkins (eds), *International Handbook of Educational Change*, 198–213, Dordrecht: Kluwer Academic Publishers.

Ignatius, A. (2016), 'What CEOs Really Worry About', *Harvard Business Review*, November. Available online: https://hbr.org/2016/11/the-best-performing-ceos-in-the-world (accessed 28 June 2017).

Inc., 'Human Resource Management'. Available online: https://www.inc.com/encyclopedia/human-resource-management.html (accessed 28 June 2017).

Inman, M. (2009), 'Learning to Lead: Development for Middle-Level Leaders in Higher Education in England and Wales', *Professional Development in Education*, 35 (3): 417–32. doi:10.1080/13674580802532654

Inman, M. (2014), 'Bringing Life to Leadership: The Significance of Life History in Reviewing Leadership Learning within Higher Education', *International Journal of Leadership in Education*, 17 (2): 237–56.

Jamali, D., G. Khoury and H. Sahyoun (2006), 'From Bureaucratic Organizations to Learning Organizations: An Evolutionary Roadmap', *The Learning Organization*, 13 (4): 337–52.

Jarvis, D. S. L. (2014), 'Policy Transfer, Neo-Liberalism or Coercive Institutional Isomorphism? Explaining the Emergence of a Regulatory Regime for Quality Assurance in the Hong Kong Higher Education Sector', *Policy and Society*, 33 (3): 237–52.

Jensen, J. M., R. A. Opland and A. M. Ryan (2010), 'Psychological Contracts and Counterproductive Work Behaviors: Employee Responses to Transactional and Relational Breach', *Journal of Business Psychology*, 25 (4): 555–68.

Johnson, J. R. (2002), 'Leading the Learning Organization: Portrait of Four Leaders', *Leadership and Organization Development Journal*, 23 (5): 241–49.

Kahn, W. A. (1990), 'Psychological Conditions of Personal Engagement and Disengagement at Work', *Academy of Management Journal*, 33 (4): 692–724.

Kahn, W. A. (2010), 'The Essence of Engagement: Lessons from the Field', in S. Albrecht (ed.), *Handbook of Employee Engagement: Perspectives, Issues, Research and Practice*, 20–30, Northampton, MA: Edward Elgar.

Karnes, R. E. (2009), 'A Change in Business Ethics: The Impact of Employer-Employee Relations', *Journal of Business Ethics*, 87 (2): 189–97.

Katzenbach, J. R., I. Steffen and C. Kronley (2012,), 'Cultural Change that Sticks: Start with What's Already Working', *Harvard Business Review*, July–August, 110–17. Available online: https://hbr.org/2012/07/cultural-change-that-sticks (accessed 28 June 2017).

Kayes, D. C. (2006), *Destructive Goal Pursuit: The Mount Everest Disaster*, Basingstoke: Palgrave Macmillan.

Keating, L. A. and P. A. Heslin (2015), 'The Potential Role of Mindsets in Unleashing Employee Engagement', *Human Resource Management Review*, 25 (4): 329–41.

Kekäle, T. and R. Viitala (2003), 'Do networks learn?', *Journal of Workplace Learning*, 15 (6): 245–47.

Kellerman, B. (2004). *Bad Leadership: What it is, How it Happens, Why it Matters*, Boston, MA: Harvard Business School Press.

Kezar, A. (2013), 'Understanding Sensemaking/Sensegiving in Transformational Change Processes from the Bottom Up', *Journal of Higher Education*, 65 (6): 761–80.

Kim, W. C. and R. Mauborgne (2014), 'Blue Ocean Leadership', *Harvard Business Review*, May, 60–72. Available online: https://hbr.org/2014/05/blue-ocean-leadership (accessed 28 June 2017).

Kolb, D. A. (1984), *Experiential Learning*, Englewood Cliffs, NJ: Prentice-Hall.

Koslowski, M., J. Schwarzwald and S. Ashuri (2001), 'On the Relationship Between Subordinates' Compliance to Power Sources and Organisational Attitudes', *Applied Psychology*, 50 (3): 455–76.

Krantz, J. (2006), 'Leadership, Betrayal and Adaptation', *Human Relations*, 59 (2): 221–40.

Krasikova, D. V., S. G. Green and J. M. LeBreton (2013), 'Destructive Leadership: A Theoretical Review, Integration, and Future Research Agenda', *Journal of Management*, 39 (5): 1308–38.

Krauss, H. H. and L. L. Critchfield (1975), 'Contrasting Self-Esteem Theory and Consistency Theory in Predicting Interpersonal Attraction', *American Sociological Association*, 38 (2): 247–60.

Krausz, R. (1986), 'Power and Leadership in Organizations', *Transactional Analysis Journal*, 16 (2): 85–94.

Kreisberg, S. (1992), *Transforming Power: Domination, Empowerment and Education*. Albany: SUNY Press.

Kujala, J., H. Lehtimäki and R. Pučetaite (2016), 'Trust and Distrust: Constructing Unity and Fragmentation of Organisational Culture', *Journal of Business Ethics*, 139 (4): 701–16.

Lafferty, G. and J. Fleming (2000), 'The Restructuring of Academic Work in Australia: Power, Management and Gender', *British Journal of Sociology of Education*, 21 (2): 257–67.

Lai, M. (2013), 'The Changing Work Life of Academics: A Comparative Study of a Renowned and a Regional University in the Chinese Mainland', *The Australian Educational Researcher*, 40 (1): 27–45.

Laksov, K. B. and T. Tomson (2016), 'Becoming an Educational Leader: Exploring Leadership in Medical Education', *International Journal of Leadership in Education*, 20 (4): 506–16.

Laloux, F. (2014), *Reinventing Organisations*, Nelson Parker, Belgium.

Leadership Foundation for Higher Education, Bespoke Leadership Programmes: Leadership Development Designed and Delivered In-House for your Institution. Available online: https://www.lfhe.ac.uk/download.cfm/docid/4FF2805A-32BF-45FC-B2FD5DF93BDBBBED (accessed 28 June 2017).

Levene, R. A. (2015), 'Capstone Project for Master of Applied Positive Psychology (MAPP)', University of Pennsylvania, PA. Available online: http://repository.upenn.edu/mapp_capstone/88 (accessed 28 June 2017).

Li, L., M. Lai and L. Lo (2013), 'Academic Work Within a Mode of Mixed Governance: Perspectives of University Professors in the Research Context of Western China', *Asia Pacific Education Review*, 14 (3): 307–14.

Lichtenstein, B. B. and D. A. Plowman (2009), 'The Leadership of Emergence: A Complex Systems Leadership Theory of Emergence at Successive Organizational Levels', *The Leadership Quarterly*, 20 (4): 617–30.

Lillis, T. and M. J. Curry (2006), 'Professional Academic Writing by Multilingual Scholars: Interactions with Literacy Brokers in the Production of English-Medium Texts', *Written Communication*, 23 (1): 3–35.

Linley, P. A., S. Harrington and N. Garcea (2010), *Oxford Handbook of Positive Psychology and Work*, Oxford: Oxford University Press

Lipman-blumen, J. (1998), 'Connective Leadership: What Business Needs to Learn from Academe', *Change: The Magazine of Higher Education*, 30 (1): 49–53.

Liu, S. (2003), 'Cultures within Culture: Unity and Diversity of Two Generations of Employees in State-Owned Enterprises', *Human Relations*, 56 (4): 387–417.

Louvel, S. (2013), 'Understanding Change in Higher Education as Bricolage: How Academics Engage in Curriculum Change', *Journal of Higher Education*, 66 (6): 669–91.

Lu, H., W. Ling, Y. Wu and Y. Liu (2012), 'A Chinese Perspective on the Content and Structure of Destructive Leadership', *Chinese Management Studies*, 6 (2): 271–83.

Luecke, R. (2007), *Manager's Toolkit: The 13 Skills Managers Need to Succeed*. Boston, MA: Harvard Business School Press.

Luthans, F., C. M. Youssef and B. J. Avolio (2007), *Psychological Capital: Developing the Human Competitive Edge*, Oxford, UK: Oxford University Press.

Lynch, K. (2014), 'Control by Numbers: New Managerialism and Ranking in Higher Education', *Critical Studies in Education*, 56 (2): 190–207.

Lynch, R. A. (1998), 'Is Power All There Is? Michel Foucault and the Omnipresence of Power Relations', *Philosophy Today*, 42 (1): 65–70.

Macdonald, I., C. Burke and K. Stewart (2006), *Systems Leadership: Creating Positive Organisations*. Farnham, England: Gower Publishing Company.

Macey, W. H. and B. Schneider (2008), 'The Meaning of Employee Engagement', *Industrial and Organizational Psychology*, 1: 3–30.

Madsen, S. R., K. A. Longman and J. R. Daniels (2011), 'Women's Leadership Development in Higher Education: Conclusion and Implications for HRD', *Advances in Developing Human Resources*, 14 (1): 113–28.

Maier, T., M. Tavanti, P. Bombard, M. Gentile and B. Bradford (2015), 'Millennial Generation Perceptions of Value-Centered Leadership Principles', *Journal of Human Resources in Hospitality and Tourism*, 14 (4): 382–97.

Maguire, S. and B. McKelvey (1999), 'Complexity and Management: Moving from Fad to Firm Foundations', *Emergence*, 1 (2): 5–49.

Malone, J. (1990), *Theories of Learning: A Historical Approach*, Belmont: Wadsworth Publishing Company.

Mann, A. and J. Hartner (2016), 'The Worldwide Employee Engagement Crisis', *Gallup*, 7 January. Available online: http://www.gallup.com/businessjournal/188033/worldwide-employee-engagement-crisis.aspx?g_source=employee%20engagementandg_medium=searchandg_campaign=tiles (accessed 28 June 2017)

Marion, R., and M. Uhl-Bien (2001), 'Leadership in Complex Organizations', *The Leadership Quarterly*, 12 (4): 389–418.

Martin, R. L. (2014), 'The Big Lie of Strategic Planning: A Detailed Plan may be Comforting, but it's not a Strategy', *Harvard Business Review*, January–February, 79–84. Available online: https://hbr.org/2014/01/the-big-lie-of-strategic-planning (accessed 28 June 2017).

Martinko, M. J., M. J. Gundlach and S. C. Douglas (2002), 'Toward an Integrative Theory of Counterproductive Workplace Behavior: A Causal Reasoning Perspective', *International Journal of Selection and Assessment*, 10 (1–2): 36–50.

Maslow, A. H. (1966). *The Psychology of Science*, New York, NY: Harper Row.

Matteson, M.T. and J. M. Ivancevich (1987), *Controlling Work Stress: Effective Human Resource and Management Strategies*, San Francisco: Jossey-Bass.

Matthews, D. (2011), 'Scholar Points the Finger at Administrators in a Case of Deadly Bloat', *Times Higher Education*, 18 August. Available online: https://www.timeshighereducation.com/news/scholar-points-finger-at-administrators-in-a-case-of-deadly-bloat/417159.article (accessed 28 June 2017).

May, T. (2006), *The Philosophy of Foucault*. Chesham, England: Acumen.

McClelland, D. (1953), *The Achievement Motive*. New York: Appleton-Century-Crofts.

McClelland, D. C. and D. H. Burnham (1976), 'Power is the Motivator', *Harvard Business Review*, March–April, 100–10. Available online: https://www.google.co.nz/search?q=%E2%80%98Power+is+the+motivator%E2%80%99&oq=%E2%80%98Power+is+the+motivator%E2%80%99&aqs=chrome.69i57j0l5.567j0j7&sourceid=chrome&ie=UTF-8 (accessed 28 June, 2017).

McGreggor, D. M. (1960), *The Human Side of Enterprise*, New York, NY: McGraw-Hill.

McPeak, M. (2001), 'Tackling Fragmentation and Building Unity in an International Nongovernmental Organization', *Non-Profit Management and Leadership*, 11 (4): 477–91.

McRae, D., G. Ainsworth, R. Groves, M. Rowland and V. Zbar (2001), *PD 2000 Australia: A National Mapping of School Teacher Professional Development*, Canberra, ACT: Commonwealth of Australia.

McRoy, I. and P. Gibbs (2009), 'Leading Change in Higher Education', *Educational Management Administration and Leadership*, 37 (5): 687–704.

Melo, A. I., C. S. Sarrico and Z. Radnor (2010), 'The Influence of Performance Management Systems on Key Actors in Universities. The Case of an English University', *Public Management Review*, 12 (2): 233–54.

Merriam, S. (2001), 'Andragogy and Self-Directed Learning: Pillars of Adult Learning Theory', *New Directions for Adult and Continuing Education*, 89: 3–14.

Mezirow, J. and Associates (2000), *Learning as Transformation: Critical Perspectives on a Theory in Progress*, San Francisco: Jossey-Bass.

Middlehurst, R. (2008), 'Not Enough Science or Not Enough Learning? Exploring the Gaps Between Leadership Theory and Practice', *Higher Education Quarterly*, 62 (4): 322–39.

Middlehurst, R. (2013), 'Changing Internal Governance: Are Leadership Roles and Management Structures in United Kingdom Universities Fit for the Future?', *Higher Education Quarterly*, 67 (3): 275–94.

Middlehurst, R., T. Kennie and S. Woodfield (2010), 'Leading and Managing the University: Presidents and Their Senior Management Team', in *International Encyclopedia of Education*, 3rd edition, 238–44, Oxford: Elsevier.

Mihut, L. A. (2014), 'Literacy Brokers and the Emotional Work of Mediation', *Literacy in Composition Studies*, 2 (1): 57–79.

Mok, K. H. (2013), 'The Quest for an Entrepreneurial University in East Asia: Impact on Academics and Administrators in Higher Education', *Asia Pacific Educational Review*, 14 (1): 11–22.

Molleman, E. and H. Timmerman (2003), 'Performance Management When Innovation and Learning Become Critical Performance Indicators', *Personnel Review*, 32 (1): 93–113.

Mondy, R. W., R. M. Noe and S. R. Premeaux (2002), *Human Resource Management*, 8th edn, Upper Saddle River, NJ: Prentice-Hall.

Myers, K. K. and J. G. Oetzel (2003), 'Exploring the Dimensions of Organizational Assimilation: Creating and Validating a Measure', *Communication Quarterly*, 51 (4): 438–57.

Myers, K. K. and K. Sadaghiani (2010), 'Millennials in the Workplace: A Communication Perspective on Millennials' Organizational Relationships and Performance', *Journal of Business and Psychology*, 25 (2): 225–38.

Nankervis, A. R. and R. Compton (2006), 'Performance Management: Theory in Practice?', *Asia Pacific Journal of Human Resources*, 44 (1): 83–101.

Nicolini, D., S. Gherardi, and D. Yanow, eds (2003), *Knowing in Organizations: A Practice-Based Approach*, New York, NY: M.E. Sharpe.

Nink, M. (2016), 'The Negative Impact of Disengaged Employees on Germany', *Gallup*, 5 April. Available online: http://www.gallup.com/businessjournal/190445/negative-impact-disengaged-employees-germany.aspx (accessed 28 June 2017).

Nixon, J. (2006), 'Professional Identity and the Restructuring of Higher Education', *Studies in Higher Education*, 21 (1): 5–16.

Nixon, J. (2012), 'Universities and the Common Good', in R. Barnett (ed.), *The Future University: Ideas and Possibilities*, 141–51, New York, NY: Routledge.

Noe, R. A., M. J. Tews and A. D. Marand (2013), 'Individual Differences and Informal Learning in the Workplace', *Journal of Vocational Behavior*, 83 (3): 327–35.

O'Connell, P. K. (2014), 'A Simplified Framework for 21st Century Leader Development', *The Leadership Quarterly*, 25 (2): 183–203.

OECD (2003), 'Changing Patterns of Governance in Higher Education'. Available online: https://www.oecd.org/education/skills-beyond-school/35747684.pdf (accessed 28 June 2017).

O'Mahoney, G., B. Barnett and R. Matthews (2006), *Building Culture: A Framework for School Improvement*, Melbourne, VIC: Hawker Brownlow.

Ordóñez, L. D., M. E. Schweitzer, A. D. Galinsky, and M. H. Bazerman (2009), Goals Gone Wild: The systematic effect of over-prescribing goal-setting. *Working Knowledge*, 28 June. Available online: http://hbswk.hbs.edu/item/goals-gone-wild-the-systematic-side-effects-of-over-prescribing-goal-setting (accessed 28 June 2017).

Organ, D. W. (1988), *Organizational Citizenship Behavior: The Good Soldier Syndrome*, Lexington, MA: Lexington Books.

Organisation Development Network, 'What is Organisational Development?', Available online: http://www.odnetwork.org/?page=WhatIsOD (accessed 28 June 2017).

Paauwe, J. and R. Richardson (1997), 'Introduction Special Issue on HRM and Performance', *International Journal of Human Resource Management*, 8 (3): 257–62.

Padilla, A., R. Hogan and R. B. Kaiser (2007), 'The Toxic Triangle: Destructive Leaders, Susceptible Followers, and Conducive Environments', *The Leadership Quarterly*, 18 (3): 176–94.

Paillé, P. and N. Raineri (2016), 'Trust in the Context of Psychological Contract Breach: Implications for Environmental Sustainability', *Journal of Environmental Psychology*, 45: 210–20.

Patel, M. (2015), 'Tough Love Performance Reviews, in 10 minutes', *Harvard Business Review*, 3 August. Available online: https://hbr.org/2015/08/tough-love-performance-reviews-in-10-minutes (accessed 28 June 2017).

Pick, D., S. Teo and M. Yeung (2012), 'Friend Or Foe? New Managerialism and Technical, Administrative and Clerical Support Staff in Australian Universities', *Higher Education Quarterly*, 66 (1): 3–23.

Pierro, A., A. W. Kruglanski and B. H. Raven (2012), 'Motivational Underpinnings of Social Influence in Work Settings: Bases of Social Power and the Need for Cognitive Closure', *European Journal of Social Psychology*, 42 (1): 41–52.

Pierro, A., B. H. Raven, C. Amato and J. J. Belanger (2013), 'Bases of Social Power, Leadership Styles, and Organizational Commitment', *International Journal of Psychology*, 48 (6): 1122–34.

Plowman, D. A., S. Solanski, T. E. Beck, L. Baker, M. Kulkarni and D. V. Travis (2007), 'The Role of Leadership in Emergent, Self-Organization', *The Leadership Quarterly*, 18 (4): 341–56.

Podsakoff, P. M., S. B. MacKenzie, J. B. Paine and D. G. Bachrach (2000), 'Organisational Citizen Behaviors: A Critical Review of the Theoretical and Empirical Literature and Suggestions for Future Research', *Journal of Management*, 26 (3): 513–63.

Pradhan, R. K., L. K. Jena and I. G. Kumari (2016), 'Effect of Work-Life Balance on Organisational Citizen Behaviour: Role of Organisational Commitment', *Global Business Review*, 17 (3): 15–29.

Raelin, J. (2011), 'From Leadership-As-Practice to Leaderful Practice', *Leadership*, 7 (2): 195–211.

Raelin, J. (2017), 'Leadership-As-Practice: Theory and Application – An Editor's Reflection', *Leadership*, 13 (2): 215–21.

Ramsden, P. (1998). *Learning to Lead in Higher Education*, New York, NY: Routledge.

Randall, L. M. and L. A. Coakley (2007), 'Applying Adaptive Leadership to Successful Change Initiatives in Academia', *Leadership and Organization Development Journal*, 28 (4): 325–35.

Randle, K. and N. Brady (1997), 'Further Education and the New Managerialism', *Journal of Further and Higher Education*, 21 (2): 229–39.

Rayton, B. A. and Z. Y. Yalabik (2014), 'Work Engagement, Psychological Contract Breach and Job Satisfaction', *The International Journal of Human Resource Management*, 25 (17): 2382–400.

Readings, B. (1996), *The University in Ruins*, Cambridge, MA: Harvard University Press.

Reeves, M., S. Levin, and D. Ueda (2016), 'The Biology of Corporate Survival: Natural Ecosystems Hold Surprising Lessons for Business', *Harvard Business Review*, January–February, 46–55. Available online: https://hbr.org/2016/01/the-biology-of-corporate-survival (accessed 28 June).

Regine, B. and R. Lewin (2000), 'Leading at the Edge: How Leaders Influence Complex Systems', *Emergence*, 2 (2): 5–23.

Reiley, P. J. and R. R. Jacobs (2016), 'Ethics Matter: Moderating Leaders' Power Use and Followers' Citizenship Behaviors', *Journal of Business Ethics*, 134 (1): 69–81.

Richards, D. A. and R. D. Hackett (2012). 'Attachment and Emotion Regulation: Compensatory Interactions and Leader-Member Exchange', *The Leadership Quarterly*, 23 (6): 686–701.

Rigby, D. K., J. Sutherland and H. Takeuchi (2016, May), 'Embracing Agile: How to Master the Process That's Transforming Management', *Harvard Business Review*,

41–50. Available online: https://hbr.org/2016/05/embracing-agile (accessed 28 June 2017).

Riivari, E. and A-M. Lämsä (2014), 'Does it Pay to Be Ethical? Examining the Relationship Between Organisational Culture and Innovativeness', *Journal of Business Ethics*, 124: 1–17.

Riley, J. (2015), 'Organisation Culture: Toxic Culture and Business Performance', 27 February. Available online: https://www.tutor2u.net/business/blog/organisational-culture-toxic-culture-and-business-performance (accessed 28 June 2017).

Robertson, B. J. (2015), *Holacracy: The New Management System For a Rapidly Changing World*, New York: Henry Holt and Company.

Robinson, S. L. and E. W. Morrison (2000), 'The Development of Psychological Contract Breach and Violation: A Longitudinal Study', *Journal of Organizational Behavior*, 21 (5): 525–46.

Rock, D. (2008), 'SCARF: A Brain-Based Model for Collaborating with and Influencing Others', *Neuroleadership Journal*, 1: 1–9.

Rogers, M. F. (1973), 'Instrumental and Infra-Resources: The Bases of Power', *American Journal of Sociology*, 79 (1): 1418–125.

Ryan, R. M. and E. L. Deci (2000), 'Self-Determination Theory and the Facilitation of Intrinsic Motivation, Social Development, and Well-Being', *American Psychologist*, 55 (1): 141–66.

Ryff, C. D. and B. Singer (2002), 'From Social Structure to Biology: Integrative Science in Pursuit of Human Health and Well-being', in C. R. Snyder and S. J. Lopez (eds), *Handbook of Positive Psychology*, 541–55, Oxford: Oxford University Press.

Saks, A. M. and J. A. Gruman (2014), 'What Do We Really Know About Employee Engagement?', *Human Resource Development Quarterly*, 25 (2): 155–82.

Salomon, G. and D. N. Perkins (1998), 'Individual and Social Aspects of Learning', *Review of Research in Education*, 23 (1): 1–24.

Santiago, R. and T. Carvalho (2012), 'Managerialism Rhetorics in Portuguese Higher Education', *Minerva*, 50 (4): 511–32.

Schein, E. H. (2004). *Organizational Culture and Leadership*, 3rd edn, San Francisco: Jossey-Bass.

Schein, E. H. (2010). *Organizational Culture and Leadership*, 4th edn, San Francisco: Jossey-Bass.

Schön, D. A. (1987), *Educating the Reflective Practitioner*, San Francisco: Jossey-Bass.

Schyns, B. and J. Schilling (2013), 'How Bad are the Effects of Bad Leaders? A Meta-Analysis of Destructive Leadership and its Outcomes', *The Leadership Quarterly*, 24 (1): 138–58.

Sefton, R., P. Waterhouse and R. Cooney (1995), *Workplace Learning and Change: The Workplace as a Learning Environment*, Doncaster, VIC: Automotive Training Australia. Available online: http://hdl.voced.edu.au/10707/138718 (accessed 28 June 2017).

Senge, P. (1990), *The Fifth Discipline: The Art and Practice of the Learning Organization*, Sydney, NSW: Random House.

Senge, P. (1995), *The Fifth Discipline: The Art and Practice of the Learning Organization*, Sydney, NSW: Random House.

Senge, P. (2006), *The Fifth Discipline*, Revised edn, New York: Random House.

Senge, P. and D. H. Kim (2012), 'From Fragmentation to Integration: Building Learning Communities', *Reflections*, 12 (4): 3–11.

Senge, P., R. Ross, B. Smith, C. Roberts and A. Kleiner (1994), *The Fifth Discipline Fieldbook: Strategies and Tools for Building a Learning Organization*. London: Nicholas Brealey.

Senge, P., C. O. Scharmer, J. Jaworski and B. S. Flowers (2007), *Presence: Exploring Profound Change in People, Organizations and Society*, London: Nicholas Brealey.

Sergiovanni, T. (1992), *Moral Leadership: Getting to the Heart of School Improvement*, San Francisco, CA: Jossey-Bass.

Shackleton, V. (1995), *Business Leadership*, London: Routledge.

Shamir, B. (2011), 'Leadership Takes time: Some Implications of (not) Taking Time Seriously in Leadership Research', *The Leadership Quarterly*, 22 (2): 307–15.

Shattock, M. (2010), 'Mangerialism and Collegialism in Higher Education Institutions', in *International Encyclopedia of Education*, 3rd edn, 251–5, Oxford: Elsevier.

Shaw, C. (2013), 'Leadership in Higher Education: 14 Pieces of Food for Thought', *The Guardian*, 5 February. Available from:https://www.theguardian.com/higher-education-network/2013/feb/05/tips-academic-leadership-career-progression (accessed 28 June 2017).

Shaw, J. B., A. Erickson and M. Harvey (2011), 'A Method for Measuring Destructive Leadership and Identifying Types of Destructive Leaders in Organizations', *The Leadership Quarterly*, 22 (4): 575–90.

Shaw, R. and D. Perkins (1992), 'Teaching Organizations to Learn: The Power of Productive Failures', in D. Nadler, M. Gerstein and R. Shaw (eds), *Organisational Architecture*, 175–92, San Francisco, CA: Jossey-Bass.

Shore, C. (2010), 'The Reform of New Zealand's University System: "After Neoliberalism"', *Learning and Teaching: The International Journal of Higher Education in the Social Sciences*, 3 (1): 1–31.

Shumar, W. (1997), *College for Sale: A Critique of the Commodification of Higher Education*, London: Falmer Press.

Sievers, B. (2008), 'The Psychotic University', *Ephemera*, 8 (3): 238–57.

Smeenk, S. G. A., R. N. Eisinga, J. C. Teelken and J. A. C. M. Doorewaard (2006), 'The Effects of HRM Practices and Antecedents on Organizational Commitment among University Employees', *International Journal of Human Resource Management*, 17 (12): 2035–54.

Smeenk, S., C. Teelken, R. Eisinga and H. Doorewaard (2009), 'Managerialism, Organizational Commitment, and Quality of Job Performances among European University Employees', *Research in Higher Education*, 50 (6): 589–607.

Smith, B. (2007), 'On Being a University Head of Department', *Management in Education*, 21 (1): 4–7.

Snowden, D. (2005), 'Strategy in the Context of Uncertainty', *Handbook of Business Strategy*, 6 (1): 47–54.

Snowden, D. and M. E. Boone (2007), 'A Leader's Framework for Decision Making: Wise Executives Tailor their Approach to Fit the Complexity of the Circumstances they Face', *Harvard Business Review*, November, 69–76. Available online: https://hbr.org/2007/11/a-leaders-framework-for-decision-making (accessed 28 June).

Sporn, B. (2010), 'Management of and in Higher Education Institutions', in *International Encyclopedia of Education*, 3rd edn, 245–50, Oxford: Elsevier.

Stefani, L. (2015), 'Stepping up to Leadership in Higher Education', *All Ireland Journal of Teaching and Learning in Higher Education (AISHE-J)*, 7 (1): 1–18.

Street, B. (2000), 'Literacy Events and Literacy Practices', in M. Martin-Jones and K. Jones (eds), *Multilingual Literacies: Comparative Perspectives on Research and Practice*, 17–29, Amsterdam: John Benjamins.

Styhre, A. (2002), 'Non-Linear Change in Organizations: Organization Change Management Informed by Complexity Theory', *Leadership and Organization Development Journal*, 23 (6): 343–51.

Szekeres, J. (2007), 'General Staff Experiences in the Corporate University', *Journal of Higher Education Policy and Management*, 28 (2): 133–45.

Tannenbaum, R. (1962), 'Control in Organizations: Individual Adjustment and Organizational Performance', *Administration Science Quarterly*, 7 (2): 236–57.

Taylor, J. and C. Baines (2012), 'Performance Management in UK Universities: Implementing The Balanced Scorecard', *Journal of Higher Education Policy and Management*, 34 (2): 111–24.

Te Pōkai Tara Universities New Zealand (n.d.), *Women in Leadership*. Available online: http://www.universitiesnz.ac.nz/aboutus/sc/hr/women-in-leadership (accessed 28 June 2017).

Te Pōkai Tara Universities New Zealand (2014, Feb 16), *Governance Changes will Undermine Role of Universities*. Available online: http://www.universitiesnz.ac.nz/node/737 (accessed 28 June 2017).

Teelken, C. (2012), 'Compliance or Pragmatism: How do Academics Deal With Managerialism in Higher Education? A Comparative Study in Three Countries', *Studies in Higher Education*, 37 (3): 271–90.

ter Bogt, H. J. and R. W. Scapens (2012), 'Performance Management in Universities: Effects of the Transition to More Quantitative Measurement Systems', *European Accounting Review*, 21 (3): 451–97.

Thoroughgood, C. N., A. Padilla, S. T. Hunter and B. W. Tate (2012), 'The Susceptible Circle: A Taxonomy of Followers Associated With Destructive Leaders', *The Leadership Quarterly*, 23 (5): 897–917.

Tsheola, J. and P. Nembambula (2014), 'Governance of the South African University Under Democracy and the Triumphalism of Managerialism over Transformational Leadership', *Mediterranean Journal of Social Sciences*, 5 (27): 1655–66.

Tsoukas, H. (1998), 'Introduction: Chaos, Complexity and Organization Theory', *Organizations*, 5 (3): 291–312.

Turnbull James, K. (2011), Leadership in Context: Lessons from New Leadership Theory and Current Leadership Development Practice, London: The King's Fund. Available online: https://www.kingsfund.org.uk/sites/files/kf/leadership-in-context-theory-current-leadership-development-practice-kim-turnbull-james-kings-fund-may-2011.pdf (accessed 28 June 2017).

Twenge, J. M., S. M. Campbell, B. J. Hoffman and C. E. Lance (2010), 'Generational Differences in Work Values: Leisure and Extrinsic Values Increasing, Social and Intrinsic Values Decreasing', *Journal of Management*, 36 (5): 1117–42.

Tyrall, D. (2005), 'The Fragmentation of a Railway: A Study of Organizational Change', *Journal of Management Studies*, 42 (3): 471–504.

Uhl-Bien, M. (2006), 'Relational Leadership Theory: Exploring the Social Processes of Leadership and Organizing', *The Leadership Quarterly*, 17 (6): 654–76.

Uhl-Bien, M., R. Marion and B. McKelvey (2007), 'Complexity Leadership Theory: Shifting Leadership From the Industrial Age to the Knowledge Era', *The Leadership Quarterly*, 18 (4): 298–318.

van Ameijde, J. D. J., P. C. Nelson, J. Billsberry and N. van Meurs (2009), 'Improving Leadership In Higher Education Institutions: A Distributed Perspective', *Higher Education*, 58: 763–79.

van Knippenberg, D. and S. B. Sitkin (2013), 'A Critical Assessment of Charismatic–Transformational Leadership Research: Back to the Drawing Board?', *The Academy of Management Annals*, 7 (1): 1–60.

Verderber, R. F. and K. S. Verderber (1992), *Inter-Act Using Interpersonal Communication Skills*. Belmont: Wadsworth.

Villa, M. D. (2012), 'The Idea of the University in Latin America in the Twenty-First Century', in R. Barnett (ed.), *The Future University: Ideas and Possibilities*, 59–70, New York, NY: Routledge.

Vincent, A. (2011), 'Ideology and the University', *The Political Quarterly*, 82 (3): 332–40.

Watzlawick, P., J. H. Weakland and R. Fisch (1974), *Change: Principles of Problem Formation and Problem Resolution*. New York: Norton.

Webb, K. (2017), 'Stop Telling People What to Do'. 10 April. Available online: https://keithwebb.com/stop-telling-people/ (accessed 29 June 2017).

Weber, M. (1954), *Max Weber on Law in Economy and Society*, Cambridge: Harvard University Press.

Webster-Wright, A. (2009), 'Reframing Professional Development through Understanding Authentic Professional Learning', *Review of Educational Research*, 79 (2): 702–39.

Weinberg, A. M. and G. Graham-Smith (2012), 'Collegiality: Can It Survive the Corporate University?', *Social Dynamics: A Journal of African Studies*, 38 (1): 68–86.

Wheatley, M. J. (2005), *Finding Our Way: Leadership for an Uncertain Time*, San Francisco: Berrett-Koehler Publishers.

Wheatley, M. J. (2006), *Leadership and the New Science: Discovering Order in a Chaotic World*, 3rd edn, San Francisco, CA: Berrett-Koehler Publishers.

Widder, N. (2004), 'Foucault and Power Revisited', *European Journal of Political Theory*, 3 (4): 411–32.

Wilber, K. (2000), *Sex, Ecology, Spirituality*, 2nd edn, Boston, MA: Shambhala Publications.

Williams, T. (2012), *The Brain-Based Boss – Adding Serious Value Through Employee Engagement*, Wellington, New Zealand: Brookers Ltd.

Winter, R. (2009), 'Academic Manager Or Managed Academic? Academic Identity Schisms in Higher Education', *Journal of Higher Education Policy and Management*, 31 (2): 121–31.

Wright, N. (2011), 'Between 'Bastard' and 'Wicked' Leadership? School Leadership and the Emerging Policies of the UK Coalition Government', *Journal of Educational Administration and History*, 43 (4): 345–62.

Xanthopoulou, D., A. B. Bakker, E. Demerouti and W. B. Schaufeli (2009), 'Work Engagement and Financial Returns: A Diary Study on the Role of Job and Personal Resources', *Journal of Occupational and Organizational Psychology*, 82 (1): 183–200.

Yielder, J. and A. Codling (2004), 'Management and Leadership in the Contemporary University', *Journal of Higher Education Policy and Management*, 26 (3): 315–28.

Yu, C. (2014), *The Reality of Counterproductive Workplace Behaviours*, Auckland, New Zealand: The University of Auckland. Available online: http://www.organisationalpsychology.nz/_content/14_12_10_Counterproductive_Work_Behaviours_White_Paper_Christine_Yu%20.pdf (accessed 28 June 2017).

Yukl, G. A. (2006), *Leadership in Organizations*, 6th edn, Upper Saddle River, NJ: Prentice-Hall.

Yukl, G. A. (2012), 'Effective Leadership Behavior: What We Know and What Questions Need More Attention', *Academy of Management Perspectives*, 26 (4): 66–85.

Yukl, G. A. and W. S. Becker (2006), Effective Empowerment in Organizations. *Organization Management Journal*, 3 (3): 210–31.

Zenger, J. (2013), 'Why Gallup's 70% Disengagement Data is Wrong', *Leadership*, 14 November. Available online: https://www.forbes.com/sites/jackzenger/2013/11/14/why-gallups-70-disengagement-data-is-wrong/#7af66c49235b (accessed 28 June 2017).

Zukas, M. and S. Kilminster (2012), 'Learning to Practise, Practising to Learn: Doctors' Transitions to New Levels of Responsibility', in P. Hager, A. Lee and A. Reich (eds), *Practice, Learning and Change: Practice-Theory Perspectives on Professional Learning*, 199–215, London: Springer.

Index